The Social Order of the Underworld

The Social Order of the Underworld

*How Prison Gangs Govern
the American Penal System*

DAVID SKARBEK

OXFORD
UNIVERSITY PRESS

OXFORD
UNIVERSITY PRESS

Oxford University Press is a department of the
University of Oxford. It furthers the University's objective
of excellence in research, scholarship, and education
by publishing worldwide.

Oxford   New York

Auckland   Cape Town   Dar es Salaam   Hong Kong   Karachi
Kuala Lumpur   Madrid   Melbourne   Mexico City   Nairobi
New Delhi   Shanghai   Taipei   Toronto

With offices in

Argentina   Austria   Brazil   Chile   Czech Republic   France   Greece
Guatemala   Hungary   Italy   Japan   Poland   Portugal   Singapore
South Korea   Switzerland   Thailand   Turkey   Ukraine   Vietnam

Oxford is a registered trade mark of Oxford University Press
in the UK and certain other countries.

Published in the United States of America by
Oxford University Press
198 Madison Avenue, New York, NY 10016

Library of Congress Cataloging-in-Publication Data
Skarbek, David.
The social order of the underworld : how prison gangs govern the
American penal system / David Skarbek.
    pages   cm
Includes bibliographical references.
ISBN 978-0-19-932849-9 (hardback : alk. paper)—ISBN 978-0-19-932850-5 (pbk. : alk. paper)
1. Prison gangs—United States.   2. Prison administration—United States.
3. Prison violence—United States.   4. Prisoners—United States.   I. Title.
HV6439.U5S557   2014
365'.6—dc23

2013041577

1 3 5 7 9 8 6 4 2
Printed in the United States of America
on acid-free paper

For Emily

Contents

Acknowledgments

I'VE BEEN EXTREMELY fortunate to have the encouragement and guidance of outstanding colleagues during the process of writing this book, and I am especially grateful to everyone who commented on drafts of the manuscript. I owe thanks to Lee Benham, Stewart Dompe, Brendan Dooley, Philip Goodman, William Keech, Gary Libecap, Benjamin Powell, Mary Shirley, and Edward Stringham for providing suggestions on individual chapters. Several people generously provided comments on the entire manuscript—many thanks to Paolo Campana, Paul Dudenhefer, Mark Kleiman, Peter Leeson, Adam Martin, John Meadowcroft, Darrell Padgett, Jason Sexton, Daniel Skarbek, and Kristen Skarbek. Michael Munger's detailed comments at an early stage of the project were tremendously helpful. Peter Boettke encouraged my academic interest in self-governance, and he has been a constant source of intellectual guidance and inspiration. Peter Leeson's research on self-enforcing exchange and criminal organization laid much of the foundation for this work. I am especially grateful for the extensive comments that he has provided to me on this and other projects. Paul Orozco deserves special thanks for sparking my initial interest in prison social order.

I presented several chapters in the Political Economy seminars at Duke University and King's College London, which generated a long list of useful comments and suggestions. Seminar participants at the Center for International Security and Cooperation at Stanford University provided excellent suggestions, as did my insightful commentator, David Laitin. Participants in the Economics of Crime working group at the National Bureau of Economic Research's Summer Institute provided important feedback. Many thanks to the directors of the working group—Philip J. Cook, Jens Ludwig, and Justin McCrary—and especially to my thoughtful discussant, Mark Kleiman.

The book builds on earlier articles that benefited from helpful suggestions by many of those listed above and by Jason Aimone, Daniel D'Amico, Eli Dourado, John Nye, Doug Rogers, Matt Ryan, Daniel Smith, Virgil Storr,

Daniel Sutter, Diana Thomas, Michael Thomas, and Georg Vanberg. I thank Elsevier for allowing me to use ideas from my article "Prison Gangs, Norms, and Organizations" (*Journal of Economic Behavior & Organization* 2012; 82(1): 96–109), which informs Chapter 2. I thank Oxford University Press for permission to use material from my article "Putting the 'Con' into Constitutions: The Economics of Prison Gangs" (*Journal of Law, Economics, & Organization* 2010; 26(2): 183–211) in part of Chapter 5. Finally, I am grateful to Cambridge University Press, which granted permission to reuse material from my article "Governance and Prison Gangs" (*American Political Science Review* 2011; 105(4): 702–716) in Chapter 6. I owe special thanks to the co-editors at the *APSR*, who went above and beyond their editorial duties in providing detailed comments on my paper and on broader issues related to this research project.

At Oxford University Press, I benefited greatly from the invaluable feedback provided by my editor, David McBride, and from the skillful work of the production staff. Two anonymous reviewers also made suggestions that helped me write a more cogent and coherent book. The Earhart Foundation provided financial support for this project, for which I'm exceptionally grateful.

My wife Emily commented on numerous drafts of every chapter, and she has been gracious and encouraging during my all-too-frequent updates on the book's status. Marrying an economist means that I am lucky enough to have someone with whom I can discuss economics nightly over dinner, and this was a great help in refining many of these ideas. I wouldn't have been able to write this book without her intellectual insights and her constant encouragement, love, and support.

I

Governance Institutions and the Prison Community

In short, in California, the question of how to manage prisons has resolved itself into the question of how to manage prison gangs.

JOHN J. DiIULIO, JR.[1]

Criminal Justice

On a warm May evening in 2009, Aaron Osheroff and his nine-year-old daughter, Melody, walked hand-in-hand through the crosswalk at the corner of San Carlos Way and San Marin Drive in Marin, California. It was about 9 p.m. A car stopped as they crossed the street; a motorcycle racing down the road did not. It sped between the stopped car and a parked car, running into Aaron and Melody. They were both seriously injured, and paramedics rushed them to the hospital. Melody died the following day at the Children's Hospital in Oakland. Aaron spent months in recovery, endured multiple surgeries, and had his right leg amputated. The Osheroff family lost their daughter, a fourth-grader who loved reading and hiking.

The motorcyclist, Edward John Schaefer, had a blood alcohol level more than twice the legal limit. He had a dozen prior convictions for driving under the influence and reckless driving. Prosecutors charged him with second-degree murder, gross vehicular manslaughter while intoxicated, mayhem, and causing injury while driving under the influence. If convicted, he faced from 17 years to life in prison. In his first court appearance, the unshaven 43-year-old made a rude hand gesture to the photographers and officials in the courtroom. He was later convicted of second-degree murder and gross vehicular manslaughter, and he received a prison sentence of 24 years to life. Officials sent Schaefer to San Quentin State Prison.

On a brisk morning in late July, only 10 days after arriving at the state's oldest prison, Schaefer walked out to the prison yard and never walked back. An inmate stabbed him seven times in the neck and chest with a seven-inch prison-made metal spear, known by inmates as a "bone crusher." It was made from a piece of a metal bunk bed. His killer, Frank Souza, was a 33-year-old associate of the Aryan Brotherhood prison gang; he wore a large "White Power" tattoo emblazoned across his entire forehead.

Schaefer's murder wasn't motivated by racism. Schaefer was white too. When authorities asked him why he did it, Souza responded, "All I got to say, nine-year-old girl." In court, he explained, "The innocence of a child will be defended at all costs."[2] He read from William Ernest Henley's poem "Invictus," wherein circumstances prey upon a man, but "under the bludgeoning of chance," he still stands tall. Good men must stand tall in the face of the tragedies that befall innocent people. Souza read from the second stanza, "My head is bloody, but unbowed."

Schaefer's death was no accident, nor was Souza's role in the murder. The prison gangs that control California's inmates carefully orchestrated the events on that brisk July morning. Racially segregated prison gangs rule over the inmate community. Sometimes they work together. At times, they wage bloody battles for control of the prison yard. No one who enters prison can ignore these gang politics. Souza enacted criminal justice at the behest of a prison gang, and in doing so, he demonstrated one of the myriad ways that gangs provide governance in the criminal underworld.

The Economic Way of Thinking

Prison gangs appear baffling. Many people associate their lifestyle, organization, monikers, activities, rituals, and customs with non-rational forces. The oddities of the criminal underworld seem attributable only to psychopathy or pure evil. Their actions raise many puzzling questions. Why do murderous prison gangs avenge the death of unknown children? Why do clandestine groups get prominent tattoos that reveal their membership? Why is prison the only place that middle-aged men join gangs? Why does racism permeate prison at a time when society is more tolerant than ever before? Why didn't gangs exist for the first 100 years of the California prison system, but now dominate them? Why do the most dangerous inmates keep the peace? Why do people join gangs that they can never leave, even after release? We cannot explain these puzzles by simply calling inmates evil, stupid, or crazy. These are not the actions of irrational men. On the contrary, the only way to understand prison gangs is to study their members as rational people. This book uses economics to explain the seemingly irrational, truly astonishing, and often tragic world of prison life.

There are two central ideas that make up the rational-choice approach. First, people are self-interested. They pursue ends that they value. This doesn't mean that each person cares only about him- or herself. People often do care more about themselves, their family, and their friends than they do about complete strangers. However, people also give to charity, save people from burning buildings, and perform acts of sacrifice for the sake of justice and honor. People pursue outcomes that they value, both self-interested and altruistic ones. One advantage of viewing the world this way is that it makes it hard to ignore social problems. If people always cared about everyone else as much as themselves, then violent crime and many other social problems wouldn't exist. People would know that these actions harm others, so they simply would not do them. Related to this point, the focus of this analysis is always on how individuals act. We cannot understand gangs, prisons, and the legal system without understanding the individuals who comprise them.

Second, people respond rationally to changes in costs and benefits. If some activity becomes more costly, people tend to do less of it. If something becomes less costly, people tend to do more of it. This does not require that each person be a lightning calculator of pleasure and pain.[3] People aren't robots. They sometimes make mistakes, get confused, satisfice, and struggle through a murky world of imperfect information and cognitive biases. However, when they recognize changes in costs and benefits, they respond accordingly. Again, this does not mean that people will not rush into burning buildings to save others. It just means that a person will be less likely to do so when the flames burn twice as hot. A person's subjective preferences determine what he or she views as costs and benefits. It is not helpful to ignore an inmate's desire for heroin just because we might not share or approve of that preference. This approach doesn't require that everyone value things in the same way or naively assume that people only want money. Economics looks at how people strive to accomplish their preferred goals, based on the costs and benefits of doing so.

The rational-choice model applies to criminals as much as it does to everyone else, possibly more so. The punishment for making errors in the underworld are often more severe, and meted out more quickly, than in traditional arenas of life. If you make a mistake in an ordinary job, you may be fired. If you make a mistake as a criminal, you may go to prison. Mistakes in prison can be fatal. This feedback makes many inmates highly attuned to their

·onment. Writing about his own experience as a political prisoner, political scientist Marek Kaminski explains, "Prison socializes an inmate to behave hyperrationally. It teaches him patience in planning and pursuing his goals, punishes him severely for his mistakes, and rewards him generously for smart action.... There is little space for innocent and spontaneous expressions of emotion when they collide with fundamental interests.... Paradoxically, much of the confusion in interpreting prison behavior arises from both a failure to understand the motives of inmates and an unwillingness to admit that outcomes judged as inhuman or bizarre may be consequences of individually rational action."[4] The rational-choice approach provides a way to understand how order emerges in the criminal underworld.[5]

A Governance Theory of Prison Social Order

Criminals lack access to many formal governance institutions: the legal and social institutions that promote social order and economic activity by protecting property rights, enforcing agreements, and facilitating collective action to provide physical and organizational infrastructure.[6] Governance institutions play a crucial role in every society. Markets, business endeavors, and nearly every sort of cooperative pursuit require well-functioning governance institutions. This includes both criminals who wish to cooperate in crime and the members of society who must cooperate to stop them. However, precisely because they are involved in illicit activities, criminals can't rely on the same governance institutions that law-abiding citizens rely on. To meet this need, criminals must create alternative, self-governing institutions. Because the theme of self-governance permeates the entire book, it will be useful to examine briefly the three components of governance.

First, governance institutions define and enforce property rights. A property right is the exclusive authority to choose how a resource is used. It determines who has the right to use it, earn money from it, transfer it to others, and enforce the exclusive control of it. Property rights are not a fixed, unchanging feature of the world. People choose how much to invest in defining and defending property rights based on the costs and benefits of doing so.[7] A person will restrict access to a resource more when it becomes cheaper to do so. For example, if the cost of a car alarm falls by half, people are more likely to install one. The car will be safer from theft, so the resource is more secure. As the value of a resource increases, it will be worth investing more to protect it. A person is more likely to buy a car alarm for a new sports car than for an old pickup truck.

Because it is costly to define and enforce property rights, not everything will have a clearly defined owner.[8] For example, no one has found it profitable to define and enforce property rights claims to vast segments of the world's oceans. It is too costly to monitor people's use of the distant blue sea, and there is often little benefit in doing so. Property rights are also more complex and nuanced than either owning something or not. A resource may have many attributes that comprise a bundle of related property rights. A person may control some of those rights, but not all of them. I may have the right to keep someone from trespassing in my home, but I might not have the right to keep planes from flying across the sky above it, broadcasters from sending radio waves through it, or own the valuable minerals buried deep below it.

Unlike normative theories of who should have property rights over something, the positive theory of property rights looks at whether someone can actually enforce a claim.[9] If I go to the store and purchase a bicycle, then it is legally mine. However, if I do not invest resources to secure it, then it won't be mine for long, especially if it is left unlocked. Even if I have a moral or legal claim, if I lack the resources to defend the claim, then in reality I don't control the property right to it.[10] An inmate can have a moral claim not to be assaulted by other inmates, but if he cannot prevent others from doing so, then he doesn't actually control that property right. People's rights differ, and they depend on one's ability to enforce such claims. Governance institutions provide a way for people to assert, define, and defend ownership claims to property rights.

The second role of governance institutions is to help people capture the benefits from trade. Voluntary exchange makes both parties better off. However, beneficial trades might not take place for a variety of reasons. The costs of finding a trading partner may be too high. The cost of learning the quality of a product may be excessive. A trader may fear that the other person won't hold up his or her side of the bargain. If people know they will have a venue for resolving disputes, then they will be more likely to engage in commercial activity. For example, a seller's reputation provides an important check on bad behavior.[11] If a seller defrauds a buyer, the buyer can expose the seller's untrustworthiness to others and reduce the profitability of the seller's business in the future. Regulation, licenses, insurance, courts, and a variety of creative market mechanisms provide the governance that address these problems and facilitate trade. This assurance gives people confidence to participate in commercial activity. Good economic governance underlies—and is the foundation of—the entire system of specialization and the division of labor that exists in a market economy. Without it, market failures proliferate.

The third function of governance institutions is to help people act collectively. Goods like national defense are difficult to produce privately because everyone enjoys their benefits once they exist. The same threat that deters a hostile country from bombing my neighbor's house protects mine too, even if I haven't paid for it. Recognizing this ability to free ride, many people won't contribute to the production of a public good. As a result, although each individual acts rationally, the public good may not be provided at all. Everyone is worse off. Collective action is also needed when people take actions that harm others, like polluting the environment. The institutions that people create to solve these types of problems are necessary for capturing the benefits of trade and establishing an orderly society. In the real world, these governance institutions take many different forms, depending on the context, resources, and people involved. Studies of a tremendous array of collective action problems from around the world reveal that governance institutions arise in "endless forms most beautiful and most wonderful."[12]

Each of these three types of governance institutions is necessary for people to live orderly, prosperous lives. People often assume that governments must create and operate these essential institutions, but that is not true. Many modern governments provide governance effectively, but none provides all of it. Private companies and organizations play an important role in protecting property and adjudicating disputes.[13] Moreover, many governments do a poor job of providing governance. The Democratic Republic of Congo's history of human rights abuses reflects the absence of secure property rights. In Zimbabwe, President Mugabe's land appropriation policies undermine commerce and the rule of law. Indeed, governments need not provide governance, and many remarkably effective governance institutions flourish outside of the control of the state.[14] Sometimes these extralegal governance institutions are more effective than state-created institutions because they can rely on local expertise and information.[15] When governance institutions work well, they solve the governance problems faced by every society. However, no one form of governance institution is best in all situations. The specific constraints of information and incentives in a particular time and place determine what context-dependent institutions will most effectively provide governance.

Criminals must rely on extralegal governance institutions. Heroin dealers cannot call the police if someone robs them. Criminals must conceal their production, transportation, warehousing, advertising, and selling of illicit goods. Assets are subject both to theft from other criminals and to confiscation by the police. The accounting services that aid legal businesses are unavailable to criminals. Criminal firms can't legally insure their assets against accidents and acts of God. Criminals can't list a company on the New York Stock Exchange, borrow funds from a local bank, or use traditional advertising to attract customers. Illegality also raises the cost of developing a good reputation. A drug dealer known for his honesty may also be well known by the police. Drug dealers must alert consumers, but not police, to their presence. It may also be more difficult to recruit employees in the criminal underworld than in the law-abiding one.[16] Criminals are more willing to violate the law and sometimes widely held moral principles. Incarceration adds to these difficulties. Correctional officers watch inmates. The imposed schedule of incarceration limits one's freedom to move about and speak to others. Criminals face an extraordinary challenge in producing the governance institutions that are necessary for illicit markets to flourish.[17]

This book examines the extralegal governance institutions that criminals create. In offering a governance theory of prison social order, I depart from the two most commonly accepted frameworks for understanding prison life that have dominated the sociology and criminology literature: the deprivation theory and the importation theory.[18] The deprivation theory contends that prison social order is a direct result of the pains of imprisonment experienced during confinement.[19] It focuses on inmates' deprivations of liberty, goods and services, heterosexual relationships, autonomy, and security. Thus, to understand the prisoner community, one must look at the nature of confinement. Prison social order has indigenous roots. The importation theory, by contrast, contends that to understand prison social order one must understand the pre-prison experiences and beliefs that inmates bring into prison.[20] The prison culture, for instance, is an extension of the criminal, working class, or drug culture in the world beyond prison walls. We can best understand the prison community by looking outside of prison.

I diverge from these theories in two ways. First, I argue that norms are not a highly rigid or inherent belief. They are neither fixed nor exogenous, and they are not primarily symbolic. Norms emerge and change to help people coordinate social interactions.[21] They are a means instead of an end. To understand prison social order—of which norms are an important part—we need to understand what problem norms arise to solve, and when they are incapable of doing so. Second, and related to this, past work on inmate deprivations has tended to downplay or ignore the fact that prisons deprive inmates of essential governance institutions.[22] Goods and services can ameliorate the pains of imprisonment, but their availability depends on the effectiveness of extralegal governance institutions. Identifying the crucial need for extralegal governance among inmates provides answers for why, where, when, and how prison gangs form and operate.[23] In short, prison gangs form to provide extralegal governance when inmates have a demand for it and official governance mechanisms are ineffective or unavailable.

Economists and political scientists should share an interest in extralegal governance institutions. Scholars have long studied prisons as microcosms of society, and understanding the development of informal institutions and conflict processes in prison provides a useful exercise in comparative politics. All around the globe people are working in informal and shadow economies. Half of the world's workers are in the informal sector: unregulated, unregistered, and untaxed.[24] They do a tremendous volume of business—$10 trillion annually. Moreover, half of the world's countries provide governance poorly or not at all.[25] Yet, the majority of political economy research focuses on formal institutions and conventional markets. We cannot fully understand political and economic outcomes without understanding how formal institutions interact with extralegal governance institutions. Informal governance institutions are of tremendous importance, and in many cases, are more important than formal institutions.[26] Prison provides a context in which to study these broader issues.

The prison setting offers an opportunity to assess the effectiveness of extralegal governance, and it is uniquely well suited for doing so because it enables me to examine a worst-case scenario and to control for a number of important characteristics that are theoretically relevant. For instance, the people who live in prison are, on average, less trustworthy and have less self-control than people in the broader population. They can't choose who to live and interact with. Inmate drug dealers can't rely on formal governance mechanisms as a last resort should extralegal ones fail (a criticism made about Avner Greif's seminal work on self-regulating trade).[27] These factors make exchange much more difficult, so prison presents an excellent environment for testing the robustness of self-governance mechanisms. More practically, if public administrators do not have a sound understanding of why prison gangs come into existence, then they will lack clear methods for mitigating their harms.

Prison Gangs

The primary focus of this book is to understand how criminal institutions form, function, and evolve, and to determine their effectiveness and robustness. Prison gangs play an important role. A prison gang is an inmate organization that operates within a prison system, that has a corporate entity, exists into perpetuity, and whose membership is restrictive, mutually exclusive, and often requires a lifetime commitment.[28] They recruit most of their hard-core members from among the most dangerous people behind bars.[29] Many gangs have elaborate written constitutions that guide their operations. Other common characteristics of prison gangs include well-defined goals and philosophies, a structured internal organization with clearly defined authority and responsibility, and widespread involvement in criminal activity both behinds bars and often on the street.[30] They vary in size, and can often include several hundred members. Nearly every prison gang restricts its membership to one racial or ethnic group.[31] Geographic and other characteristics often matter too. For instance, in California, Hispanics from Northern California (known as *Norteños*, Spanish for Northerner) and Southern California (*Sureños*, for Southerner) affiliate with different Hispanic prison gangs. Some have operated for decades and have substantial influence in the criminal community. Compared to street gangs, prison gang members are typically more organized, entrepreneurial, covert, selective, and strict.[32]

Gangs have had an increasingly important presence in jails and prisons across the United States. Prison gangs did not exist prior to the 1950s. By 1985, prison gangs were active in 49 states, with 114 different gangs and nearly 13,000 members.[33] By 1992, national prison gang membership had tripled to roughly 46,000.[34] A recent study estimates that there are about 308,000 gang members in U.S. prisons.[35] Prisons in California and Texas hold about 70 percent of all prison gang members in the United States, so it is a useful context to study, to understand their origin and operation.[36] In 2002, a high-ranking official testified that there were 40,000 to 60,000 gang members in California prisons.[37] Another estimate suggested that 75 percent of California inmates were gang members.[38] Importantly, the number of prison gang members underestimates their actual influence, because gangs have substantial influence over other inmates. A gang investigator at Wabash Valley Correctional Facility in Indiana described the gangs' control: "What people don't realize is that almost everything that happens in a prison setting has some sort of gang involvement, whether it be extortion, intimidations, trafficking narcotics. There's nothing that goes on that at least one gang member is not involved with...nothing."[39]

Compared to research on street gangs, criminologists and sociologists have done relatively little work on prison gangs. The most widely cited article on prison gangs reports that there have been only a few in-depth studies.[40] Two leading criminologists describe prison gangs as the final frontier of gang research.[41] Ethnographic research on prison social order in the United States more generally is in decline. In 2000, one scholar observed that studies of prison social organization have largely ceased since 1980.[42] Sociologist Loïc Wacquant writes that detailed ethnographic studies of "the everyday world of inmates in America have gone into eclipse just when they were most needed on both scientific and political grounds."[43] Fortunately, there has been some renewed interest in studying prison social order, but none focuses on the role of extralegal governance.[44]

The absence of useful data is the major obstacle to studying prison gangs. Data on gang-affiliated inmates remain some of the most elusive figures in corrections.[45] According to a recent study, "there are no national (or state) longitudinal data tracking street gang expansion in state and federal prisons, and prison gang growth over the three decades of prison expansion."[46] From the mid-1990s to 2005, the California Department of Corrections and Rehabilitation even closed down its research unit.[47] Moreover, there is little or no coordination of information management systems among the hundreds of criminal justice–related agencies that track offenders in California.[48] When officials collect data, the data set often isn't useful because it is "confounded by definitional variability and variation in disciplinary policies."[49] People in different corrections departments measure and count things differently, so we can't compare them. Moreover, data are often only for departmental use because officials consider the information too sensitive or confidential to make public.[50] Of course, unlike the study of mainstream businesses, we cannot use gang's financial statements and accounting records.[51]

There are several additional obstacles to collecting qualitative evidence. Prison gangs enforce a code of silence.[52] Staff can revoke an inmate's privileges if they validate him as a gang member.[53] Even if a gang member is willing to talk, he may exaggerate his claims or lie. Unlike studies of other deviant communities, no one has conducted field studies on prison gangs.[54] One difficulty is that the same walls that keep inmates locked in also keep researchers out. Getting evidence on the inmate community, and specifically prison gangs, therefore presents a substantial challenge.

In my work, I rely on wide-ranging types of evidence. First, I use the best academic research available, much of it from criminology and sociology. Rebecca Trammell's work on prison violence has been especially useful, as have classic works by Donald Clemmer, Gresham Sykes, and John Irwin.[55] Second, I have collected data on California's inmate population, going back in some cases to the 1850s. Much of this information comes from annual reports and periodic studies released by the California Department of

Corrections and Rehabilitation.[56] I have supplemented it with information obtained in other sources, like histories of the state's prisons.

I have also made extensive use of legal documents related to California's prison and street gangs. This includes indictments, criminal complaints, court orders, and testimony. In addition to histories and descriptions of gangs, these items give detailed lists of alleged overt criminal acts and reveal the inner workings of numerous street and prison gangs. While legal documents provide a tremendous amount of information, courts of law have not yet vetted many of these allegations. Law enforcement is not without its own biases. Police want to make arrests, and prosecutors want to get convictions. One way that I leverage these court documents is to see what appellate court judges think about the quality of the evidence. They review and describe the evidence presented in the original case, assessing its reliability and validity. This provides a relatively impartial and judicious assessment of the evidence. A related source of evidence is declassified files from the Federal Bureau of Investigation. Numerous agents working on different projects over several decades created these documents. Because they are primarily internal correspondence, they tend to be informative and are likely to be fairly accurate.

Personal memoirs and biographies of former law enforcement officials who investigated prison gangs in California also provide insights. Some of these people spent decades scrutinizing prison gangs, others served long tenures as correctional officers. In addition, prison gang members who have dropped out and testified against their former colleagues have written about them. Prison gangs kill former members who tell their secrets, so the people involved appear to consider informants' accounts accurate enough to warrant serious action. A gang investigations supervisor I spoke with described these works as highly informative and reliable. I supplement these with conversations with correctional officers, gang investigators, gang experts, police officers, and former inmates. I have visited some of the prisons discussed in this book, including minimum-, medium-, and maximum-security facilities in California and elsewhere.

I have also taken advantage of documentaries and media reports on prisons. This is a nontraditional, but useful, source of evidence. Clearly, the producers of these reports do not randomly select the prisons they go to, the people they speak with, and the clips they air. These sources do not single-handedly provide generalizable results. However, they do coincide strongly with findings from both the academic literature and my own interviews. They also offer texture, detail, and perspective that complement other sources. They add to the rich mosaic of qualitative evidence, and they help paint a compelling picture of prison life. I would prefer to rely entirely on scholarly observational studies, but as Loïc Wacquant sadly notes, "with social science deserting the scene, one is forced to turn to the writings of journalists and inmates to learn about everyday life in the cells and dungeons of America."[57]

Each of these types of evidence is imperfect, yet together they provide a compelling picture. Their authors come from both sides of the law and from many academic disciplines. Judges have vetted and assessed much of it. It is qualitative and quantitative. I hope to show that the synthesis of these diverse sources provides an accurate and convincing picture of the criminal underworld.

Finally, economics helps us identify the mechanisms that underlie social interactions, but it neither condones nor condemns the people involved. Just because we understand why something happened doesn't mean that it is desirable. Clearly, many prison gang members have participated in heinous, deplorable crimes and have left in their path a wake of innocent victims and shattered lives. (I document this in some of the vignettes throughout the book, which provide vivid illustrations of issues related to gangs and governance.) If we have any hope that we can improve the problems associated with crime and incarceration, then we must believe that people are not inherently and immovably committed to violence and racism. Criminals, like all people, respond to incentives.

Men's Central Jail

BUILT IN 1963, the Men's Central Jail in Los Angeles is one of the oldest county jails in California. Officials claim it's the largest jail in the world. It is also one of the most controversial. The jail is overcrowded. Its antiquated design reportedly makes it dangerous for both inmates and staff. Over the last several years, inmates, visitors, and the American Civil Liberties Union have raised serious concerns about the behavior of the jail's deputies.

In December 2010, Juan Pablo Reyes was serving a short sentence in the Men's Central Jail for making a criminal threat. He had threatened his wife during a domestic dispute. He is a native Spanish speaker and knows "a little English." Because he was neither a gang member nor a serious offender, staff assigned him to a job as an inmate worker and to a cell that housed only inmate trustees. He spent his days delivering bag lunches to inmates, sweeping and mopping floors, picking up trash, distributing mail, and cleaning the staff bathrooms and deputies' desks. This is a relatively comfortable way to serve a sentence at Men's Central because an inmate gets to spend lots of time outside of his cell and is not housed among the most dangerous inmates. However, according to Reyes's legal deposition, his incarceration experience quickly changed for the worse.

While at work on December 10, Reyes found a piece of mail on the ground. It didn't appear to be trash, and he claims that he was going to return it. Before he could do so, however, a deputy saw Reyes holding the mail and accused him of stealing it. Reyes objected, saying that he had just found it. The deputy didn't believe him, and said that he would "deal with him" on his next shift.

On Sunday, December 12, two deputies approached Reyes while he was in his cell. They told him that if he identified inmates who had cocaine and crystal meth, they would forgive him for stealing the mail. Reyes told them that he didn't know anyone with drugs. This displeased the deputies. They ordered him to switch out of his green inmate clothes (which indicated he was an inmate worker) into blue clothes (for regular inmates). They had fired him. The deputies then ordered him out of his cell and told him to stand with his face against the wall. They put on plastic gloves. Then the beating began.

According to Reyes's translated deposition, "They punched me in the eyes, body, back and ribs, and one of their punches broke my eye socket. I could feel my face breaking as they beat me. The beating was extremely painful, and I felt upset, confused and helpless. Two other deputies, whom I cannot name at this time, joined in the attack, and continued to punch me as well. I did not strike back, but tried to cover myself up as I fell to the ground. Once I had fallen, the deputies proceeded to kick me with their leather steel toed boots. I cried out for them to stop, but they refused, and were laughing."[1]

After the beating, officers took Reyes to a holding area and made him undress. They were moving him to the housing unit reserved for gang members. Not being a gang member, this was an unusual housing decision, and for Reyes, much more dangerous. They walked him up and down the tier of the gang module, naked, and spoke in English about Reyes being a homosexual. As Reyes walked past the row of inmates in the gang module, one of the deputies spoke over the intercom so that all of the inmates could hear: "Aqui va un maricon caminando." Translation: "Here goes a faggot walking." The deputies and some of the inmates were laughing as they marched him around.

Reyes entered a four-man cell occupied by three gang members, two Hispanics and one black. Hispanic gang members follow "gang rules" that require them to assault *Paisas*, inmates from Mexico and Central America. The deputies closed the cell door. Almost immediately, and without warning, the Hispanic gang members began to beat Reyes. He explained, "I do not know whether they beat me because of whether they thought I was gay, or because I was a Paisa, or the fact that I was paraded naked by the deputies gave them license to beat me, but they proceeded to punch me and hit me on my back, face, chest, and stomach." Sadly, this was not the end. "The beating started midmorning, and continued on and off all day for hours. Deputies would walk by doing their cell checks and feeding the inmates, and they ignored my cries for help and my appearance. They refused to respond to my cries to take me out of the cell. One time when [the deputy] walked by the cell, I begged him to take me out. I told him that I was being attacked. He said I deserved the attacks by the inmates and walked away." At night, his cellmates took turns raping him.

When the cell doors opened the following morning, Reyes fled. He ran into a holding area and cried out for help. A female chaplain heard his cries and contacted a sergeant. Officials took him to an interview room. The deputy who beat Reyes was in the room when the sergeant asked him what happened.

Reyes told them about how the inmates had beat and raped him, but he didn't mention the beating he received from the deputies. He feared retaliation.

He received medical care at the jail that day, and about two weeks later, he spent several days in the county hospital. The doctor told him he needed eye surgery. Instead, officials released him from the hospital directly to the street, two months earlier than expected. Since he didn't receive the surgery and doesn't have insurance, his eye remains unrepaired.

The American Civil Liberties Union alleges many more disturbing instances of neglect and abuse by deputies in the Los Angeles Jail system.[2] It is important to note that this is not the experience of all inmates or the actions of all deputies. Moreover, the legal system has not yet examined these allegations. Nonetheless, there has been a growing awareness of corruption and misconduct in Men's Central Jail. These complaints come not only from inmates but also from court-ordered monitors, jail chaplains, and former Los Angeles Sheriff's Department jail supervisors. This disturbing incident illustrates one of the reasons why inmates often seek out alternative forms of governance: they cannot always rely on the guards.

2

The Convict Code

One might tend to suspect that a group of rebels—muggers, rapists, forgers—confined together would exist in a perpetual state of anarchy. Far from the case; the inmate society is surprisingly orderly and organized.

VERGIL WILLIAMS AND MARY FISH[1]

Without order we have anarchy, and when we have anarchy people die here.

Inmate, Corcoran State Prison[2]

I've always fought for what's white, and what's right with our people. And I believe in stabbings. I believe that some people should be stabbed. Child molesters, rapists, and all that. We have to live by a set of standards in prison. It would be a free-for-all if we didn't.

Inmate, Corcoran State Prison[3]

Inmates Require Self-Governance

Dangerous, violent criminals fill American prisons, and it can be quite treacherous living among them. As an inmate explains, "You don't have to do anything to become a victim, and there's no one man who is strong enough to come against a group of five or six. And, if someone gets a wild idea in their mind that they want to do something obscene or what-have-you, there's nothing I can do if they catch me in the wrong spot at the wrong time."[4] In 2011, of the male inmates in California's prisons, 64 percent had been convicted of violent crimes, such as rape, assault, and murder; 16 percent had committed property crimes, such as burglary and theft. Many of these men are experts at deception and guile, and some are capable of monstrous acts of brutality and violence. The correctional system rates each inmate's security risk—from Level I (low) to Level IV (high)—based on his criminal history, violence, gang involvement, sentence length, and several other factors.[5] In 2012, about 57 percent of inmates in the California prison system were either Level III or Level IV inmates.[6] One inmate at Kern Valley State Prison summarizes incarceration simply as "predatory. Prison is predatory."[7]

However, despite the population's characteristics, prisons can be quite orderly. Objectively, order exists when the inmates experience relatively few overt acts of violence, such as assaults, rapes, riots, and murders; subjectively, an orderly prison is calm, stable, and predictable.[8] By these measures, prison social order has improved over the last four decades. Riots have become much less common. In the 1970s, it was unexceptional for there to be more than 40 riots per 100,000 inmates per year. In the 1990s, there were often fewer than five riots per 100,000 inmates per year.[9] The rate of inmate homicides declined 94 percent between 1973 and 2003, at which time the homicide rate in state prisons was actually lower than that in the general population.[10] The inmate suicide rate has roughly halved since 1980.[11] From 1984 to 2000, inmate-on-inmate assaults fell from 43 to 29 per 1,000 inmates.[12] A national survey in 1997 asked state prison inmates how safe they felt from being hit, punched, or assaulted by other inmates. The majority of inmates chose the two safest responses, with 20.4 percent of respondents reporting they felt "somewhat safe" and 48.6 percent feeling "safe."[13] By these measures, prisons are orderly.

Given prisons' inhabitants, the relatively orderly nature of prisons requires explanation. People often assume that officials provide most of this order, and to some extent, this is certainly true.[14] Correctional officers punish inmates who attack or steal from others. Sharpshooters in guard towers monitor prison yards. When violence erupts, they use a variety of lethal and less-lethal weapons to stop bloodshed. Inmates who kill their cellmates, attack staff, and carry out numerous other offenses are subject to a host of punishments. Inmates may lose privileges, such as time out of their cell, the opportunity to participate in work or education programs, and loss of good-behavior credit for early release.[15] Offenses that are more serious can lead to additional criminal charges and new prison sentences. The physical layout of a prison also creates order. The same bars that keep an inmate locked in his cell also keep others out. Panopticon-style prisons allow officers to watch over many inmates at once.[16] Prisons appear to be total institutions, where the state watches for and punishes all misdeeds.[17]

Yet, it is not that simple. Officers provide only a portion of the governance of inmates' lives. Correctional officers cannot protect all of the inmates, all of the time. During an inmate's incarceration, he will interact with hundreds, and perhaps even thousands, of other inmates in a variety of situations. In many of them, social dilemmas arise in which the rational actions of each individual leads to a situation where everyone is worse off.[18] Inmates might pilfer others' cells or extort money from weaker inmates. During a prison drug deal, an inmate might not pay, pay late, or pay less than agreed on. Inmates can choose to cooperate during one of these interactions by respecting other inmates' safety and property and by acting honestly. Cooperation benefits both inmates. However, there is also a chance that an inmate won't cooperate. Instead, the inmate may choose to take advantage of the other person. Inmates can act uncooperatively and cause physical, psychological, economic, and social harm. This includes disrespect, rape, theft, assault, murder, betrayal, and opportunism when exchanging contraband.[19] Social dilemma models in which people have imperfect information and cannot rely on third-party enforcement of agreements suggest that inmates will often rationally take actions that lead to less desirable social outcomes overall.

The chief psychologist at the federal prison in Leavenworth describes the uniqueness of the environment. He explains, "When you are small and need help, you run to your parents. When you get older, you run to a priest, a minister, a psychologist. If you have a legal problem, you hire an attorney. If someone threatens you, you call a cop. In prison there is no one to turn to, no one to solve your problems for you. If you go to the guards, you will be known as a snitch and that can get you killed. So you are on your own, perhaps for the first time in your life, and you are forced to deal with your own problems. Believe me, the guy demanding that you drop your drawers isn't going to be a good sport and simply let you walk away. You must either be willing to fight or you must give in."[20]

Gresham Sykes's pioneering study, *The Society of Captives,* describes the dilemma facing inmates. Each inmate must decide if he will, "bind himself to his fellow captives with ties of mutual aid, loyalty, affection, and respect, firmly standing in opposition to the officials. On the other hand, he can enter into a war of all against all in which he seeks his own advantage without reference to the claims or needs of other prisoners."[21] This depicts a state of nature where people lack the formal institutions that constrain violence and predation. In this anarchic jungle, the shared strategies, norms, and rules that inmates adopt will determine whether the inmates' existence is solitary, poor, nasty, brutish, and short.[22] In Thomas Hobbes's classic 1651 work of political philosophy, *Leviathan,* people in a state of nature rely on a sovereign to save themselves from the destitution and chaos of statelessness.[23] Leviathan punishes those who violate others' property rights, and without it, order or peaceful exchange could not prevail. The sovereign solves the social dilemma by punishing people who do not cooperate. In the prison context, the state seems practically omnipresent. Why don't inmates rely entirely on the state to solve their social dilemmas?

First, correctional officers have limited resources. According to one study, inmates learn that "no amount of supervision, no physical barriers, can prevent their being the object of threats and advances ranging from simple pleas to physical violence."[24] A facility with thousands of inmates means that officers can't watch and protect everyone. At San Quentin State Prison, after an attack left an inmate with multiple stab wounds and a large slash across his head, a correctional officer explained, "When you got this many guys out on the yard, they can pull this stuff off without being seen."[25] One inmate explained, "They [correctional officers] can't really protect you in here from rape. They got their hands full. When you got 64 guys in one dorm and we're all moving around, one's [a guard] in the shower, one's in the bathroom, one's talking to the free man, you know, by the time he'd know it's done [a rape]."[26] A former inmate explained that officers "can't see half the shit that goes on. They don't know dick about this stuff. We knew exactly where to go to fight and how to get away with it."[27] When officers learn of an assault, uncertainty about what happened may make it infeasible to do anything. Inmates sometimes falsely accuse others of theft or assault, and officers often have little information to judge the veracity of such claims. Inmates might intentionally harm themselves in order to get time away from a prison job or to move to a more preferred cell block.[28] Inmates who inform on others are often subject to ostracism, severe beatings, and even murder. This makes many inmates—even those who are subject to violence themselves—hesitant to provide information about misconduct.

Second, correctional officers may shirk their responsibilities. Many correctional officers are highly proficient at their job, and there is, of course, much variation in job performance.[29] However, just like everyone else, not all officers work as hard as they can at every moment. Supervisors cannot monitor correctional officers perfectly, and some officers find ways to avoid work. It takes time to file a discipline report against an inmate. Punishing one inmate can generate blowback from the inmate or his friends. If these efforts don't directly benefit the officer, then he may think twice about giving it his all. Many inmates believe that correctional officers are stupid and lazy. One former inmate complained that they are "fucking useless.... They are always standing around, doing nothing, or they say shit to us to piss us off.... If some guy is hassling me, I'm supposed to go to the guards?"[30] One inmate complained to a correctional officer that an inmate was threatening him, only to be told that "there is nothing that we can do about it, and there is nothing that the brass can do about it, so hit him [the hostile inmate]."[31] A guard at the U.S. Federal Prison in Leavenworth explains, "Most of us have wives and kids or grandkids. You tell me: Are you going to risk your life by stepping in front of a knife when you have one lousy piece of shit trying to kill another lousy piece of shit?"[32] Frankly, some inmates don't do much to endear themselves to correctional officers. They insult and assault staff. In some cases, they even "gas" officers by throwing feces and urine on them. As sociologist Donald Cressey describes it, the guards "have withdrawn to the walls, leaving inmates to intimidate, rape, maim, and kill each other with alarming frequency."[33]

Inmate victimization may also occur because of guards' inexperience rather than laziness. A deputy's first job out of the training academy is often to work in the county jail. The least experienced officers enter a world occupied by menacing people, complex social relationships, and gang politics. Training occurs beforehand, but the classroom doesn't teach many of the most important skills necessary for rookies to negotiate these interactions. Inmates are master manipulators and constantly attempt to "get one over" on correctional officers.[34] It takes time to learn the potential pitfalls, and "merely being hired does not make one a guard in the truest sense of the word. The new guard must first become 'con-wise.' That is, he must come to have an understanding of the inmate culture, certain expectations of inmates, and a method of interacting with them that is common to guards."[35]

In addition, sheriff's departments often send deputies accused of wrongdoing on the job—from bar fights to more serious corruption claims—to work at the county jail, to keep them away from the public. This means that, in many jails, the people responsible for protecting inmates and maintaining a safe facility are those with either the least experience or histories of misconduct. Perhaps it shouldn't be surprising to learn that deputies have smuggled in contraband. The California Legislative Analyst's Office reports that prison employees are the main source of smuggled cell phones in prison.[36] In one instance, a Los Angeles County Jail deputy received thousands of dollars to smuggle in phones, private messages, and cigarettes.[37] In another case, officials caught an officer smuggling a heroin-filled burrito to an inmate.[38] Recently, allegations have been made that officers at the Los Angeles County Jail use unwarranted violence against inmates, and they have allowed (and even encouraged) inmates to assault and rape others.[39] Officers reportedly enforce a code of silence that makes whistle-blowers hesitant to step forward. Not all correctional officers engage in this egregious behavior, and many inmate complaints about correctional officers are total fabrications. Yet, the evidence suggests that officers, on occasion, break the rules.

While inmates value physical safety, contraband markets may be a more important sphere of self-governance. A flourishing illicit trade within jails and prisons supplies contraband.[40] However, prison regulations state that "an inmate may not exchange, borrow, loan, give away or convey personal property to or from other inmates."[41] As such, inmates must self-regulate exchange. Some inmates desire items that they are allowed to possess in certain quantities, but for which anything over a certain limit is forbidden. For example, regulations forbid an inmate from having more than two books of stamps. If he wants to purchase more, he will have to rely on illicit markets. An inmate need not be an avid letter writer to want more than the permissible allotment of stamps. Since the California Department of Corrections and Rehabilitation banned smoking in 2005, stamps have replaced cigarettes as the medium of exchange.

Inmates also demand goods and services that are legal in the free world but prohibited behind bars. Such items include money, tattoos, coded messages, computer disks, and catalogs that sell products "lacking serious literary, artistic, political, educational, or scientific value."[42] Inmates can't have maps of nearby areas or pornography. More recently, cell phones have become a serious contraband problem. Inmates have called friends, victims, and witnesses. Officials even confiscated two cell phones from notorious cult-leader Charles Manson.[43] Officials seized more than 15,000 cell phones from California inmates in 2011.[44] If we assume an interdiction rate of 25 percent, that implies there are 60,000 cell phones behind bars. At an interdiction rate of 10 percent, there's nearly enough phones for every inmate in the prison system. Moreover, many inmates have SIM cards and simply rent phones from others. During 11 days at one California prison, officials used a smartphone-tracking device and detected more than 25,000 unauthorized calls, texts, and Internet requests.[45] Inmates are clearly taking advantage of this, and many other, illicit markets.

Another important type of contraband is controlled substances. Despite notable efforts to stop the smuggling and trafficking of drugs, county jails and state prisons remain inundated with them. Warden Patrick Arvonio explained, "Nobody can convince me that there's a county jail, a prison, a juvenile detention center, or any other place where you have drug addicts locked up, that there's not drugs in the facility. There is no such place."[46] Drug-dealing in prison generates substantial profits, and prison drug dealers cannot rely on official forms of social control to ensure that their businesses run smoothly.

Gresham Sykes and Sheldon Messinger note that for contraband markets to operate, "a large share of the 'extra' goods that enter the inmate social system must do so as the result of illicit conniving against the officials, which often requires lengthy and extensive cooperation and trust."[47] Inmates cannot rely on official mechanisms to establish trust while trading contraband. Extralegal governance mechanisms must elicit cooperation.

Economists and political scientists have offered several potential solutions to social dilemmas. The most obvious solution is to appoint a third party to punish defection, but officials cannot do so because of their own resource and motivation constraints and inmates' peculiar and illicit needs. Economists have offered a second solution, which is that people can become more cooperative when they interact repeatedly.[48] Gordon Tullock refers to this as the "discipline of continuous dealings," because the benefits of future interactions—the allure of profit opportunities—constrain one's bad behavior in the present.[49] This works especially well when two people's interactions are indefinitely repeated because there is an endless bounty of benefits to be had—or lost. However, indefinitely repeated games do not necessarily guarantee a cooperative outcome.[50] Inmates might still find uncooperative behavior profitable. In reality, people often choose their strategies by coordinating on focal choices—a choice that seems natural, special, or relevant.[51] In conflict situations, cultural, historical, and social factors play an important role in determining which choices are focal.[52] Many individuals in the inmate population have disturbing histories, vocalize a culture of mayhem, and praise those who act violently, which will tend to undermine coordination on cooperative outcomes.

Even if people want to act cooperatively, the discipline of continuous dealing is premised on several conditions that are not likely to be present in prison. First, the allure of future benefits is ineffective when people do not anticipate exchanging in the future. If I only act cooperatively because I want to benefit from future exchanges, then in the last exchange we make, I'll defect. Since you know that I think that way, neither of us trusts each other and we don't make that trade. We then realize that the previously second-to-last exchange is now the last, so we again both plan to defect. The problem, of course, is that we both know the other will defect, so that exchange does not take place either. This unravels all the way back to our first exchange, so we never trust each other, and we don't exchange at all.[53]

If people do not know ex-ante when the interactions will stop, they can still establish a self-enforcing equilibrium in which both cooperate with each other.[54] However, in prison, many inmates have unambiguous release dates, which are often public knowledge. When inmates know this, they get mean. Inmates often challenge those who are approaching their release date because fighting back can lead to additional charges or loss of good-time credit. The pending absence of future beneficial exchange makes cooperation less profitable.

A second way to get around this problem is to allow people to choose with whom to interact. If people can choose to live or trade only with those they trust, then people have an incentive to establish good reputations.[55] Honest people only trade with other honest traders. Cheaters never prosper. Two problems arise here. First, if honest traders do not trade with cheaters, then cheaters have no incentive to be peaceful once they have a bad reputation. They might as well plunder rather than produce. Second, in the prison context, inmates have very little control over who they will live with. The very nature of incarceration is that people are forced to live in an environment that they did not choose—an involuntary association.

A third characteristic that makes the discipline of continuous dealing more effective is when both parties are patient. Patient people are willing to wait to enjoy the benefits of future interactions. Impatient people discount future benefits highly, so those benefits are less likely to deter the short-term, immediate benefits of uncooperative behavior. In surveying the economic approach to crime and punishment, economist Edward Glaeser explains, "crime may be more appealing to people who live in the present; crime seems to offer immediate rewards, and the costs of crime, especially lengthy prison sentences, are paid for only over time."[56] On average, people in prison are less patient and therefore less likely to cooperate. John DiIulio explains that crime-prone youth are "radically present oriented" and that they are "almost completely incapable of deferring gratifications for the sake of future rewards."[57] Kenneth Avio refers to the "widely held belief that offenders as a whole tend to discount the future more heavily than non-offenders."[58] Self-enforcing solutions to social dilemmas don't come easily.

Norms and Organizations Provide Governance

Inmates have a need for governance, but they cannot fully rely on third-party enforcement (the correctional officers) or the discipline of continuous dealings to solve their problems. Inmates use two alternative sources to official mechanisms: norms and organizations. Norms identify the permitted, obliged, and forbidden behaviors of people with particular attributes in a given context.[59] Norms are a familiar part of our daily lives. They tell us to cover our mouths when we cough and to hold doors open for others. They are guidelines for how to act in society. They tell us the behaviors that we may do, must do, and must not do. Appreciation for norms arises through interactions with others in a community. Norms are not a fixed, immutable feature of society. They change according to the needs and resources of people in a particular context.[60] Norms arise to coordinate people's actions, and as people's needs for coordination changes, norms change in response. They differ between communities when those communities face different problems.

An important attribute of norms is that there is no individual designated to punish someone who violates a norm. Punishment is decentralized. When I walk through a door, I'm supposed to hold it open for the person entering after me. If I fail to do this, there is no designated person to publicly shame me. No commission or bureaucracy has determined the appropriate punishment. People have an idea of what a proportional punishment entails, and it is up to them to choose to apply it. There is no designated person to impose a punishment and no venue for discussing what the punishment is and how it will be implemented.

Norm-guided governance is relatively inexpensive. Norms do not require that everyone meet in a large auditorium and then decide—perhaps after vigorous debate and voting—that it is rude to cough on someone. To engage in collective decision-making for every possible social interaction would be tremendously burdensome. Moreover, to assign a group of people to monitor for and identify when these norm violations occur and to punish them would be quite costly—certainly more than the benefit of reducing mildly and moderately discourteous behavior. In many instances, decentralized punishment is efficient. In some cases, however, it is worth the time and effort to be careful and clear about which behaviors are acceptable.

An alternative mechanism to limit bad behavior is an organization. Like norms, organizations delineate the behaviors that one may, must, and must not do. However, in addition, the rules that organizations create also designate specific individuals to punish rule violations. There is a rule-making process for establishing the range of punishments, one for assigning the authority to punish, and a procedure for imposing the punishments. Organizations create rules that have a clear "or else" threat.[61] Someone exists to monitor for rule violations and to carry through the threatened punishment. Organizations define and enforce the standards of acceptable behavior. The term *organization* encompasses a wide range of groups. Clearly, the government creates rules through its legislative, regulatory, and judicial actions. However, the government is not the only rule-maker. Self-governing communities can have their own sanctions and enforcements.[62] Homeowners associations, stock exchanges, bridge clubs, businesses, and universities each develop rules that govern people's actions and have a threat of punishment when people violate the rules.

Organizations that enforce rules are relatively costlier than norms because it takes time, effort, and resources to decide on the appropriate punishment, assign the authority to punish, and allow the punisher to do his or her job. Rule-making is costly. The community needs to establish ways of generating information about rule violations, designate who should punish the offender, what the punishment should be, and communicate to others that the punishment has been meted out. Organizations that establish rules, therefore, must also create mechanisms of information transmission and enforcement. These improve the effectiveness of governance but cost more than norms. Both norms and organizations have governed the hidden world of the inmate social system, so it provides an excellent context to understand how norms and organizations arise, operate, and evolve to create order.

The Era of the Convict Code

For as long as people have researched the prison social system, they have found that inmates follow a "convict code."[63] Researchers have referred to this code by numerous names, including the "inmate code" and the "prisoner code." Many inmates themselves refer to "the code" or the "convict code." Despite numerous names, they all refer broadly to the same basic set of norms. In surveying the literature on the informal subcultures of inmates, Lee Bowker finds that the code arises in many prison contexts; "all studies of prisoner subcultures describe the same basic sociocultural system, regardless of the location and characteristics of the institution."[64] One penologist reports that the convict code "is not peculiar to our prison, but exists in all prisons as well as in the culture of the underworld."[65] A more recent study describes prison culture as having "transmitted similar interpretations of sociosexual life over generations of inmates. Those same interpretations have been documented by prison researchers since the 1930s."[66]

The convict code describes the inmate norms that dictate how to interact with each other and with officials. Donald Clemmer's seminal study of inmate life, *The Prisoner Code*, explains it as follows: "the fundamental principle of the code may be stated thus: Inmates are to refrain from helping prison or government officials in matters of discipline, and should never give them information of any kind, and especially the kind which may work harm to a fellow prisoner. Supplementary to this, and following from it, is the value of loyalty among prisoners in the dealings with each other. This basic idea constitutes the prisoners' code."[67]

The code suggests a number of praiseworthy behaviors.[68] Never rat on a con. Don't be nosy. Don't have a loose lip. Don't put a guy on the spot. Be loyal to the cons. Don't lose your head. Do your own time. Don't exploit inmates. Don't break your word. Don't steal from cons. Don't sell favors. Don't be a racketeer. Don't renege on debts. Don't weaken. Don't whine. Don't admit guilt. Don't be a sucker.

The convict code reduces conflict with other inmates by coordinating people's actions and expectations. This norm-based coordination mitigates the difficulties of imprisonment. In general, inmates recognize this, and they believe that the best way to accomplish their goals in prison is by following the convict code. Sykes and Messinger reported that, although inmates often fall short of the code's commands, "observers of the prison are largely agreed that the inmate code is outstanding both for the passion with which it is propounded and the almost universal allegiance verbally accorded it."[69]

A study from 1974 explains, "the inmate social roles set up a system of mutual care and protection. The mutual obligations created within the inmate culture strengthen inmate morale and, more significantly, protect inmates engaged in illicit activities.... [T]he strongest tenet in the inmate code of behavior is the rule that one inmate must not interfere with another inmate's participation in illicit activity."[70] The convict code provides "the legal environment of the sub rosa system. The code approves any kind of abuse against the prison administrators, who represent the society that rejected and imprisoned them; conversely, the code does not tolerate abuses of one member of the culture by another member."[71]

The need for institutions to facilitate social cooperation is of great importance. For contraband markets to operate effectively, inmates must find ways to secure property rights, make agreements, and resolve disputes. Stealing from others, failing to repay one's debt, or failing to hand over contraband goods are important ways that illicit markets can fail, and inmates cannot look to official mechanisms for solutions. Inmates punish people who violate the norms, creating an incentive to reform one's behavior. By providing this governance, the code provides "satisfactory solutions for obtaining illegal goods and services to mitigate the prison poverty imposed upon the inmates."[72] "The strength of the inmate culture," write Vergil Williams and Mary Fish, "functioning around a code, is the guarantee of that cooperation."[73]

An inmate's adherence to the code determines his place in the social hierarchy. Sykes and Messinger report that "conformity to, or deviation from, the inmate code is the major basis for classifying and describing the social relations of prisoners."[74] John Irwin, penologist and former inmate at Soledad Prison, explains that the inmate society is "arranged in a hierarchy of prestige, power, and privilege."[75] The inmate's social ranking is determined by the extent to which inmates support the code and adhere to its dictates. If an inmate follows the convict code, inmates respect him. If he violates the code, inmates relegate him to a low-status position. An inmate's obedience to the norms determines his status and, in turn, how comfortably he lives.

An inmate's history also influences his standing in the social hierarchy. Bowker explains, "the assignment of prisoners to roles in the subculture is not random, nor is it based merely on personality characteristics. Preprison criminal career is an important determinant of prisoner role occupancy."[76] Child molesters and informants rank low in the inmate hierarchy, and these inmates often face a presumptive threat of assault.[77] Inmates claim that assaulting child molesters is, in part, a way to establish the social hierarchy. Assaulting someone is a clear signal to other inmates that one is not associated with the individual and does not approve of his actions. Inmates use violence to create social distance between themselves and undesirables.

Though murderers typically rank high in the inmate social order, the nature of their crime can undermine that status. The warden at San Quentin, Louis Nelson, claims that inmates view killers poorly if they victimized women. Even for Charles Manson, Nelson explained, "it would be dangerous to put a guy like Manson into the main population, because in the eyes of other inmates he didn't commit first-class crimes. He was convicted of killing a pregnant woman, and that sort of thing doesn't allow him to rank very high in the prison social structure. It's like being a child molester. Guys like that are going to do hard time wherever they are."[78]

Because crimes committed in an inmate's past partly determine his status, the social hierarchy is not completely fluid. Prison officials Lloyd McCorkle and Richard Korn, writing in 1954, described the prison community as having a "rigidly hierarchical character.... The number of roles an individual may play are severely limited and, once assigned, are maintained—particularly at the lower status levels—with enormous group pressure."[79] Nevertheless, one's place is not completely fixed, either. Inmate behavior provides opportunities for promotion and demotion, and Clemmer notes, it "is quite possible for a man in the middle group to rise to the upper group through behavior which bears the stamp of the prisoners' approval, such as assaulting an officer or refusing to give information to authorities, even though punished. Similarly, a member of the elite class may lose case and no longer be treated as a social equal by his former companion through behavior which is contrary to the class code."[80]

There is some debate over how much differentiation exists in the inmate social hierarchy. Some scholars argue that the key distinction is simply between "convicts" who follow the code and "inmates" who do not.[81] Others argue for a more fine-grained distinction between numerous inmate classes.[82] The most important points to recognize are that there is a hierarchy, it is not perfectly mobile, and it is determined by the evaluations of other inmates.[83]

Ignoring the code would relegate an inmate to a low rung on the social ladder. Moreover, while inmates might resist the code or violate its precepts, the code's importance is evidenced by the fact that inmates conceal behavior that violates it. Inmates do not announce loudly to others when they inform on someone or pilfer someone's cell. Clemmer argues that the code's persistence, "in spite of violation and the fact that it does control conduct in many instances and tends to control it in other instances, shows its vigor. The fact that most violations of it are hidden and secret is further emphasis of its controlling force."[84] The existence of the norms places an obligation on an inmate. Bowker notes that "for one prisoner to make behavioral demands on another prisoner that are based on these norms is considered proper."[85]

Punishment of norm-violators takes place in several ways. Disesteeming someone provides a low-cost, decentralized method of doing so. Gossip is most effective against people who wish to be viewed well by the gossiper. The norm-violator may not be aware of the gossip, but he will still be punished, as people are less likely to interact with him or are more likely to challenge him. Quite often, gossipers intend to be heard, so the punishment comes in the form of the disrespect and shame of being spoken of poorly. Gossip can also help an inmate discover which inmates have friends who will defend his character.[86]

An elaborate prison argot aids gossip, and it is helpful in distinguishing social status and defining others' status. Inmates develop slang with precise meanings that help define the relationship among inmates.[87] For example, some terms—*rapo, lame, cho mo* (prison parlance for a rapist, a naïve or stupid inmate, and a child molester)—carry strong connotations because they are the labels of the most despised classes of prison inmates. An inmate at San Quentin got into a fight just a few days before his parole date because someone insulted him. He explained, "I was supposed to parole on Monday. I did everything I could to avoid the situation. I did everything I could. When people say certain words in prison—*punk, bitch, lame*—things like that, it's an automatic fighting word."[88] Particular words in the prison argot carry clear meanings, and using them is an attempt to assign an inmate to a particular class of inmates. As such, gossip and name-calling can be quite effective.

Ostracism is a second form of decentralized punishment. An individual who does not approve of an inmate's behavior can avoid interacting with him. He won't share cigarettes or food. He won't share a cell with him. He won't defend him if he is attacked. According to Clemmer, some of the benefits of having a group to interact with include the "exchanges of confidences, the sharing of luxuries, the toleration of annoying conduct," and the willingness to accept punishment for others.[89] Ostracism is an easy way to impose costs on someone who doesn't follow the convict code. It requires little or no coordination with others. Each man chooses to impose these costs at his own discretion.

While gossip and ostracism can be effective, some transgressions merit more severe punishment. Violence is a powerful mechanism for punishing norm violations. There are many attractive features of using violence to punish wrongdoers. First, it has many gradations.[90] Punishment can entail a slap, punch, kick, beating, group assault, stabbing, slashing, rape, or murder. Inmates can punish increasingly serious offenses in increasingly stronger ways. Second, violence communicates information to other people about an individual's loyalty to the code. For example, an inmate who receives a beating for a relatively minor violation will recover in a few days. There is not necessarily a permanent tarnish to his reputation. However, if inmates want to communicate a stronger message about someone's character, they may slash the person across the cheek. "It's fairly common," says San Quentin's Sergeant Thompson, "that they'll try to cut each other in the face. Just another way in prison of knowing that somebody is no good. He's in bad standing. He has a cut mark across his face."[91] The scar communicates that someone had a serious complaint about that person's behavior. Killing someone provides the ultimate check on bad behavior.

Individuals and informal groups have enforced the convict code in an incredibly decentralized fashion. Prior to the 1960s, inmates mostly grouped together in small factions based on pre-prison acquaintances and cultural similarities.[92] Groups improved the effectiveness of gossip and ostracism. Group activity was also necessary when inmates deemed a substantial amount of violence as suitable, or when they required coordination to prevent official reprimand for using violence. When inmates grouped together with other inmates, they typically did so with those who shared the same status in the inmate hierarchy. One inmate describes the remarkably casual nature of the informal groupings in the 1930s: "Prisoners, when there is a chance to do so, divide naturally into groups of not more than four or five men, unless they are players or spectators at some game, and most of the groups are smaller—three men or four are accustomed to walk together or sit together in their spare time."[93] A study of 177 inmates from this era found that only 17.4 percent of the inmates claimed to have had a strong affiliation with a distinct group of inmates. Forty-two percent of inmates were ungrouped.[94]

Informal groups, often called "tips" or "cliques," helped resolve disputes. Irwin describes them as "extended social networks or crowds that were loosely held together by shared subcultural orientations or preprison acquaintances. Most of the tips were intraracial, and they were overlapping and interconnected. An individual could be involved in more than one tip and usually was related to other tips that connected with his own."[95] When conflicts arose, inmates relied on these loose networks. He recounts an incident about a white inmate incarcerated in the 1950s:

> Me and this Chicano dude got into it at work and it got pretty hairy. After we called each other a sack of mother fuckers, he told me I better have my stuff (knife) next time we meet. I split and went around locating a shiv, but I also swung by and talked to a Chicano who I did time with in Lancaster. We were still tight and I thought he might know this other dude and be able to straighten it out without us getting it on. I told him what had happened and asked him who this other Chicano was in a way to kind of let him know that I would be happy to have it cooled. Well, it worked and in a few hours I got the word that everything was all right and why didn't we just forget it.[96]

Sometimes people who were influential among a cohort would take on leadership roles, but they played a very limited part. "Prison leaders, except in conflict situations, have no definite program," explains Clemmer, "The only objective which the group and leader share is to make the time pass as agreeably and as comfortably as possible."[97] A leadership role was limited because groups were small and transitory. Leaders would lose their positions when "the bonds in a group, seldom very strong, weaken.... [T]he prison group leader may be considered as a person who, for a relatively short period of time, guides and controls the less important opinions and behavior of his group in a minor way by behavior which they tentatively approve."[98]

In stark contrast to modern prison gangs, there were no hierarchies to ascend, no votes to win, no coalitions to organize, no politicking to achieve a leadership role, and no grand use of power. Leadership was transitory and carried few privileges and responsibilities. Membership was not mutually exclusive or permanent. An inmate might intermingle with people from several different groups, based on race, hometown, or personal interests. Participation was voluntary, and no expectation of continued association lasted, especially beyond prison walls. There were no well-established internal structures and few, if any, collective decision-making mechanisms. Groups were small. Each of these characteristics of informal inmate groups is a notable departure from modern prison gangs.

No group of inmates met and decided that the convict code was the acceptable standard of behavior. No group was charged with evaluating everyone's behavior, establishing an accurate social ranking, and punishing misdeeds. Punishment was decentralized. Norms emerged to solve the particular problems faced by inmates. The convict code facilitated social cooperation and diminished social conflict. It helped establish order and promote illicit trade. People who followed the code made life in the community easier, and inmates respected them for this. People who violated the code caused conflict and disrupted order in the inmate social system. Inmates who didn't live up to the convict code were ostracized, ridiculed and mocked, challenged, assaulted, stolen from, and killed.

The Weakening of the Convict Code

The convict code provided the foundation for a reputation-based governance system. However, beginning in the 1950s, it started to fall short of inmates' needs. Irwin writes that by 1970, "there [was] no longer a single, overarching convict culture."[99] By that time, the "reverberations from the 1960s [had] left most men's prisons fragmented, tense, and often extremely violent. The old social order, with its cohesion and monotonous tranquility, did not and perhaps [would] never reappear. The prisoners are divided by extreme differences, distrust, and hatred."[100] Norms were no longer the dominant source of governance. Instead, Irwin writes, violent inmates, "who, in the pursuit of loot, sex, respect, or revenge, will attack any outsider have completely unraveled any remnants of the old codes of honor.... [V]iolence-oriented groups dominate many, if not most, large men's prisons."[101] In 1975, James Jacobs wrote that "the old picture of the prisons as an inclusive normative and moral community toward which the individual had to take a stance is no longer accurate. The prison is now a conflict-ridden setting where the major battles are fought by intermediate level inmate groups rather than by staff and inmates or by inmates as unaligned individuals."[102]

The convict code was the foremost self-governance mechanism prior to the mid-1950s and, according to Irwin and Jacobs, had become ineffective by the mid-1970s. The principles of the code continue to receive verbal support today—and many of the code's behaviors are enforced by gangs—but the decentralized, norm-based governance that existed in the earlier era is no longer sufficient to provide the governance that inmates demand. Past work on norms suggests several specific empirical predictions about why norms fail. Most important, key changes in inmate demographics upset the order created by the convict code.[103]

First, norms can be remarkably effective at facilitating social cooperation when there are relatively few people involved.[104] It is easier to communicate reputations in small groups. In a close-knit community, everyone knows how someone has acted in the past. If someone cheats, everyone knows this and can refuse to interact with the person. With fewer people in a community, it is possible to know how trustworthy everyone is. However, the more people there are, the more costly it is to learn and remember information about others.

In addition, the number of possible interactions increases as the population grows. For instance, as the division of labor increases with the extent of the market, people will specialize more narrowly and trade more broadly. With greater opportunities for interactions, there are more opportunities for others to defect. Because information costs increase in larger groups, it is more difficult to identify how reliable and honest other people are. With less information about any random inmate, people become more cautious about interacting with others. Inmates spend more time and energy learning about a particular person. This increases the transaction costs of doing business and therefore reduces the volume of trade. In large groups, one person can violate the norms and still have plenty of other people who don't know his reputation with whom to trade. In small groups, opportunism is costly because it drives away potential trading partners. The desire to trade keeps people honest.

Norms are also less effective when communities are large because punishing norm violations provides a public good to others. It is costly for someone to observe a norm violation, punish the person, and communicate that information to others. Doing so benefits the community because it deters future violations of the norms. The problem is that producing this public good suffers from the free-rider problem. Because others enjoy much of the benefit of punishing norm violations, each individual may choose not to. In small groups, it is easier to monitor for free-riding and to punish it when it occurs, and each person's contribution is more decisive. Larger groups, by contrast, will prove to be less observant and less informed, meaning that norms provide less information and produce less governance. In short, norms will be effective at providing governance when the inmate population is relatively small, but as it grows, norms will break down.

Consistent with this argument, the California prison system underwent unprecedented growth in its inmate population during the time that the convict code weakened. The population of the entire system (measured at the end of each year) was relatively small for nearly 100 years (Figure 2.1). Before 1948, it never exceeded 10,000 inmates, and before 1924, the total inmate population was always less than 5,000. From 1851 to 1900, the average annual inmate population was less than 1,000 inmates. Despite a quickly growing state population, the average year-end inmate population in its first 100 years (from 1851 to 1951) was still less than 3,400 inmates. Starting in the late 1940s, however, California began to incarcerate many more people. Between 1945 and 1970, the population increased from 6,600 to almost 25,000 inmates—a 378 percent increase. The prison system experienced 24 years of sustained growth in the inmate population, and it grew larger

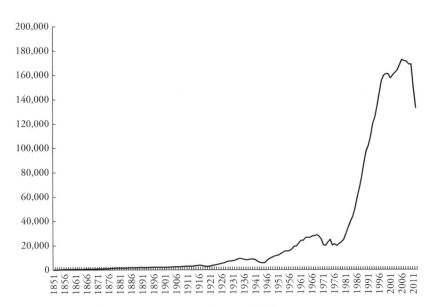

FIGURE 2.1 Total year-end inmate population in California, 1851–2012

Source: California Department of Corrections and Rehabilitation, Annual Reports

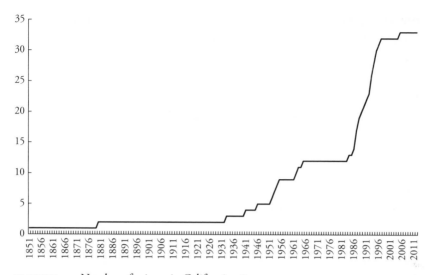

FIGURE 2.2 Number of prisons in California, 1851–2012
Source: California Department of Corrections and Rehabilitation, Locations Statewide

than ever before. The 1980s and 1990s saw an even more incredible prison buildup. In 2007, there were more than 170,000 inmates in the California prison system. Moreover, the total number of prisons increased from 5 in 1950 to 33 facilities in 2012 (Figure 2.2).

The populations were also increasing remarkably quickly at both of California's two oldest prisons, San Quentin and Folsom. In 1900, their combined inmate populations were 2,131 inmates. By 1963, their populations had risen to 7,478. Although the state built more prisons to hold the swelling number of inmates, they did not build them fast enough. From 1945 to 1963, the average number of inmates per facility increased from 2,135 to 3,009 (Figure 2.3). In 2012, facilities held an average of roughly 4,000 inmates. Wave after wave of new inmates undermined the small, close-knit community where a reputation-based governance system had previously worked well. The convict code could not provide governance as well because it required that people's reputations be widely known. In this massive new population, it was not possible for decentralized information transmission to communicate reputations effectively.

These changes didn't diminish the need for governance; in fact, they amplified it. Not only did the prison system house more inmates, it incarcerated more violent offenders. From 1951 to 1980, the percentages of inmates serving time for a violent offense increased from 43.6 percent of the population to 63.5 percent. The ratio of violent to nonviolent offenders increased

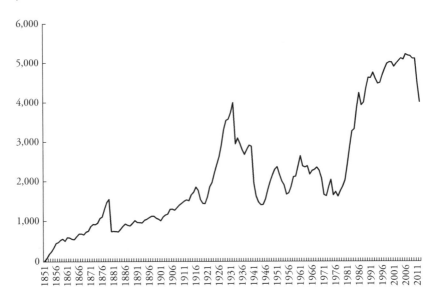

FIGURE 2.3 Average number of inmates per facility in California, 1851–2012

Source: California Department of Corrections and Rehabilitation, Annual Reports and Locations Statewide

from 0.62 in 1961 to 1.74 in 1981 (Figure 2.4). The spike in the presence of violent offenders, combined with the surge in inmate population, undermined the convict code as a governance mechanism.

Imagine that all of the inmates who entered the prison system in a particular year did so on the same day, and you—a nonviolent offender—are one of them. If violent offenders are more likely to assail nonviolent offenders, then you are in a more perilous situation the greater the proportion of violent offenders. There is a greater chance that you will become a target. But it would also be reasonable to care not just about the proportion of violent inmates but also about how many violent offenders surround you. The number of inmates arriving into the prison system for violent crimes increased during the period from 1951 to 2011 (Figure 2.4). In 1951, only 973 violent offenders would enter prison alongside you. By 2010, 13,816 violent offenders would enter prison at your side. This environment does not engender honest, trustworthy behavior. Inmates needed even more governance than in earlier periods, when there were smaller, less violent populations, but it was precisely at this time that norms were likely to be least helpful.

Entering prison means learning a new set of norms. Donald Clemmer describes the process that new inmates face as "prisonization."[105] Inmates who

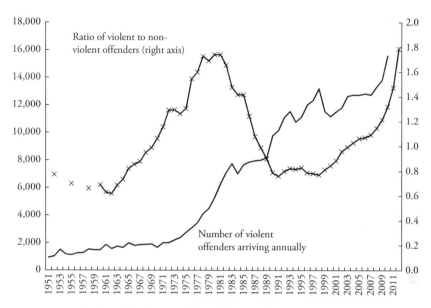

FIGURE 2.4 Violent offenders in California prisons, 1951–2011
Source: California Department of Corrections and Rehabilitation, Annual Reports

have served a sentence before are more likely to know the code, to abide by it, and to enforce it. At one prison, hard-core believers in the convict code had twice as much previous incarceration experience as those inmates who were less strongly committed to the code.[106] Some new inmates may be ignorant of the norms, but as they spend more time behind bars and interact with inmates, prisonization increases their awareness. Some inmates will have knowledge of these norms before they enter prison. Relatives and friends may communicate this information to them before their arrival.[107] Some inmates will enter the prison in ignorance but quickly learn the norms. Other inmates may never fully grasp the norms. When ignorant new inmates blunder into the society of captives, they undermine the social order.

Ignorance of the norms will be greatest when inmates arrive in prison for the first time, so norms will be less effective when a greater proportion of arriving inmates have never served a prison sentence. In 1951, about half of the inmate population had served a prior prison sentence (Figure 2.5). By 1984 (the last year for which I have data), that number had fallen to 43 percent. By 1975, when Irwin argues a unified convict code no longer existed, only 35.6 percent of inmates in the prison population had already served a prior prison sentence. In 1951, nearly 60 percent of inmates arriving at prison had served a

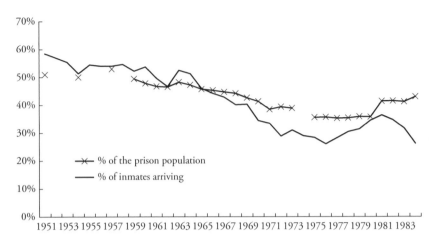

FIGURE 2.5 Inmates in California with a prior prison commitment, 1951–1984
Source: California Department of Corrections and Rehabilitation, Annual Reports

prior prison sentence, but only 26.8 percent had by 1984. If inmates don't know and enforce the convict code, then it cannot be used to govern.

Norms are also more effective in communities with substantial ethnic and cultural homogeneity.[108] There is greater consensus among inmates about the norms. It's easier to converge on the accepted standard of behavior and the proper sanctions for infringements. Members of homogenous groups may have other-regarding preferences, so that inmates value the benefits others receive when one enforces the norms. People share the same cultural materials—language, experience, and mental models—that improve the effectiveness of communication, monitoring, and enforcement efforts. Homogenous groups may be more tight-knit, which means it is easier to find and punish norm violators, and their frequent interactions transform the environment from a one-shot interaction into a repeated interaction.

There were notable changes in the ethnic and racial background of the inmate population during the period of the code's decline. In 1951, white inmates dominated the prison population—two white inmates for every minority (Figure 2.6). However, each subsequent year the percentage of blacks and Hispanic inmates grew larger. By 2011, there was one white inmate for every three minorities. In 1950, 972 minority inmates entered the system alongside nearly 2,000 white inmates. By 2009, almost 10,000 white inmates arrived amid 27,000 minorities. This dramatic change in ethnic and racial group challenged long-held inmate privileges and ways of life.

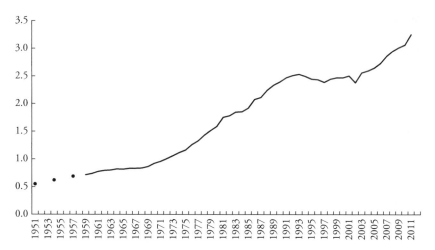

FIGURE 2.6 Ratio of minority to white inmates in California, 1951–2011
Source: California Department of Corrections and Rehabilitation, Annual Reports

Previously, there was relatively little conflict between races and ethnic groups. According to Irwin, based on his incarceration experience, inmates of different races "were somewhat hostile toward each other and followed informal patterns of segregation, but there was commingling between all races and many prisoners maintained close friendships with members of other racial groups."[109] Edward Bunker, an inmate at San Quentin in the 1950s, explains that "although each race tended to congregate with their own, there was little overt racial tension or hostility. That would change in the decade ahead."[110] During this transformative period, when the ethnic and racial composition inverted, an inmate's obligations and interactions became markedly different. Bunker describes it as a race war. His former friends were now rival combatants, so "what I did for a black friend in the mid-fifties is something I would never have even considered a decade later."[111] By 1990, "race [overrode] all of these particular identities and influence[d] every aspect of prison life."[112] During a time when civil rights were being advanced in society, inmates were in the process of crystallizing and solidifying racial segregation.

Research in a broad range of situations finds that greater ethnic and social diversity is associated with lower contributions to public goods and collective goods.[113] Greater ethnic and racial differences reduce public-good provision, making norms less effective. Ethnic fractionalization measures the approximate probability that two randomly drawn individuals from the population belong to different ethnic groups (in this case, white, black, Hispanic, and other).[114] From 1951 to 1975, ethnic fractionalization of the prison population increased from 52 percent to 64 percent. In 2011, ethnic fractionalization stood at 69 percent. The convict code failed to overcome the increasing ethnic and racial heterogeneity.

While the prison system grew in size and diversity, it did not grow older. The resident population was becoming younger. Young people create problems for norms.[115] To understand the effect of younger inmates, researchers interviewed older, serial offenders about their experiences behind bars. Inmates referred disparagingly to young inmates as "boys trying to become men."[116] One inmate described them as the "Pepsi Generation," defined as "the young shuck and jive energized generation. The CYA [California Youth Authority] mentality guys in a man's body and muscles can really go out and bang if they want. They are the youngsters that want to prove something—how tough and macho and strong they are. This is their whole attitude. Very extreme power trip and machismo. The youngsters want to prove something. How tough they are. And there is really very little remorse."[117] Young inmates tend to be more disruptive and rowdy. One inmate observed that young inmates are "more violent. They are more spontaneous. I think they are very spontaneous. They certainly don't use TBYAS [think before you act and speak]. I think their motivation is shallower than it was years ago."[118]

Another inmate explained that young inmates' inexperience in prison meant that they don't know or follow the convict code. Youngsters lack "a juvenile record or anything like that, and so that when they come in they have no sense of what it is to do time.... Which means, for instance, that if they can get out of something they will go ahead and give somebody up or they will go against the code."[119] Young inmates make doing time more difficult, "there are so many children and kids in prison it is hard to do time now. It is not like it used to be where you can wake up one morning and know what to expect. But now you wake up and you don't know what to expect, anything might happen."[120] Disruptive young inmates also show "little or no respect for the older inmates, many of whom had long histories of prison life which normally would have provided them with a high degree of status."[121]

Young males spurned the convict code. With fewer people respecting the norms and fewer people choosing to enforce its edicts, it was less effective. From 1950 to 1981, the percentage of young male inmates steadily increased. By 1975, more than half of the inmate population was under the age of 30, and those aged 24 or younger composed about a quarter of the population. By contrast, in 1951, 39 percent of inmates were younger than 30. In 1950, only 799 inmates under the age of 25 entered the prison system. In 2011, more than 11,000 inmates under the age of 25 entered the California prison system.

Prisons in Turmoil

The prison population today is remarkably different from the prison population a century ago. The changing inmate demographics have played a critical role in altering how the convict code provides governance to the criminal underworld. These changes explain why the foremost governance mechanism weakened substantially over the span of less than two decades. The code became ineffective because there were more inmates, more violent offenders, more first-time inmates, and more young inmates. There was also a radical shift in the ethnic and racial background of inmates. Each of these demographic changes is associated with a weakening of decentralized governance mechanisms that rely on reputations.

The data do not exist to test the independent effect of each of these demographic changes on how they changed inmate governance institutions. The data show that the proportion of violent offenders and the percentage of young offenders in the population cannot give a full explanation for the weakening of the code. Both of these increased during the era of decline but later reverted to earlier levels. They may be necessary to the convict code's effectiveness, but they are not sufficient. Based on qualitative accounts, the rise of both violent and young offenders strained the inmate social system. In addition to disrupting established orders, young offenders also contributed less to producing decentralized governance. Both of these factors weaken norm-based governance. The inmate population has continued to swell. Past studies of norms identify the size of the population as a key factor in the viability of reputation-based governance. However, there is not enough variation in the size of the inmate population to test whether or not the population alone is sufficient to explain when norms are effective. By 2010, the male inmate population was nearly eight times larger than it was in 1970. Rather than make strong claims about which factors matter most and by how much, these data indicate that, taken together, demographic changes were an important reason for the convict code weakening when it did.

As norms failed, violence erupted. A report by the California Department of Corrections indicates that inmate violence was on the rise from 1960 to 1973.[122] Inmate-on-inmate stabbings, for example, increased from 28 to 179 during this period. Assaults against staff members rose from 32 to 84. In order to understand the rise in violence, the department studied what facility-level factors were associated with violence. They found that both smaller building and ground area and larger prison populations correlate strongly with increased prison violence at the facility level. This is consistent with the argument that larger populations cannot rely as much on norm-based governance. In addition, the department found no measurable impact on violence at the facility level from increasing the number of custody staff.[123] This implies that, on the margin, formal mechanisms of social control are not perfect substitutes for extralegal governance mechanisms. Each variable's relative importance in explaining facility-level violence was scored on a scale of 0 (weakest) to 100 (strongest). A facility with a high concentration of inmates incarcerated for violent crimes received the highest score, 69.6, with the next most important factors receiving much lower scores. The size of the inmate population (score of 8.7), having more minority inmates (7.2), the degree of overcrowding (5.8), and having more young inmates (8.7) all have some explanatory power.

This study supports the two main arguments laid out in this chapter. First, the data suggest that inmates do not rely entirely on official governance mechanisms. There is no distinguishable effect in this study from the number of custody staff on violence at the facility level. If, on the margin, inmates relied primarily on officials to prevent violence and resolve disputes, then we would expect to find that increasing the number of officials is associated with less violence. That is not the case. Second, the study finds that the same factors that reduce the effectiveness of norms are associated with more violence. Since norms resolve disputes and constrain violence, we would expect there to be more violence when they are less effective. That is precisely what the study finds: larger prisons, with more young inmates and a changing racial mix among the inmates, are more violent. As the convict code became ineffective, violence increased, and inmates sought new ways to protect themselves, their property, and the underground economy. As the next chapter will show, inmates turned to prison gangs for governance.

Death Row

AT 7 A.M. ON AUGUST 30, 2012, two San Quentin correctional officers were escorting a condemned inmate from the shower to his cell. When they opened the shower door, the inmate stabbed and slashed the officers on the head, necks, and arms with a razor blade that had been fashioned into a weapon. Officials subdued the inmate. The correctional officers received notable, but not life-threatening injuries. The assailant was a convicted murderer and gang member from Los Angeles named Timothy McGhee.[1] McGhee was a shot caller for a gang in Northeastern Los Angeles called Toonerville Rifa 13, a gang that has existed since the 1950s. A wanted poster issued by the Department of Justice described him as 5'11", 190 lbs., with gang tattoos on his chest, head, neck, and back. He earned his way to death row through a series of brutal, and sometimes random, murders in the Atwater Village neighborhood of Los Angeles.

In 2002, the U.S. Marshalls Services sought McGhee in connection with 12 murders. The victims included rival gang members, witnesses, and strangers. At the time of his arrest, he was on the U.S. Marshall's list of the 15 most wanted fugitives. More than two dozen officers arrested the 29-year-old in Bullhead City, Arizona, where he was living in a doublewide mobile home. Officials described McGhee's gang as highly regimented, and McGhee had a strong influence over the gang, even while incarcerated and on the run.

McGhee has been in and out of prison for most of his adult life. He served time for assault with a firearm in 1989. He was locked up in 1994 for assaulting a police officer. After three years in prison, the state released him, but he was returned on a parole violation a short time later. In 1999, he again experienced freedom, but it was short-lived, and he returned to prison in 2000. After yet another release, he lived with his grandmother in Pomona and enrolled at a local college, where he studied criminal justice. Authorities believe that he wanted to understand how the police conduct criminal investigations so that he could better evade detection and capture.

Detective Andy Teague described McGhee's apparent joy at killing, saying, "it's his high, and he does it for kicks."[2] Officials believe he first killed in 1997, when he murdered a rival gang member. In 1999, he was suspected of being involved in the murder of a rap artist's bodyguard. He was convicted of killing a 16-year-old in 2000, for the simple reason that the two young men shared the same street name. In 2000, two Toonerville gang members were engaged in a high-speed chase with Los Angeles Police Department officers. McGhee monitored a police radio scanner and coordinated a multiperson ambush on the officers. They threw a washing machine and other debris in front of the pursuing police car, forcing the officers to swerve into the gang's gunfire. Police believe that, in addition to orchestrating the ambush, he was one of the triggermen. Later that year, McGhee was suspected of killing a 17-year-old in the Los Angeles riverbed. A homeless man was shot and killed nearby that night, and police believe McGhee also killed him because he witnessed the young man's murder. In 2001, police believe he shot and killed a 21-year-old, and in the process shot and permanently brain-damaged his pregnant girl-friend. The following month, he killed three people (including a woman and her 64-year-old mother) because the daughter had allegedly told police that McGhee's sister was dealing drugs out of her house.

After his arrest in February 2003, McGhee was extradited to California and held in Men's Central Jail.[3] In January 2005, a riot occurred in the A-Row of the 3300 block, the highest security area of the jail. According to the appeals court ruling, McGhee "was the inmate leader of A-Row, i.e., he was the 'shot caller.' Thus, other inmates would ask appellant permission for various things."[4] On the afternoon of the riot, deputies noticed that another inmate, Mr. Gonzalez, was highly intoxicated. They wanted to extract him from his cell, but to avoid resistance they told him that his attorney was waiting to speak with him. The inmate complied and deputies escorted him in handcuffs down the tier past McGhee's cell, but McGhee intervened. According to the appellate ruling, McGhee "had not given Gonzalez permission to leave, [so] Gonzalez started to return to his cell."[5] At that point, the deputies started to remove the inmate forcefully. McGhee "shouted orders directing other inmates to throw liquids at the deputies. [McGhee] and other inmates...began pelting the deputies with apples, oranges, urine and bleach." The inmates began breaking up their sinks and throwing the porcelain and other items at the deputies. They started fires. It took several hours for the Emergency Response Team to quell the riot.

In 2007, McGhee was convicted of three counts of first-degree murder and four counts of attempted murder. Law enforcement officers believe that he committed other murders for which he was not convicted. During the sentencing, the judge speculated that McGhee seemed to find killing to be "some kind of perverse sport as if he was hunting human game."[6] During the trial, jurors heard some of McGhee's rap lyrics:

> Here I come last chance to run
> Killer with a gun out to have some fun
> In my dreams I hear screams
> Pleasure I feel is so obscene

The judge sentenced him to death. McGhee was shipped to the Condemned Unit at San Quentin, where he now waits to die. Even while incarcerated, he continues to harm people.

Dangerous men occupy the state's prisons and jails. Other inmates must find a way to survive while living among them.

3

The Rise of Prison Gangs

*The Mafia is, essentially, nothing but the expression of a
need for order, for the control of the State.*

JUDGE GIOVANNI FALCONE[1]

The Business of Private Protection

Before the mid-1970s, the convict code had provided governance relatively
effectively. Reputations were known in the inmate population, and the fear of
gossip, ostracism, and assault constrained much predatory and opportunistic
behavior. However, the convict code began to break down once large demographic changes occurred within the prison system. Inmates still voice respect
for the code today, but it cannot provide the governance that they require,
and it is not the preeminent governance institution. As demographic changes
made decentralized governance less effective, violence erupted and inmates
sought alternative sources of social control. Inmates turned to organizations—
prison gangs—to provide protection in the inmate social system. These organizations required effort to operate effectively, but if inmates did not bear
these costs, they would continue to suffer the consequences of disorder. By
recognizing inmates' demand for governance, we can identify why governance
institutions became more centralized and explain where and when prison
gangs form.

Like many other mafia groups, prison gangs originated to provide protection. Historically, organized crime has played a crucial role in producing governance in the underworld. In fact, what makes mafia groups unique is not
that they engage in crime in an organized and sophisticated fashion but that
they govern crime. They enforce the rules of the game that allow people to
participate in illicit markets. In surveying the interdisciplinary research on
organized crime, economist Stergios Skaperdas has found that "the defining
economic activity of organized crime is the provision of *protection* or its more

respectable variation, *security*."[2] Seminal work by Diego Gambetta examines the formation of the Sicilian Mafia during the 19th century, a time when state enforcement of property rights was uncertain and bandits preyed on the property of new landowners.[3] Landowners had a demand for private protection that the government did not satisfy, and the end of the feudal system meant that soldiers were available to offer their services as private rights-enforcers.[4] These men became mafiosi. They expanded into a number of other rights enforcement activities, including acting as third-party adjudicators of disputes, enforcing contracts, and punishing criminals.[5] Similar organizations arose in other parts of Italy—such as the 'NDrangheta and Camorra mafias in the Calabria and Naples regions.[6]

It is common for organized crime to form when newly established property rights have no effective state-based mechanisms to secure them. For instance, Federico Varese has shown that when the Soviet Union collapsed, property rights enforcement was incomplete and uncertain, and businesspeople had a strong demand for protection. Supplied by the abundance of now-unemployed Russian soldiers and secret police, the Russian Mafia stepped in to sell protection to businesses.[7] Surveys conducted in three Russian cities examined why shopkeepers purchase governance from private protection organizations. Respondents explained that their demand for these services stems from their activity in the informal and illicit economy, which they participate in to avoid strict government regulations.[8] Shopkeepers view these organizations as an alternative to the failing and ineffective state-based courts and police system. Surveys of Russian and Polish businesses in 1998 revealed three key facts that help make sense of private protection organizations.[9] First, merchants rely on private protection more when they participate in informal economic activity. Mafias provide a substitute to official mechanisms that people in the informal economy cannot rely on. Second, managers recognized that these organizations are costly and far from ideal, but they often consider private protection services to be beneficial. Third, merchants confirmed that rather than providing protection only from rival sellers of "protection," these organizations provided protection from real threats of theft and predation. This was not merely a protection racket.

In Japan, the Yakuza provides property rights protection to make up for inefficiencies "in formal legal structures, including both inefficient substantive law and a state-induced shortage of legal professional and other rights-enforcement agents."[10] The number of Japanese organized-crime firms is negatively correlated with the number of civil cases filed in district court, reported crimes, and loans outstanding. This suggests that the Japanese mafias "play an active entrepreneurial role in substituting for state-supplied enforcement mechanisms and other public services in such areas as dispute mediation, bankruptcy and debt collection, (unorganized) crime control, and finance."[11] Similarly, China's transition toward a more market-oriented economy includes land reforms and massive privatization of state-owned and rural enterprises. These changes have obscured property rights assignments. Uncertainty, systemic corruption, and weak judicial institutions left people in need of governance. Chinese mafia groups arose to adjudicate commercial disputes and facilitate cartelization of industries.[12]

Ethnographic studies of American street gangs in multiple major metropolitan areas have found that the gangs provide an important source of protection to its young members.[13] Gang members frequently report that they join street gangs because they need the protection that gangs supply, and "interview data have documented consistently that gang members are drawn to these groups for their perceived protective quality."[14] Individual-level data on gang membership and victimization are difficult to collect. One study, however, examined the relationship between the number of gang members in Los Angeles and the violent-crime rate. The conventional wisdom holds that gangs cause violent crime, but the evidence does not support this view. In fact, gang membership increases after increases in violent crime, rather than before it. This is consistent with the claim that people join gangs for protection from the violent crime that is occurring in their communities, not that they join gangs to participate in violent crime.[15]

Mafias do not materialize and come to power at random. They form in power vacuums where people cannot rely on state enforcement of property rights. They often control relatively small areas because it is too costly to keep out competing mafias.[16] Three potentially chaotic situations are typical. First, people might be so geographically isolated from the government that they are not protected. It isn't worth the government's effort to set up police departments and courts in remote areas that have few valuable resources, a primitive or languishing economy, or a small tax base. In the state's absence, people turn to local mafias for protection.

Second, people participating in prohibited trades, such as drugs, gambling, and prostitution, are excluded from using state-based legal institutions to secure governance. The illicit nature of the business forces them to seek alternatives. In the United States, the mafia came to power in the freewheeling alcohol markets of the Prohibition Era. They ended up playing a far-reaching and important role in enforcing agreements and settling disputes in the criminal underworld.[17] In addition to governing illicit markets, mafias often

help businesses manipulate legal markets. For example, local building con-
tractors might hire a mafia to enforce a restrictive cartel within an industry.
The mafia deters cartel members from offering lower prices and new firms
from entering the market.[18]

The third potentially chaotic situation is when politically contentious
areas subject to instability from revolutions, riots, and rebellion give rise to
power vacuums and a corresponding need for protection. After both the
demise of the Soviet Union and the collapse of the Italian feudal system, the
number of private property holders increased dramatically, but the availability
of conventional property enforcement mechanisms either remained constant
or declined. In short, mafias form when the state cannot or will not provide
governance and a long-term demand for governance exists.[19]

With the decline of the convict code, the inmate social system experienced just this type of power vacuum. Inmates had a need for self-governance
that was met by neither official mechanisms nor the norms that previously
ruled the community. Gangs formed to meet the demand for protection, for
both one's person and property, but also to protect the security of transactions
in the prison's underground economy. Identifying the changes in the supply
and demand for governance explains why prison gangs form. While mafias
exist in a wide range of situations and form to solve a very general problem, the
particulars of their origin and operation depend on the unique, contextual
details. To understand the rise of prison gangs, we turn to the California prison
system and the inmate society in the actual facilities where they surfaced.

The Origins of California Prison Gangs

In 1945, the California legislature approved the building of the Deuel
Vocational Institution (DVI). Earl Warren, the famed jurist who later served
as the 14th Chief Justice of the United States, was California's governor at
the time. He believed in the progressive approach to incarceration, the "new
penology" devoted to rehabilitative ideals. He appointed Richard McGee,
also a proponent of the new penology, to lead the Department of Corrections.[20] They believed that scientific bureaucracies could educate and train
the criminally minded so that these individuals could return to society and
lead productive lives. The purpose of DVI was to do just that. It was built in
Northern California in the San Joaquin Valley, in the small, dusty farming
town of Tracy.

Its doors opened in 1953, and as one employee at the time remarked, its
walls and buildings reflected the "current correctional attempts to bring the

total forces of contemporary rehabilitative and management techniques to bear on the individual offender."[21] This facility provided room for 1,250 "young and trainable (i.e. salvageable) inmates" and included "the programs necessary for their resocialization as constructive members of the free community."[22] From the start, DVI's mission was to teach inmates how to make an honest living. The facility provided vocational training and a complete elementary- and high-school–level educational program that met all of the state's curriculum requirements.[23] DVI combined an educational element with a custodial setting, but it was still a prison. According to a former staff member, its construction "represent[ed] a monument in concrete and steel to society's failure to discover acceptable alternatives to the 'pains of imprisonment.'"[24]

One observer quipped that it was a "progressive school for bad boys."[25] But this description wasn't perfectly accurate. The inmates who took residence at DVI were not just minors. Whereas other custodial facilities held either juveniles or adults, about half of the inmates at DVI were youths and half were adults.[26] Juvenile facilities sent youth to DVI for a variety of reasons, but the most important was to control inmates considered "management problems."[27] Prisons sent adults to the facility because they were either "skilled workmen" or "young and trainable."[28] As a result, the inmate population at DVI held both the most disruptive young inmates and a large number of adult offenders. Officials hoped that this innovative facility would be the key to unlocking the mystery of rehabilitation. Instead, it provided a fertile environment that gave birth to a new form of organized crime. These gangs would grow to an unprecedented scale and place of power in the criminal underworld.

During this period, changing inmate demographics across the entire prison system were frustrating the effectiveness of the convict code. More inmates, more young inmates, more violent offenders, and more first-time inmates undermined the ability of reputation-based governance mechanism to operate successfully. The inmate population at DVI eclipsed these broader trends, for several reasons. First, the number of inmates grew rapidly. Ten years after opening, the population had reached 1,600 inmates, nearly 130 percent of the designed capacity.[29] Second, because of the unique philosophy undergirding DVI and the corresponding inmate selection process, the inmates were much younger than at other prisons. The median age of inmates at DVI was only 24.1 years, compared with the median for all of the state's prisons of 31.9 years.[30] Third, there was a higher percentage of people at DVI incarcerated for crimes against persons. Compared to other juvenile facilities, twice as many of the youth were incarcerated for violent offenses.[31] Finally, inmates at DVI were much less likely to have served a prison sentence—only 39.6

percent compared to 46.2 percent for the entire prison system.[32] The same demographic factors that made norms less effective at the system-wide level were even more pronounced at DVI. It is precisely at this facility that we would expect to see decentralized governance fail and violence to erupt.

At DVI, prison gangs sprang violently into existence.[33] From the beginning, it had not been an orderly prison. Violence and periodic race riots plagued inmates at the facility.[34] People referred to it as "Gladiator School."[35] Robert Morrill, a member of California's first Prison Gang Task Force and a nearly 50-year veteran of law enforcement explains that prior to the 1950s, "there were groups of Mexican-American inmates that had become prey to larger and usually stronger groups of Black and White inmates in California prisons."[36] In 1957, young Hispanic inmates formed the first California prison gang—the Mexican Mafia.[37] According to a variety of sources, these inmates formed the gang for protection. Morrill writes, "At the inception of the Mexican Mafia, it seemed to be only a self-protection union, or a surrogate family used only to protect its members and their possessions. This is how most prison gangs begin."[38] The Mexican Mafia, "like all Security Threat Groups which formed afterward, initially started out as a self-protection group. They wanted to survive in the prison environment and protect their private property from being taken."[39] A former prison gang member reports that the Mexican Mafia formed when "several Latino inmates organized a protection group and dedicated themselves and their resources to equal and fair treatment for Mexican-American inmates."[40]

The founding members of the Mexican Mafia were relatively young—including some as young as 15 years old—and typically were members of Los Angeles street gangs.[41] They sought to reduce conflict among the rival gangs from Hispanic neighborhoods. Instead of having multiple street gangs fighting against each other, they consolidated their power. A former prison gang member explains that the budding gang "aggressively recruited newly arrived Mexican-American inmates to boost its membership....New recruits were instructed to lay all vendettas and conflicts from the streets to rest."[42] The prison gang's goals were multifaceted. According to a Department of Justice study, the gang members "gave up their street gang identity for the collective purposes of mutual protection, to run illicit businesses in the prison, and to gain power over other inmates."[43] A former Mexican Mafia member explains that to accomplish these objectives, the founding members began "establishing their reputation of terror."[44]

In the early 1960s, officials transferred many of the founding members of the Mexican Mafia to other prisons (primarily San Quentin, Soledad, and

Folsom) to disturb their operations.[45] Officials intended to discourage their disruptive and violent behavior by mixing them with hardened adult convicts.[46] However, rather than dividing and conquering this group, the dispersal of Mafia members throughout the prison system helped them recruit new members and spread the gang's influence.[47] In these prisons, the Mexican Mafia reacted to disrespect from inmates with quick, brutal acts of violence. Still, that wasn't the only reason they shed blood. Within days of being transferred to San Quentin, Mafia members stabbed "unsuspecting" inmates to death on two different occasions, for no apparent reason. A gang member who was active in the early years of the Mexican Mafia notes that violence was committed in public places and in a dramatic fashion for the specific purpose of making the biggest display possible. These murders, he explains, were "committed for no reason other than to make a statement to the general population at San Quentin."[48] As with all other mafia groups, violent acts established the gang's reputation and allowed it to credibly provide protection.[49]

Some of the members felt that the group's name didn't suitably reflect their Latino heritage. They agreed to adopt an additional name for the organization, *La Eme* (pronounced lah EH-*meh*), the Spanish letter *M*.[50] The gang recruited the most dangerous Hispanic inmates, regardless of street gang affiliation, and early members came from both Northern and Southern California neighborhoods. While their official membership numbers were relatively small, according to some accounts, by 1965 La Eme controlled nearly every California state prison.[51]

The gang was different from the inmate groups that had existed in the past. Before the Mexican Mafia, Morrill reports, there had "always been smaller groups of inmates that banded together...but they never had any real meaning other than close friendship or a mutual business arrangement while in prison."[52] Past inmate groups centered around inmates' street gangs and neighborhoods. The Mexican Mafia transcended that. The member's allegiance was to the prison gang, and membership required a lifetime commitment.

The Mexican Mafia developed internal rules to govern its operations and to maintain order among its members, but it did not provide governance to all inmates. In fact, as their power grew, they increasingly preyed on others. A former Mexican Mafia member claims that the gang members "began robbing inmates of their possessions—prison ducats, canteen goods, and drugs—while making examples of those that would dare oppose their demands."[53] Inmates who were not affiliated with the Mexican Mafia had "to surrender their prison luxuries and items of comfort such as wrist watches, rings, shoes and anything that could either be enjoyed by [the Mexican Mafia] or sold on the prison black market."[54] Some of the Mexican Mafia members looked down on Hispanics from small, Northern California towns.[55] According to a former Mexican Mafia member, "in sharp contrast to their more regimented and streetwise counterparts from Los Angeles, they were very unorganized and lacked the aggressiveness and street savvy that was necessary to survive in the prison jungles."[56] Mafia members referred to them derogatively as "farmers" and "sodbusters." They did not consider them "true gangsters, or *veteranos*, but merely potential victims."[57] The Mafia "was quick to forget its origins and, once its members began losing sight of their true purpose, they, too, began to prey on their own people."[58] La Eme had formed to fight against predatory inmates, but they had now become a dangerous predator.

Other inmates were not blind to the Mexican Mafia's threat. John Irwin notes that their abuse "aroused and consolidated a large number of 'independent' Chicanos, who planned to eliminate the Mafia members."[59] Many of these inmates were the Hispanics from rural farming communities who had suffered their abuse. In 1965, at Soledad State Prison, they grouped together and fought back.[60] To defend themselves, they "formed their own alliance for self-protection."[61] The group would come to be called *La Nuestra Familia*— Spanish for "our family."[62] A former member notes that the Nuestra Familia "took a firm stance against oppression or other types of unjustifiable practices proven detrimental to La Raza [all those of Latin descent] within the penal system."[63] They began recruiting inmates to protect themselves and the Hispanic inmate population in general.

The primary objective of Nuestra Familia (NF), according to a former member, was "to protect and defend its members and/or La Raza against any outside aggression, especially from the EME....Many Latino inmates suffered a great deal of unnecessary hardship and indignity, as did inmates of other races."[64] The NF leadership "vowed that familianos would no longer passively allow the EME to victimize the very people they had solemnly sworn to protect."[65] Like the Mexican Mafia, the NF formed for protection; one of the founding members is claimed to have said, "La Nuestra Familia must be the voice of the people, not only in Soledad, but throughout the prison system."[66] They adopted the Huelga bird symbol, the same logo chosen by the National Farm Workers Association, led by César Chávez. The Nuestra Familia's stated aim was to help its members while incarcerated. Their founding document, a written constitution, states that the "primary purpose and goals of this O [Organization] is for the betterment of its members and the building up of this O on the outside into a strong and self-supporting *familia.*"[67] Recent internal gang documents reveal that the gang promotes itself as a warrior for justice, noting that members "challenge all those who oppose our unity and advancement towards equal justice.... Those who seek to destroy and undermine our raza's efforts to rise above their standards of living have through their own actions made it possible for us and other groups like us to come together."[68]

The Mexican Mafia and the Nuestra Familia were the first two prison gangs to form in California, and they were not the last. As they rose to power, inmates of other races and ethnicities formed gangs as well. Morrill explains that, in the following years, inmates "who formed these other gangs felt they had to in order to protect themselves."[69] In the late 1950s and early 1960s, white inmates formed the Blue Bird Gang. Little is known about this organization, but by the late 1960s, the Federal Bureau of Investigation reported that it had become "apparent to other white inmates that a more powerful gang was needed to protect white inmates from the Black and Mexican prison spawned gangs that were in power in the California Department of Corrections prison system."[70] The Aryan Brotherhood prison gang formed in 1967 with the explicit purpose of protecting white inmates from black and Hispanic gangs.[71] Hispanics from Texas did not align with either the Mexican Mafia or the Nuestra Familia.[72] As a result, the Texas Syndicate prison gang formed in California in 1976, and their primary purpose was to protect themselves from other inmate groups.[73]

At around the same time, black inmates formed the Black Guerilla Family, to protect themselves from the Mexican Mafia.[74] A Black Guerilla Family member describes how they "controlled the line [mainline prison population] there, by offering protection of numbers, protection of comradeship."[75] Membership made other benefits available as well. He went on to explain, "you would never really want for anything. Your little smoking habits were taken care of if you were a good soldier. We had private stores—cigarettes, candy, pies, canned food, canned meat. If you were short you could get stuff from us and you wouldn't have to double up [pay interest on borrowed goods]. Or we'd get someone to write to you from out on the streets, keep you from getting lonely. When you're going out, we have community officers who have contacts with people on the streets."[76]

Prison gangs continue to provide their members with protection, mutual aid, and the ability to participate in the lucrative prison drug trade. A federal indictment notes that Nuestra Familia provides "protection and security for its members and associates from rival organizations and gangs both inside and outside California correctional institutions."[77] Studying the Nuestra Familia in Colorado, former inmate Robert Koehler reports that they offer valuable support and supplies. The gang operates as a mutual aid society and "provides *Familianos* [members] with physical protection from rival gangs and supplies them with store goods at low cost or on low credit, and Familia serves as their emotional family."[78] A gang in Texas with more than a hundred members even calls itself the "Self-Defense Family."[79] The histories of numerous prison gangs, including the Aryan Circle, Border Brothers, G-27, 211 Crew, the Puro Tango Blasters, the Texas Aryan Brotherhood, and the Mexikanemi reveal that they all formed to provide protection.[80]

Those who argue that prison gangs provide protection are not mere fringe observers. People who interact with these gangs on a regular basis, such as correctional officers and gang investigators, agree with this assessment. A correctional officer at Corcoran State Prison notes, "When you come to prison, you have to join a gang. You have no choice. If you don't join a gang, you'd better pack up. Go into the sergeant's office and tell him you're ready to leave the yard. Because there's just no options. You have to be in a gang."[81] A national survey of prison administrators by the Department of Justice found that protection is the sixth most frequent activity that prison gangs engage in.[82] A veteran correctional officer claims that "most gangs in prison originally started out as protection groups from other gangs and act as a welcoming committee for new prisoners after their intake into the system."[83] A Federal Bureau of Investigation memo in 1973 describes prison gangs' goal as "self-protection."[84] Prison gangs provide governance by protecting their members, providing mutual aid, and creating organizational structures that allow them to flourish in the underground economy.

Outlaw Economics

Today's prisons are very different from the prisons of the early 20th century. They now comprise booming illicit marketplaces. There are several reasons for this. First, with more people behind bars, the demand for contraband has increased. More people means there are more trading opportunities available in underground markets. Starting in the 1970s, inmates had another big reason to demand more governance—the prison drug trade. Previously, California had imprisoned few drug users. However, in the wake of President Nixon's Comprehensive Drug Abuse Prevention and Control Act of 1970 and subsequent legislation, there was an unprecedented rise in the number of inmates arriving for drug-related offenses. In 1959, 1,450 of the inmates arriving into the prison system admitted having a drug or narcotics addiction, including marijuana (Figure 3.1). That constituted 26 percent of new inmates.

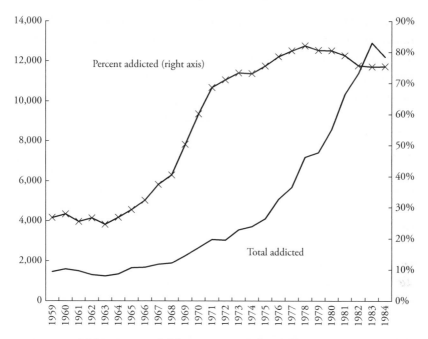

FIGURE 3.1 Male inmates in California arriving with an addiction, 1959–1984
Source: California Department of Corrections and Rehabilitation, Annual Reports

The percentage of addicted inmates arriving in prison stayed relatively stable for the next decade, at an average of 27 percent. This figure increased dramatically after 1970. From 1970 to 1980, the average percentage of addicted inmates rose to 59 percent, reaching a recorded high of 82 percent in 1978. The total number of inmates addicted to drugs increased as well. From 1955 to 1984, the number of inmates arriving in the state prison system who were addicted to drugs and narcotics increased more than eight times, from 1,450 to 12,205. In 2002, 83 percent of all jail and prison inmates in America were heavily involved in drugs or alcohol.[85] In 2006, 56 percent of all California inmates were deemed to have a "high need" for drug treatment and 80 percent had a drug problem.[86] Inmates' demand for controlled substances is substantial.

The number of inmates arriving for drug-related offenses provides another useful measure of the magnitude of drug-involved inmates. People who go to prison for drug-related offenses may not be drug users, and many people incarcerated for non-drug-related offenses use drugs. However, one study found that 81 percent of adults arrested for selling drugs tested positive for drugs at the time of arrest.[87] Nonetheless, to the extent that people sentenced for drug-related offenses are users or are knowledgeable participants in the

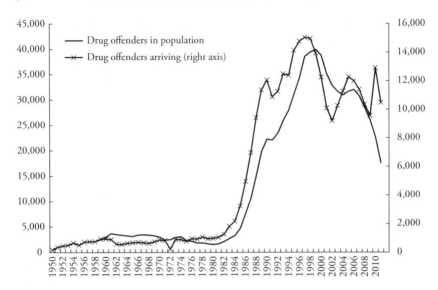

FIGURE 3.2 Drug offenders in California prisons, 1950–2011
Source: California Department of Corrections and Rehabilitation, Annual Reports

drug trade, this provides an informative complement to the previous figure. In 1951, there were only 168 inmates entering the prison system for narcotics-related offenses (Figure 3.2). By the 2000s, that number was regularly over 10,000 inmates per year. The number of people in prison for drug offenses increased from 525 in 1951 to more than 26,000 in 2009. In other words, by the end of that period, there were 50 times as many inmates in prison for drug offenses.

Inmates with drug connections on the street aid prison drug dealers. Drug smugglers find numerous ways to traffic drugs into jail and prison. A common method is for visitors to pass drugs to inmates during visits. The warden at San Quentin explains, "A lot of drugs come in through the visiting room, a lot of drugs."[88] A lieutenant concurs: "It's prison and these guys are pros at doing this stuff, to get it in. They want it and a lot of it comes through the visiting rooms, unfortunately."[89] People also smuggle drugs in through inmate mail and concealed in legal documents.[90] Inmates can transport drugs into the system by swallowing drug-filled condoms and retrieving them later. Drugs can also be "keistered" in an inmate's anal cavity.[91] People throw bags of contraband over prison walls to incarcerated accomplices. Corrupt guards and employees smuggle contraband in, too.[92] According to a court-appointed observer, in the Texas prison system, "the major source of drugs comes from prison staff, particularly correctional officers who are young, single, and inexperienced."[93] In one instance, the drug and alcohol staff counselor was fired for smuggling in alcohol for inmates.[94] A correctional officer at Corcoran notes that for "gang members, their number one source in making money is through narcotics. Out on the street and in the institution. They can make just as much money in the institutions as they can on the streets."[95]

For a prison drug dealer to make money, he must overcome two important obstacles: (1) deterring theft, assault, and opportunism from other inmates, and (2) ensuring the quality of his product to consumers. Traditional businesses in the free world can rely on contracts, courts of law, the police, and regulations to provide this governance. In their absence, inmates must devise self-enforcing governance mechanisms. Prison gangs have a comparative advantage in self-enforcing exchange in the underground economy.

A sole proprietor faces substantial obstacles to participating in the drug trade. As an individual, other groups of inmates who sell drugs can threaten to kill him if he lures their customers away. Other inmates can steal his drug inventory or force him to give it to them. A sole proprietor needs to traffic drugs into the facility, which requires trusting at least one other person to deliver the drugs and to not inform on him. If, as is common behind bars, a drug dealer allows people to buy drugs on credit, then he risks that they might not pay him back.[96] If he isn't particularly fearsome, then an inmate won't pay what he owes. Another problem is that a customer can cancel his debt by killing the sole proprietor. Moreover, consumers may doubt his trustworthiness. Some customers might want to buy drugs, but they don't know if he will take advantage of them. He might sell them low-quality drugs or rat poison. He might meet them in an isolated area to make the deal but instead of giving them the drugs, just strong-arm the payment from them. Uncertainty abounds.

Each one of these problems is potentially ruinous to an individual who wants to trade in self-enforcing markets. The organizational attributes of a prison gang, however, overcome these challenges. First, a gang strong enough to protect its members and property is strong enough to credibly threaten others. A prison gang is effective because people realize that it can and will use violence. If you steal from a prison gang, they can kill you. They can lure away someone's customers without being intimidated. Because they are effective protective associations, they can effectively deter predatory competitors.

They also have an advantage in the selling of drugs on credit. Their information transmission and enforcement mechanisms (discussed at length in Chapter 4) make it easier for them to hunt down and assault people who default. Unlike sole proprietors, they have networks that provide information about inmates in many prisons. Gang members are in place to search out and punish delinquent debtors. As a result, prison gangs can sell drugs on credit and have a greater likelihood of repayment. Moreover, having a corporate identity that exists into perpetuity provides an important advantage: Prison gangs eliminate the incentive for debtors to kill their lenders. Killing one prison gang member doesn't erase the obligation to the organization. As a Texas prison gang member explained, "Say I get killed and a snitch or somebody is responsible. No matter where they go, we got people on every farm [prison], and the one that's running it there will tell the leaders what went down. They'll pay for what they did."[97] One of the mottos of the Aryan Brotherhood reads, "An Aryan Brother, Never need fear. For his death shall be avenged, By his Brothers still here."[98]

Gangs with lifetime commitment requirements have yet another advantage: When their members are released to the streets, they remain obligated to the gang. An important way that a released gang member will assist the gang is by finding ways to smuggle drugs into prison. The Aryan Brotherhood provides one example. According to the Federal Bureau of Investigation, "The rule of thumb is that once on the streets, one must take care of his brothers that are still inside. The penalty for failure to do so is death upon the members return to the prison system. Some of the paroled members' duties would be to supply his brothers inside with drugs, or to make hits on the street as commanded by his brothers."[99] Unlike many sole proprietors, the Aryan Brotherhood has trustworthy and devoted members of the gang that help supply their inventory.

Prison gangs have a powerful ex-ante mechanism that makes them more effective than the sole proprietor: reputation.[100] Selling drugs as part of a prison gang means that the gang's reputation is on the line. The good name of the gang is held hostage, so if they sell low-quality drugs, their reputation is tarnished. If they rip people off, inmates will turn to other sellers. The gang's investment in its reputation is a large sunk cost, so they have an incentive to maintain their reputation as a high-quality drug seller.

As prison gangs formed and established their place of power, they quickly got involved in the underground economy. After officials transferred Mexican Mafia members out of DVI in the 1960s, the gang realized the profits available in the drug trade, especially for heroin. Many inmates find that heroin eases the experience of incarceration, and it proved to be a reason for the gang's rise to power.[101] In 1964, inmates who made loans and dealt in contraband at San Quentin were typically sole proprietors. When the Mexican

Mafia arrived, they became a major player in loan sharking, drugs, and any other type of profitable contraband.[102] John Irwin notes that with the appearance of gangs, "the individual entrepreneur faded or disappeared. Anyone with a rich stock of valuable commodities and without protection from a group [would] be threatened and robbed."[103] Former Prison Gang Task Force investigator Robert Morrill explains, "the prisoners soon learned that they could not play handball, use the weights, play checkers or engage in any type of recreation [without] paying a fee."[104] A Nuestra Familia gang member described his rival's control of the underground economy, noting that the Mexican Mafia was "in charge of every drug transaction and prison pleasure."[105] An ethnographic study of San Quentin's inmate social system at this time reported that the Mexican Mafia "virtually controls the illegal economic activities" of the prison.[106] Likewise, in a Rhode Island prison, the emergence of gangs led to a situation where "individual 'merchants,' largely white, [had] been driven out of business by 'racketeers' backed by large gangs."[107]

The Mexican Mafia's permanence made it a more reliable seller of drugs and allowed them to collect debts with greater effectiveness. Anthropologist Ted Davidson writes that the Mexican Mafia in San Quentin

> has an unquestioned stability because it has the power and means to collect and pay legitimate debts from one prison to another (or even on the streets)....This makes dealing with [the Mexican Mafia] a very positive, secure, yet serious matter. For example, [the Mexican Mafia] *will* collect or pay a legitimate debt, regardless of where the debtor or debtee might be transferred—even if he is released to the streets. In contrast, if a prisoner has financial dealings with an inmate, there is the constant threat that the inmate will be transferred to a different prison (or even be paroled or charged to the streets)—which would present serious difficulties in tendering payment or collecting a debt.[108]

The gang's violent reputation deters fraudulent and deceptive behavior by consumers:

> Anyone who consciously deals with [the Mexican Mafia] knows the seriousness with which members regard [the Mexican Mafia] activities and the extent to which they will go to protect [the Mexican Mafia]. Non-[Mexican Mafia] individuals who function on the lower levels of the prisoner culture understand the rules of the game, and even the

extreme act of death to a snitch may seem justifiable to them. The mere possession of this knowledge usually is sufficient to keep prisoners from crossing [the Mexican Mafia] in any way....Members [of the Mexican Mafia] know very well that their group could never survive without such severe protective measures.[109]

Because prison gangs are not transitory sellers, they have an incentive not to abuse their power. Doing so would drive customers away. As a result, the Mexican Mafia has become "the financial institution of the prisoner economy."[110]

Officials confirm that the Mexican Mafia ran the drug trade in San Quentin and Folsom prisons in the early 1980s.[111] Davidson suggests that the Mexican Mafia's role in the inmate economy improved market opportunities more broadly. The prison gang reportedly "increased the routine volume of goods available for all prisoners, making more goods available at lower prices than would be otherwise," and "the conditions of many Chicanos and convicts has been significantly improved. Many Chicanos claim that they are in a better position than any other group inside prison."[112]

Gangs continue to be an important participant in contraband markets throughout California. In fact, prison gangs' prominent role in drug trafficking behind bars is an important reason for correctional officials' attempts to disrupt them.[113] Drug trafficking is the second most frequent criminal activity engaged in by prison gangs, and prison gangs are responsible for the majority of drug trafficking.[114] Administrators report that "almost without exception...the gangs are responsible for the majority of drug trafficking in their institutions."[115] A former gang member has noted that "the basis of Familia is capitalism... economic ventures allow Familia to counter the perceived hegemony of the guards/prison system and the threat of rival prison gangs."[116] And a lieutenant at Corcoran adds, "The gangs inside the prison control drug trafficking, extortion, any kind of crime that you can think of that happens on the street, happens in the prison system."[117] An official at Soledad confirms that "they attempt to control most narcotic contraband 'business' within the prison."[118] In short, prison gangs govern the underground economy and promote illicit markets.

Alternative Explanations

The governance theory of prison gangs diverges from several more common and well-accepted explanations of prison gang formation. Understanding why the current explanations are incomplete or unsatisfying lends support to the governance theory.

Although prison gangs now exist throughout the United States, there is substantial variation in when and where prison gangs formed. Table 3.1 shows the long time span over which officials in each state first identified prison gang activity in their facilities. Gangs formed as early as 1950 in Washington, but not until the 1980s (and later) in other states. A useful theory of prison gangs should not substantially contradict this long and varied history. However, many of the current explanations of prison gangs fail to make sense of it.

A common argument is that prison gangs arise when street gangs import their operations behind bars.[119] For example, "super-gangs" in Illinois were so large that it was relatively easy for them to import their organizational structure into the prison system.[120] There are two empirical problems with this explanation. First, not all states had this experience. Texas prison gangs formed and proliferated in prisons. During the 1980s, all eight gangs identified by Texas correctional officials began in prison, not on the street.[121] In a national survey in 2010, prison officials estimated that 52 percent of inmates who are currently gang-affiliated were not in a gang when they were admitted to prison.[122] They are not simply importing their street gangs into prison.

This theory also suggests that prison gangs will form earliest in those states with a substantial street gang presence. This did not happen. California and Illinois loosely support this prediction because of their long history of street gangs and the early emergence of prison gangs. However, the prediction fails when we look at other states. States without serious street gang problems

Table 3.1 Year that Prison Gangs Began Operating in a State Facility

Year	State	Year	State
1950	Washington	1974	Virginia
1957	California	1975	Arizona
1969	Illinois	1975	Texas
1970	Utah	1977	Federal System
1971	Pennsylvania	1978	Wisconsin
1973	Iowa	1980	West Virginia
1973	Nevada	1981	Missouri
1974	Arkansas	1982	Kentucky
1974	North Carolina	1983	Indiana

Source: Camp and Camp 1985, 20–21

had prison gangs forming very early, including Utah, Pennsylvania, Iowa, Nevada, Arkansas, North Carolina, and Virginia. Likewise, in 1985, Pennsylvania, Missouri, and Arizona ranked among the top five states with the largest number of prison gang members.[123] Even in California, modern street gangs existed in the 1930s (and perhaps as early as the 1910s), but prison gangs did not form until the late 1950s and 1960s.[124] If the presence of street gangs explains prison gang formation, then we shouldn't observe a 20- to 50-year lag. Moreover, the Mexican Mafia was not formed by the members of a single street gang who imported their organizational structure but by rival gang members who created a new and unique organization. Founding members of the Nuestra Familia were specifically not gang members but rural agricultural workers from farming communities. Prison gangs were not simply importing their gang structure or gang culture behind bars. Supply-side answers alone do not suffice.

A second argument suggests that judicial interventions affected the administration of corrections departments and gave rise to prison gangs. Prior to the mid-1960s, an inmate lost all legal rights when incarcerated. He or she experienced a "civil death" that made the person a "slave of the state."[125] Federal and state courts followed a hands-off doctrine and generally refused to hear cases about poor prison conditions.[126] However, Earl Warren (serving on the Supreme Court) and others participated in a process of legal reform that extended legal rights to inmates. Courts became more confident about intervening in state-based institutions after gaining experience implementing school desegregation.[127] This corresponded with the rise of public law litigation, and lawyers sought and obtained court-ordered reform for schools, mental health facilities, prisons, and jails.[128] The Civil Rights Act of 1964 gave inmates more procedural rights with which to complain about prison administration.[129] Members of the American Civil Liberties Union and the National Association for the Advancement of Colored People also challenged poorly run prisons systems in the courts.[130] As a result, the number of legal suits filed against corrections officials increased from 219 in 1966 to nearly 10,000 annually by the late 1970s.[131] By the mid-1980s, 45 states had some part of their correctional system under a court order.[132] This increasing interference by federal courts, it is argued, tied the hands of correctional officials, preventing them from controlling their facilities effectively (and perhaps in a cruel manner), so that they were unable to manage inmates and subdue gangs.[133]

If U.S. Supreme Court rulings or the Civil Rights Act affected prisons in all states, then we would expect to see prison gangs forming across the United States at the same time, not across a span of more than three decades and not prior to the 1960s. This is not what we have seen. If judicial intervention mattered, it would have to be in a more context-specific way. This is plausible because many court rulings affected the operation of a specific prison or prison system. However, past work has rarely identified the mechanism that leads from judicial intervention generally to the formation of prison gangs in a specific location. James Jacobs notes that the court intrusions have had a "subtle and indirect" effect, making any sort of empirical testing difficult to conduct.[134] It is not clear how much judicial intervention matters and in what way.

The most compelling case for the importance of judicial intervention comes from Texas. Ben Crouch and James Marquart examined the implications of *Ruiz v. Estelle* (1980), a far-reaching lawsuit on prison conditions that required major changes in the state's corrections department.[135] Arguably, it had the most substantial impact on a state corrections system out of any court order in U.S. history. Unlike past work on prison systems, the authors identify the mechanism through which the court ruling gave rise to gangs. Specifically, an important part of the court order disbanded "building tenders," an informal inmate assistant to officials. Building tenders resolved disputes and informed officers about what was occurring among the inmates. They provided a source of extralegal governance that supplemented formal mechanisms of social control. After the ruling, officials could no longer rely on building tenders, creating a governance vacuum. Officials lost control of their prisons, leading to higher rates of violence. Gangs formed as prisoners exploited the decline in traditional controls.[136]

It would be a mistake, however, to interpret Crouch and Marquart's study as making a general argument for why gangs form, and their findings do not imply that judicial intervention is either necessary or sufficient. In some states, like California, there were no major court rulings that precipitated gang formation. Judicial intervention is not a necessary precursor to gangs. In fact, the Texas example does not demonstrate that judicial intervention is sufficient to do so, either. By the end of 1979, Texas held 26,522 inmates. This was the largest state prison population at the time—3,900 more inmates than California.[137] The large prison population confounds the effect of court actions on gangs. This case does not tell us if the same type of judicial intervention in a small prison setting would have led to gangs.[138] Moreover, large court interventions often don't lead to gang formation. Between 1970 and 1985, federal courts issued orders against 12 state prison systems.[139] These orders constituted major interventions, but by 1985, prison gangs did not exist in 10 out of 12 of these prison systems. Of the two prison systems where gangs were active, gangs formed both before the court decision in one state and after the court decision in the other. In short, court intervention is not sufficient to prompt prison gang formation. Rather, the courts are one factor among many that can influence governance institutions. Changes in inmate demographics also affect inmates' demand for extralegal governance. Judicial intervention is better understood as an important part of a broader governance theory of prison social order.

Likewise, John DiIulio has argued that formal governance mechanisms matter a great deal, and corrections management can differ substantially across states and facilities. He has looked at prisons in Texas, California, and Michigan to gauge the effectiveness of formal prison governance. Many factors that people assumed would be important for determining the level of order, amenity, and service in a prison did not appear to be influential, including the violent characteristics of the inmates, high inmate-to-staff ratios, architecture, and repressive corrections tactics. DiIulio argues that prison leadership is the key to creating stable, safe prisons. Formal mechanisms of social control clearly affect inmates' demand for governance and the ways in which it is supplied. When prison officials can effectively protect inmates, they have less demand for gangs to do so.

There is relatively little research on prison social order around the world. While measuring and comparing formal governance across departments and countries may be infeasible, the limited evidence available is consistent with the argument that gangs emerge to provide extralegal governance.[140] Latin American prisons are typically governed less effectively by formal mechanisms, and news accounts suggest that gangs are often in charge of the inmate community. According to one report, 60 percent of Mexican prisons and jails were "self-governed."[141] Bolivia's San Pedro Prison is governed entirely by the inmates, with guards only present at the gates to prevent escape.[142] Prisons in the United Kingdom, by contrast, hold a much smaller inmate population than in the United States. Officials also appear to be more concerned with controlling contraband and they are therefore more restrictive. Both of these factors suggest that inmates may have less demand for extralegal governance.[143] Consistent with this argument, prison gangs rarely operate in U.K. prisons, and when they do, they are significantly less powerful, permanent, or influential than those in the United States.[144] Finally, in the United States, prison gangs are most prevalent in the two states with the largest prison systems: California and Texas. This fits the argument that large prison systems undermine reputation-based governance regimes. It also helps to explain the variation in prison gangs across the United States. These international examples also suggest that factors that are unique to the United States—such as the history of the Civil Rights movement, specific court interventions, and the drug war—are not necessary to explain the formation of prison gangs.

A third theory of prison gangs focuses on government policy changes at the state level. For instance, California implemented an indeterminate sentencing regime from 1944 to 1977. The system sentenced an inmate to prison for a range of years (for example, 1 to 15 years for forgery or second-degree burglary) and left it to an administrative board to decide when the inmate was rehabilitated.[145] The California Department of Corrections conjectured that indeterminate sentencing created uncertainty that frustrated inmates, who then lashed out against the system and formed gangs.[146] Alternatively, inmates may have increasingly violated the convict code by informing on their peers to improve their chance of early release.[147] The timing of this explanation works well. However, if this were the key factor, then we would have seen gangs forming among all inmates who were subject to indeterminate sentencing practices, both males and females. This did not happen.

Female prison gangs do not exist in the California prison system.[148] A woman incarcerated for drug possession notes that "women don't form gangs…we're not into it."[149] Another woman explained, "There's more of a formal system with the men; they assume their roles and they know their positions. With women, it's not like that."[150] Yet another woman comments, "We are not like the men, because we learn to live with each other. We communicate. It is not a racial thing in here."[151] Female inmates come together in pairs or small "families." A woman takes on a specific role in these nuclear family units, as either a mom or dad, and these "parents" sometimes have "kids" whom they mentor and for whom they watch out.[152] For the most part, women do not segregate themselves by race. These families lack the defining characteristics of prison gangs. They have no internal rule-making institutions and no explicit mechanisms for punishing bad behavior in the prison community. Membership is not permanent or mutually exclusive. They do not have a corporate form or exist into perpetuity. These prison families are much smaller than prison gangs. They lack lifetime membership requirements. They do not engage in organized criminal enterprises that extend beyond bars. Female inmates do not typically fight as often or as seriously as male inmates do, and they rarely make or use prison weapons.[153]

The organization of the female inmate social order supports the argument that gangs form to provide governance. Male inmates in California created gangs because demographic changes undermined norms. This didn't happen among females, for whom norms continue to work well. The highest recorded female inmate population to exist in the California system is a meager number, fewer than 12,000 inmates in 2009. Historically, the female population has always been much smaller than the male inmate population. In fact, the male population exceeded this size prior to the 1950s, before prison gangs formed. The female population has never grown as large as the male population had at the time that the convict code declined. Moreover, female inmates have less demand for protection, since fewer of them are incarcerated for violent crimes. In 2009, only 35.2 percent of the female population was serving time for crimes against persons, compared with 57 percent of incarcerated males. In the late 1990s, fewer than 14 percent of females were categorized as Level III or Level IV security risks, substantially fewer than in male facilities.[154]

With a small inmate population, norms are effective, and we should not observe the formation of prison gangs. It might be that female prison gangs don't form for some other reason—and the data do not rule out all of those alternative explanations—but the lack of gangs is consistent with the governance theory. It also casts doubt on alternative explanations that appeal to state-level changes in correctional philosophy or practice as the primary causal factor.

A fourth approach to understanding prison gangs incorporates demand-side factors, such as inmates' desire for protection or camaraderie. One article in this vein infers a five-step process of prison gang formation, based on observations of inmates in the Texas prison system.[155] The first stage begins when an inmate enters prison and he finds himself alone and afraid. The second stage occurs when he seeks out a clique of inmates with whom to associate who provide a sense of belonging. A clique resembles the informal groupings described by Donald Clemmer: they lack a clear group identity and have no formal rules, leaders, or membership requirements. Some cliques evolve into self-protection groups, which have a group identity but few or no internal rules, and have no involvement in illegal activities and do not engage in unprovoked acts of violence. The self-protection group turns into a predatory group once it begins to restrict membership, disrupt the official operation of a facility, assault staff members, and participate in illegal activities and leaders emerge. The final stage occurs when the predatory group graduates into a full-blown prison gang.

This process of prison gang development identifies why inmates demand gangs—as a source of belonging, protection, and control of resources—but it provides no explanation for why these demands change over time. It treats preferences and demand as a black box. It may be true that inmates join prison gangs out of a sense of belonging and camaraderie, but without elaborating on why inmates' desire for camaraderie changes in a way that makes sense of the temporal and spatial variation of prison gang formation, this approach is incomplete. Some inmates will always seek out groups for camaraderie; in order to account for the absence and then dominance of gangs, however, we need to explain why the marginal prison gang member's desire for camaraderie changed so dramatically.

A related literature offers cultural explanations for changes in prison social order. Two prominent arguments focus on the idea of male domination and on inmates' adherence to a hypermasculine ideal. The former seeks to explain prison life by identifying a general tendency to, or desire for, male domination and to understand how it is constructed and reproduced in prison.[156] Given the absence of females to subjugate, men must find alternative forms of domination, and "an obvious answer is that incarcerated men create gangs and use physical violence to control each other."[157] The problem, however, is that male domination is not explained. Throughout nearly the entire history of American incarceration, prisons have segregated males and females. Why then has male domination not always given rise to gangs? Without explaining what determines the form of male dominance, this explanation cannot make sense of the historical and contemporary evidence.

Similarly, in a fascinating study of Los Angeles County Jail, Sharon Dolovich argues that the gay and transgender housing unit is free of gang politics because its residents do not embrace a hypermasculine identity.[158] The latter claim may be true, and this explanation seems consistent with the finding that female inmates do not form gangs. However, it does not explain why male inmates didn't previously form gangs, and it offers no explanation for why gangs do not exist to the same extent in all prison and jails. L.A. County Jail has the second highest percentage of jail inmates affiliated with gangs in the United States—why is hypermasculinity so important there?[159] To attribute changes in the inmate social system to camaraderie, male domination, or hypermasculinity—but not provide an explanation for these changes—offers relatively little explanatory power of variation in prison gang activity.

Consistent with the governance theory, however, several characteristics of the gay and transgender dorms predict that norms will govern them well. It is a relatively homogenous population. If the absence of hypermasculinity is associated with less violent behavior, then these inmates will indeed have less need for governance over potentially violent disputes. Unlike the general population at Men's Central Jail—which officials claim is the largest jail in the world—it is also small, with an average of only about 100 inmates per dorm. Its residents have a high recidivism rate, which leads to greater stability in the community and perpetuation of reputations. Most inmates entering the general population of the jail will know few or no people, whereas residents of the gay and transgender dorm return to "familiar and even friendly faces."[160] Formal governance mechanisms reportedly operate much more effectively in this unique dorm than in the general population. For nearly the entire history of the unit, it "has been run by the same two officers, who have treated unit residents with respect, evenhandedness, and concern for their well-being," so inmates have less demand for centralized extralegal governance.[161] The costly information transmission and enforcement mechanisms that gangs create are not necessary in this environment. Interestingly, one-on-one fights with other inmates are much more common in the gay and transgender dorms than in the general population, where inmates have few, if any, such fights.[162] This suggests that gang-created governance may be more effective than norm-based governance.

A related argument explains prison gang formation and activity by inmates' desire to promote hateful, racist ideologies.[163] It is true that many gangs use racist language and symbols to identify their groups, which are racially segregated. By this account, inmates have a preference for racism, and gangs help them satisfy this desire. There are two problems with this explanation. First, without a theory of preference formation, it does not provide falsifiable predictions. It does not explain why prison gangs are more active in, say, California than in Rhode Island or Wyoming. Second, and related to this point, a seemingly straightforward prediction would be that the rise of gangs reflects an increase in racial prejudice in society. Yet, across a wide range of measures, racially discriminatory behaviors and beliefs have been declining since at least the 1940s.[164] If society is becoming more tolerant, then we should see a decline rather than an increase in gangs whose purported purpose is to promote racism.

It wouldn't be surprising to find that the public believes, based on television shows and movies, that blood-thirsty, sadistic killers form gangs to cause chaos. Sensational stories sell. Law enforcement might exaggerate a group's dangerousness with the hope of receiving bigger budgets. The California Department of Corrections and Rehabilitation says that gangs "promote violence," suggesting that violence is the end in and of itself.[165] They describe gang members as having a "violent nature" and an "agenda of violence."[166] It is without a doubt true that some prison gang members kill and destroy with great injustice. The problem with this explanation is that violent people existed long before prison gangs did. Why didn't they form prison gangs? In fact, as the rate of incarceration has gone up, it is likely that the marginal inmates entering prisons are less deviant. The worst offenders commit more serious crimes more often, so we would expect that they would be the first to fill prison cells, not people who commit relatively less serious crimes, less often. Finally, if inmates join gangs to promote violence, then we would expect to see an increase in the rate of violence in prison as the number of prison gangs and gang members increases. Instead, there has been a substantial decline in prison violence since the 1970s—the same period in which gangs proliferated.[167]

The United States Department of Justice estimates that only 15 percent to 20 percent of prison gang members are hard-core participants who have a vested interested in the organization and leadership.[168] Most gang members are not dedicated to crime. Joining a gang is a way for them to do their time more easily. In a study of gang dropouts, only 25 percent of respondents admitted to engaging in gang-related violence at all. According to the authors of the study, this contradicts the claim that gang members have a proclivity for violence.[169] A study of the Aryan Brotherhood in Arizona found that a member's criminal record, use of controlled substances, age, childhood delinquency, and violent incidents in prison are not statistically significantly different from those of non-gang members.[170]

Data on inmate violence during the 1960s also challenge the conventional wisdom. As discussed in Chapter 2, inmate-on-inmate stabbings were on the rise at the same time that norms were failing. The California Department of Corrections conducted a study to understand the cause of this upsurge in violence. Looking at two issues, what they found is illuminating. First, they wanted to know why some facilities are more violent than others. Not surprisingly, they found that there were more stabbings in crowded facilities with more young, violent offenders.[171] There was more conflict where we would predict norms to be less effective.

Second, they wanted to understand what factors make a particular person more likely to be a "stabber." This is where things get interesting. When they examined which inmates actually became a stabber, they found no relationship between being imprisoned for a violent offense and being a stabber. In fact, their study determined that a violent-commitment offense was the least important factor out of the 12 variables they looked at.[172] The second most important factor in determining who would become a stabber was if the person had an association with a prison gang.[173] The people most likely to become stabbers are gang members not incarcerated for a violent offense who live among lots of violent offenders. People join prison gangs in dangerous environments to shelter themselves from violence. People become stabbers not because they are violent offenders but because they live among violent offenders.

Inmates interact in a remarkably large sphere of relationships that must be self-governing. They cannot rely on officials to resolve all disputes and to protect them at all times. Prior to the 1960s, inmates relied on the force of norms to control people's baser instincts. As demographic changes altered the inmate social system, the convict code became less effective. The social sanction of disesteem is not useful in anonymous populations. Ostracism is not costly if an inmate can find new allies and trading partners in a large population. The failures of decentralized governance opened up a governance vacuum in the inmate social system, and inmates formed prison gangs to fill this void. Like mafia groups around the world, they are in the business of private protection, and inmates have a strong demand for their services.

My Brother's Keeper

AT THE CALIFORNIA State Prison in Sacramento, two inmates in Cell 3216 had a fight. Once it ended, Julian Barajas lay dead. Correctional officers found his body during the inmate count that night. His cellmate, Robert Canchola, was standing over Barajas's bloody body (which was hog-tied on the floor), drinking from a quart container of *pruno*, or prison-made wine. Barajas had been stabbed at least 19 times; there were large lacerations across the forehead; the throat had been crushed; and he reportedly displayed signs of sexual assault. The man had been tortured before his near-decapitation.

This wasn't an ordinary cellmate murder. The bizarre twist to this gruesome killing comes from the two men's histories. Eleven years earlier, following an argument outside of a party, Barajas had killed Canchola's 19-year-old brother on the streets of Los Angeles. How did these men end up sharing a cell? The district attorney argued that Canchola "maneuvered to get the victim into his cell as his cellmate for the express purpose of killing him in revenge for the murder of the defendant's brother."[1] Canchola was in prison at the time of the killing, and he had been at the Sacramento prison for roughly three years before Barajas arrived, more than a decade after the murder. He claims that his family never told him who killed his brother.

When a new inmate arrives, it is common for inmates who come from the same neighborhood to welcome him to the yard. An inmate with the moniker "Wicked" grew up in the same area as Barajas, so when he arrived at the prison, Wicked gave him a gift basket that included toiletries and snacks.[2] Wicked and Canchola were cellmates, but several weeks later, they decided that they didn't want to cell together anymore. According to prison staff, an informal inmate group called *La Mesa* plays an important role in running the prison yard.[3] The group's primary purpose, officials explained, is to resolve conflicts among Sureño (Southern Hispanic) inmates, including facilitating housing changes. Officers spoke with members of La Mesa to find new cellmates for both men. They said that Barajas and Canchola were a good fit. Because inmates housed in maximum-security facilities tend to be dangerous, officers take housing changes there seriously. Before moving the two inmates in with each other, officers got approval from all of the inmates involved, and they all approved the switch in writing, including Barajas. Supervisors signed the order as well.

Canchola claims that Barajas pulled a knife on him as soon as he got in the cell. He explains, "He came at me…running at me, swinging at me. I tried to get a hold of what he was swinging at me. I bit him. I clawed at him.…I couldn't get it away from him at that point. We're bouncing all over the cell.…I grab a pen and start stabbing at him.…[Barajas] kept telling me, 'You know what's up.'" With both men exhausted, the fight ended in a draw. However, because the yard was on a modified program with restricted inmate movement, both men had to wait in the cell. They watched each other. Canchola claims Barajas taunted him: "He told me, 'You know what I'm busted for,' and I told him, 'No, I don't.'…He told me, 'Quit acting stupid. You know what I'm busted for. I'm busted for killing your brother.'"[4] Several other cell fights took place. Nine days after moving in together, Canchola won their final battle, and Barajas lay dead.

Canchola denied knowing prior to the cell switch that Barajas killed his brother. He admitted that they had had three violent fights during the short time that they were cellmates. He told the deputy district attorney, "I thought it was an issue I could take care of, that I could control. My injuries weren't that serious. I thought it was something we could work out as cellies."[5] He denied orchestrating the cell switch, explaining, "I'm asking myself the same question. How is it that something like that can transpire?" Interestingly, officials had, in fact, booked Barajas into the prison under an alias. Canchola also denied committing the murder. He explained to the deputy district attorney, "Ma'am, I didn't kill him. He died." He eventually received a sentence of 45 years to life for second-degree murder.

Violent men can settle disputes with shanks and garrotes, but in a society where one man's actions affect others, they find ways to limit its harmful effects. A 27-year veteran of corrections who worked on the yard believes that La Mesa orchestrated the cell change so that the two men could resolve the dispute in private.[6] Canchola wanted to avenge his brother's death, but doing so in a public forum would have caused problems for other inmates. A murder on the yard would have disrupted the prison drug trade. Officials might have locked down the yard entirely. Barajas knew that he would have to fight for his life in cell 3216, but to enter protective custody would have been a shameful act. Despite Canchola's denials, officials believe he knew exactly what was going on, and that he conspired to orchestrate the cell change. The sentencing judge described the murder as "truly and obviously…planned, premeditated and deliberate."[7] Though they take place in the shadows, prison gang politics are always at work.

4

Governance in the Society of Captives

*To say that man is a social animal is also to say that man
never lives in a world completely of his own choosing.*
GRESHAM M. SYKES[1]

*It was my responsibility on the yard to ensure that...our
people were not harmed by another race. I took care of the
drug debts. If one of our people became delinquent in a drug
debt to another race, it was my responsibility to either cover
their drug debt or have them stabbed. In which case, we
would send one of ours to stab him.*
Inmate, Corcoran State Prison[2]

The Community Responsibility System

Merchants in the late medieval period faced a serious problem. They knew
that it would be profitable to trade with strangers from foreign lands, but they
didn't know whom they could trust. Impersonal exchange means that a
merchant (1) doesn't know how trustworthy a potential trading partner is;
(2) doesn't expect to have future interactions with the trader; and (3) has no
way to tarnish someone's reputation by telling other people if he acts dishon-
estly. This is a risky trading situation. The shadow of the future doesn't discourage defection. A merchant cannot deter opportunism by threatening to
drive away a corrupt merchant's future trading partners. In addition, merchants often could not rely on fair and impersonal foreign courts. In anticipation of costly commercial disputes, merchants do not trade. Self-enforcing
exchange appears infeasible.

Inmates today face the same problem of impersonal exchange. An inmate
might wish to buy drugs from someone whose reputation he doesn't know.
He must interact socially with strangers. In a large prison population, an
inmate can't alert everyone else if he is defrauded. It might be costly to do so,

or controls on his movements in a facility might limit his access to others. Some people might not believe his complaints. If he doesn't know the other inmate, he doesn't know if he will be around for continued dealings or is soon being released. And, of course, there are no official, independent, and fair courts to resolve disputes over drug deals in prison. Whenever inefficiencies like this arise, there is a profit opportunity available to someone who can solve it. Inmates overcome this impediment to trade in the same way that medieval merchants did.

Historically, people who sought to participate in impersonal exchange have often developed a "community responsibility system" to establish order and promote trade.[5] In such a system, all members of a community are responsible for the actions and obligations of any other member. Consider two communities. These could be communes in medieval Genoa and London, but for the sake of familiarity, let's consider two of the most prominent American fraternal groups: the Knights of Columbus and the Elks Lodge.

Imagine that a member of the Knights wants to buy a car from a member of the Elks, but he doesn't personally know the seller. In a community responsibility system, if the Elk fraudulently sold the Knight a lemon, then all members of the Elks Lodge would be responsible for his actions. The Knights of Columbus could demand that the Elks Lodge either force the Elk member to refund the money or they could do it themselves. The Knights have a credible threat to make these demands. If the Elks do not make restitution, then all members of the Knights of Columbus boycott all members of the Elks Lodge, not just the fraudulent one. They hold the community responsible. If the Elks Lodge members wish to be on good terms with the Knights of Columbus, then this is a serious threat.

The community responsibility system provides a clever solution to the problem of impersonal exchange. All that a person needs to know about a potential trading partner is the reputation of his community, rather than the individual's personal history and reputation. It is less costly to obtain this information. If the community has a reputation for upholding each member's obligations, then a member of the Elks can trade in good faith with a member of the Knights whom he doesn't know. He knows that if a Knights member takes advantage of him, then the Elks can impose costs on the Knights.

For this type of system to operate effectively, each community must establish structures that allow non-members to verify a person's affiliation. These signals should be difficult to fake, so that non-members can't free ride on a community's good reputation. If someone could easily claim to be an Elks member, then he could trade with Knights and defraud them. The community must also be able to monitor its members. They exclude people from their community who they think will be delinquent or opportunistic in their dealings. A key reason for the success of the community responsibility system is that it creates incentives for those who can more easily observe peoples' behavior to certify their trustworthiness and punish wrongdoings. While it is costly for a stranger to learn about a particular person, the community members themselves can more easily assess a member's reliability by relying on their personal knowledge of the individual. As members of each community select and monitor their members, trade among groups becomes easier.

In today's prisons, gangs perform the same assurance role that exists in a community responsibility system. An inmate who wants to buy drugs may not know if a gang member is trustworthy, but he does know the gang's reputation. All members of a gang are responsible for each member's actions. Gangs work in a community responsibility system to encourage peace among inmates and to facilitate a flourishing impersonal trade in contraband. Inmates have structured their community to fulfill the two requirements of a functional community responsibility system. First, it is easy to determine which group an inmate is affiliated with. They rely, in large part, on race to identify a person's affiliation, and they use prominent gang tattoos to make further distinctions. Each gang has a variety of logos and insignia that indicate one's membership.[4] An unaffiliated inmate puts his life at risk if he gets a gang tattoo without their permission. Second, each gang has procedures for assessing the quality of a potential member and mechanisms for monitoring his actions. This helps the gang demand good behavior from its members and protects its reputation. This system provides the foundation of self-governance by prison gangs in the society of captives.

The Role of Race and Ethnicity in Group Formation

In California, there are three levels of gang affiliation in the community responsibility system.[5] The California Department of Corrections and Rehabilitation designates the most active, hard-core gang members as falling into the category of "Security Threat Group I." This category includes members of the Aryan Brotherhood, Black Guerilla Family, Mexican Mafia, Nazi Low Riders, Northern Structure, Nuestra Familia, and Texas Syndicate. These are some of the oldest and most notorious prison gangs. To both officials and inmates, these gang members are the most serious, "made" members of prison gangs. "Security Threat Group II" includes inmates associated with other groups and street gangs that are lower in the gang hierarchy, including members of the Crips, Bloods, Norteños, Sureños, White Supremacists, 2–5's, and Northern Riders. Many other gangs and inmate groups at this level exist. These inmates are members of criminal gangs on the street, and in prison, these gangs often play a supportive or subordinate role to the elite prison gang members. For example, Norteños and Sureños act as soldiers for the Nuestra Familia and Mexican Mafia. A Norteño is not a full-fledged prison gang member, but as a Norteño, he is affiliated with the Northern Hispanic inmates who are controlled by the Nuestra Familia. When members of street gangs enter the prison system, they set aside their rivalries and align with their respective prison gang group. These inmates are involved in the gang politics of the prison, even if they are not officially members of one the traditional prison gangs.

The least involved inmates are those with no street gang affiliation. These people align with broader racial and ethnic groups, primarily as blacks, whites, Hispanics from Southern California, Hispanics from Northern California, Paisas, American Indians, and Asians. (Among inmates, each of these groups are referred to as "races," even if they do not fit the formal definition of the term.) All inmates are expected to affiliate with their racial or ethnic group, which in turn is governed to different degrees by the gangs above them in the hierarchy. These people are not prison gang members per se, but because race, ethnicity, and gang are so closely linked, when inmates use phrases like "gang politics," "gang membership," and "gangbangers," they are also referring to these broader racial and ethnic groups.[6] For example, a Hispanic from Northern California with no street gang ties would affiliate with Norteño inmates and follow their gang rules, even though he is not a gang member. Full gang membership is not required, but all inmates must affiliate with some inmate group, most commonly one's race.[7] (Accurately accounting for this distinction is one factor that undermines the reliability of data on prison gang membership.) Race, ethnicity, and gang membership are thus intimately interlinked, and one's race and ethnicity play a major role in determining one's place in the prison social system.

Prison gangs have become influential participants in the inmate social system. "Shot callers" run the gangs and make demands of the inmates who affiliate with them. Their decisions affect inmate's daily lives in a number of surprising and important ways. For instance, understanding prison gang politics helps explain today's widespread racial segregation in prison. Despite the California Department of Corrections and Rehabilitation's policy of full racial integration, race permeates nearly all aspects of the inmate social system.[8] A white inmate at the Los Angeles County Jail explains, "I never wanted to get involved in racial problems. When I went to prison, I didn't hate blacks. I didn't hate Mexicans. I didn't hate Indians. I didn't hate anybody like that. But when you go to these prisons, by the time you do 10 years, like me, if you are even half way sane, it's a miracle."[9] A white inmate sitting at a table in one of San Quentin's dorms explained the racial politics of where one can sit: "There's just certain races that you can play [card] games with right here [at this table]... Don't ask me why. But we can't play with the black folks. I would get beat up. You'd get in a fight over it. That's just the way it is. There's more racism here than there is in civilization, for sure. And if you don't come in prejudiced, you might leave prejudiced."[10] Inmates only have their hair cut by someone of the same race, and only with clippers that other races have not used.[11] A white inmate at Pelican Bay State Prison described the obligatory nature of segregation, explaining, "to talk to a black would cause problems with my own race.... I grew up totally colorblind so it's a big adjustment, you know, but that's just how it is.[12]

People with no history of racism, who may actually hold no racist beliefs, must live in a segregated world. One inmate reports that many people who appear to hate others are just adopting the rules and behaviors necessary for survival. He described the prison community: "That's how the whole system runs. I mean, everything is broken into little groups. I mean, and theoretically, you know, a lot of people hate [and] hate. And, you know, it's all about hate and this and that. But it's not, really. What it's about is mainly, you come into an environment and you're surrounded by a thousand killers and every one of them is a stranger. So naturally, you're going to find people that you have things in common with and you're going to group up because you have to."[13] A black inmate at Pelican Bay notes, "I've never been a racist person, and I will never be a racist person. But there are realities in each environment that dictate its own response, whether we like it or not. In a violent institution, I have to find a way to shelter myself from that violence or respond to it when it becomes necessary. Not because it's my mentality but it's necessary to survive."[14]

An inmate has an obligation to defend his own race when interracial violence erupts. A black inmate described what was required of him: "If it's a racial situation, you got to respond according to your racial background. If I'm standing next to this man here, and he's suddenly attacked by another racial group. Even if I don't know him, he's black. I'm obligated by myself to assist this man."[15] A white inmate at Folsom Prison echoed this rule: "If it's a white thing, you know, you get in it. If it's with the whites and another race or something, then you got to be a part of it. If it's something else, I just turn my head. I don't even want to see it."[16] If it's a "white thing," a dispute between a white inmate and an inmate of another race, then he has an obligation to aid the white inmate. The associate warden at Pelican Bay testified that inmates group up by race when violence erupts, because "if they didn't, they would be disciplined, so to speak, by their own race."[17] Self-policing by race is widespread.

Gangs require inmates to support their group when violence takes place, but they do not enforce segregation in every situation. A black inmate who served eight years for manslaughter explained how the "official" rules (official among the inmates) work: "The races don't officially mix. That's true, but you can buy drugs from whoever, and the leaders control that stuff. I've had a cig-arette with some white guys, and the Mexicans, the Southerners, are mostly good guys. Their leaders are, well, some of them are flexible with their boys. It's not as cut and dried as you think. But if a fight breaks out, then yes, the races stick together. If the blacks and whites go at it, I'm in and I'm taking down some white guys."[18] A white gang leader noted that when he was incar-cerated, even though some interracial interactions were acceptable, housing had to remain segregated: "We have to keep control on the race thing. I was fine with the boys playing cards or dealing meth to the blacks and the Southerners and stuff, that's fine. Celling-up is another story... if he told me he was going to the blacks to cell up, then I check him."[19]

Inmates learn about segregation quickly when they arrive at prison, and both the correctional officers and gang members tell them about it. An officer at San Quentin explains that it's easy to identify inexperienced inmates. "You can always spot a guy that's not used to prison—a new inmate. Because he'll come out. He'll wander around. He won't go with his own group. He's just looking. And, usually what will happen is one of the gangsters will go over and snatch him up and bring him over and run the game down to him. Tell him this is what you got to do, this is where you got to be. You can only hang out with your own people. We don't want to see you talking to people of other races. And, that happens real quick, real quick."[20] Officers also tell new inmates about the segregation.[21] An inmate who served a five-year sentence for assault with a deadly weapon explained, "I'm a white guy, so I can only hang with white guys in prison. The COs told me that I would only run with the white guys. I knew that going in, but they told me too. A guy, a white guy, came up to me right away and told me to get with the skins and I'd be okay. I got some ink, some white power stuff."[22] A Public Enemy #1 (PEN1) gang member notes, "When I got in, the other guys took me under their wing. They showed me where to go and what to do.... Most of the guys going in don't have a clue, so you talk with your cars [people from your county], you figure out what to do. It's not hard."[23] Up until 2005, inmate reception forms even explicitly asked inmates to report which gang they affiliated with.[24] For example, at one prison, a Hispanic inmate could identify his gang affiliation as Northerner, Southerner, Bulldog, or Paisa.

According to the *Johnson v California* (2005) Supreme Court ruling, inmates held in double cells at prison reception centers had "pretty close" to zero percent chance of being housed with someone of a different race. This makes it more likely that an inmate will affiliate with his racial group. The initial receiving officer may even warn new inmates about the state of gang politics. One officer told the inmates who just arrived, "Just some friendly advice, men. Whites, Brothers, Northerners, Southerners, Paisas, listen up. The Bulldogs [a Hispanic, Fresno-based prison gang] are bombing on you. They don't care—three on one, four on one, it doesn't matter to them. So keep your eyes open. You don't have any problems with the cops here. You got problems with the dogs. Now I'm not giving you a green light to go and retaliate, but go talk to your peoples and see what's up."[25]

For the community responsibility system to operate effectively, inmates need new arrivals to integrate with the existing groups. Each race expects the other groups to educate new inmates about the system. When inmates are affiliated, leaders can assert influence on group members to limit disruptive behavior. When this happens, the system works well, so each group wants others to inform new inmates about how the system works. A white inmate who served 10 years for robbery complained, "The black dudes were slow at training their new guys. When they [white inmates] come in, we have a talk and set them straight. My boys were on it; you cannot fuck around and let this slide. The Mexicans, they know what's what and they were quick, but the black guys, that's a different story. I had to remind them several times, you know, 'You have a new boy on the yard' and stuff."[26] In a study of reception centers, sociologist Philip Goodman noted, "One officer at Central told me that there were very few 'Unaffiliated Hispanics' at reception center Central because of extreme pressure and violence by Fresno 'Bulldogs' who, according to the officer, will not 'tolerate' 'Unaffiliated Hispanics.'"[27] As each race brings new inmates into the fold, they establish well-defined groups, solidify segregation, and assert their power over the inmate population. New inmates quickly find a place in the community responsibility system. If gangs served solely a predatory or war-like function, then we wouldn't expect white inmates to encourage black inmates to become affiliated, as this would serve to strengthen their adversary. Instead, inmates want everyone to affiliate because it facilitates the governance provided in a community responsibility system.

Prison Gangs Create Order

To understand why inmates cannot opt out of the community responsibility system, it is necessary to understand the extent to which these groups control prison life. Each gang claims territory, basketball courts, toilets, showers, workout equipment, tables, benches, and other common property. There are rules for when each race can use the showers and in what order they will go to lunch. A correctional officer at San Quentin describes it in terms of a battle: "This is a turf war here. Everybody's got their own turf. And they're not going to let anybody else take it from them. Inmates segregate theirselves out here. And the reason being that the gangs want it that way. So a man has no choice but to go with his own type of people."[28]

Violence is an important mechanism for allocating resources. Gangs fight for something as simple as where one congregates in the prison yard or who controls the TV at specific times. A former gang member relayed the intensity of these battles: "If a new yard opens up, you're going to fight for that handball court, you know, you're going to fight for some tables.... If you ain't a Northerner [Norteño] and you come into that areas, you're going to get stabbed. It's a whole different lifestyle in here. And it can get complicated sometime."[29] Another inmate noted that officials have little say in what happens in the yard: "Somebody wanna control this basketball court or that basketball court. Or this weight bench or that weight bench. CO has nothing to do with that. That's amongst the inmates, the convicts. Sometimes you can maybe talk it out, get it settled without the violence. Sometimes you have to bring the violence."[30] Sociologist Brian Colwell relays a white inmate's account of an altercation that took place over control of a common resource. The white inmates were allied with Southern Hispanic inmates, and the inmate explains that he approached several black inmates who were playing checkers on the Southerners' workout bench:

> I came over and said [in a subdued tone], "Excuse me, could you do me a favor. These are the "Southerners" [Hispanics from southern California] benches. I know they aren't here now, but when they aren't here, they become our [the white inmate groups] responsibility and nobody else is supposed to drive on them when they aren't here. You can finish up your game, but when you're done I'd appreciate it if you could move on up to those other tables that are made to be used to play games on. That's what they are for." They didn't even look up at me, they didn't even pay me that respect when I was talking to them. One

just said, "We're not moving and we're going to do both, white boy." Well, I picked up a weight bar; I was weaker back then so I didn't do it fast enough so he was able to block it with his hand when I was bringing it down on him. Then madness. The whole scene popped off. The riot lasted for 30 minutes, which is a long time for a riot in here.[31]

It is important for gangs to control these common areas and resources in the yard because this is the arena in which much illicit business happens. An officer describes inmates' yard time at San Quentin: "They're down there passing drugs, they're down there passing information, there are orders on who's to be hit, who's supposed to be holding weapons, who's supposed to be holding drugs. And, you know, it's their time to do their business."[32]

In addition to the direct benefits derived from controlling these resources, some areas of a prison yard also provide strategic advantages. The physical layout of a yard can make it difficult for one group to launch an attack against another group without warning. Some areas allow inmates to monitor other inmates more easily or to be more concealed from direct observation by correctional officers.

One of the gangs' most important jobs is to resolve conflicts among inmates, the most common causes of which are disrespect, disputes over drug deals and drug debts, and theft.[33] The shot callers watch out for problems and work to resolve them when they arise. A shot caller is typically someone who has been incarcerated (often in that housing area) for a relatively long time, knows the facility and common problems to arise, and has the skills needed to resolve disputes. A former inmate explained, "A shot-caller is someone that runs the whole tank or module. Pretty much, people that know a lot about incarceration cuz they've been in prison for a while. They run it and they run the section."[34] Another former inmate described the two main functions that the shot caller performs: "So here's the deal, you got old guys like me who have been in prison forever and have shot-callers do their job, keep peace and run the action. That's why we have shot callers so when a couple of idiots get into it in the yard, instead of letting them kill themselves, the shot-caller goes out and works it out. He talks to these guys and finds out what happened, who did what to who, it's very simple."[35]

Each gang is responsible for their members' actions, so they have an incentive to monitor their members to ensure they maintain their collective reputation. Interacting with unknown people from different gangs is possible because each inmate knows that the other gang's reputation is on the line and each gang faces relatively low costs of demanding good behavior from its members. A white inmate at Folsom Prison explained that if an inmate from your county acts poorly, it reflects poorly on you, so you are the obvious person to handle the problem. He noted, "Like if you get somebody who has been an informant from your county, you know, or a child molester or something, somebody in your car (that's your county).... You got to handle it. Somebody's gotta handle it or the whole car is shunned. You know your whole car will be put on shine, you know, lame status."[36] To protect their reputation, groups punish members who violate the rules of the inmate social system.

If someone starts trouble, the shot caller can punish him or make him apologize. A white inmate who served eight years for robbery and assault explained how the gang worked to keep white inmates in line: "I knew this guy that ran his mouth a lot, made lots of problems, called people names and stuff. He called these Mexican guys a bunch of greasy wetbacks. He's a loose cannon, he's going to cause trouble you know what I mean, we work hard to keep that race shit calm and here is this prick causing trouble, no one wants that so we had to check him. We took him down a peg or two, it came right from the top, the asshole needs a lesson."[37] A black inmate described his initial surprise at the gang policing of interracial violence. After he disrespected a white inmate, "the next thing I know, I'm told to make it right with him. I have to man up and take care of my shit. At first I thought, you gotta be kidding me. No way am I going to tell this guy that I'm sorry. Then they told me that I have no choice. That's the rule, you do what you're told. They made a very good argument about how I need to fall in line. Okay, so I made things right."[38] A Northern Hispanic inmate explained, "Pretty much we respect other groups. You aren't supposed to be disrespectful or do anything...like disrespecting you to just get everybody in a wreck. If I was just to say, 'Fuck you' just because, that is not tolerated."[39] One inmate elaborated on how things might unfold if an inmate felt disrespected by an inmate of another race. He would go to "the guy with the most power or seniority over the car (group). Then they hold court and decide what discipline is to be had. Maybe run, they'll make the guy run laps, [as opposed] to stabbing him. That doesn't happen very often. It's got to be a big deal for a guy to get stabbed. It's usually just something so they see it. The other side. They see it and know we have unity. We show everybody we go down together and this guy got disciplined."[40]

A white inmate who served 16 months on a drug charge explained, "If someone pisses me off, you know starts trouble with me, he has to answer to his own people. They decide if it's worth fighting over you know? If they decide that he's just a big dick and he needs to apologize to me for being a dick then he will tell me he's sorry. That's how it usually ends. Nothing too dramatic."[41] One inmate described the process of intergroup dispute resolution: Members of other races "aren't going to communicate with you for no reason unless they are trying to prevent problems. There is no doubt who is right or wrong. Some guy starts saying 'Man I didn't do this or that'; it's like 'Shut up.' It's not going to be, 'He's lying.' Cuz for one there's going to be other people that seen it. People will be talking about, 'Yeah we saw him do this to that white guy, disrespecting him.'"[42]

Another inmate described how each group monitors and punishes its own members: "We need to keep the boys in line. If one of our guys is a hot head or something and is always shooting off his mouth it can get everyone into trouble. We don't want a lockdown, we don't want a riot so I've had to beat down my own guys to control the bigger picture. If one of my guys is messing up then we either offer him up to the other guys or we take him down ourselves. Like I had a guy that ran up a big drug debt, he owed money to the woods [peckerwood skin-head gang] and I had to turn him over to them. They took him to a cell and really beat the shit out of him. We had to do it. If not, then everyone fights which is bad for business and bad for us."[43]

For illicit markets to operate effectively, there has to be an arena in which inmates can resolve commercial disputes. If an inmate owes someone money, the lender can work with their gang to be paid. A PEN1 gang member described how they worked together: "My leader tells me to talk with their Lieutenant and set up the rules. There's really no problem here, and no one is jumping me or anything. It would be a lot worse if I did not know what was going on with the brothers, you know? We have to talk. I remember this one time, the colored guys owed us some money, so I go to their guys and say 'Hey, man, I want to work with you, but I'm not a punk, you need to pay up.' They were totally cool, their guy was like, 'That's cool man, I get it, we'll talk with the boys.' Stuff like that. I have to tell you, I do not like the blacks; I know that's not cool, but I don't like them. That doesn't mean that I won't talk to them. If the time is right and they owe me money, they will pay up if I explain that it's about business. Everyone is fine with that."[44] Despite the fact that inmates segregate by race, have racist tattoos, and vocalize their hatred of others, they work together to establish order so that they can gain from trade and live together more peacefully. When there are profits available, people find ways to overcome prejudices.

Gangs don't always make their members do the right thing, and disputes still happen. A white inmate described one such instance: "I got into a fight with this guy; he owed me money. I told his boys that they need to talk with him and they were like, 'What can we do about it?' which means that I gotta go get the money myself. I go talk with him, and he spits on me. What the hell? I wasn't going to beat him up, but now I have to on principle alone.... If he was cool, nothing would happen. Instead, he has to be a total dick and spit at me. Who does that? What are we, 10 years old?"[45]

Typically, gangs must authorize the use of violence because spontaneous, unplanned violence causes problems for other inmates. An inmate who did eight years for manslaughter explained, "You can talk with the leaders if you want to fight, that's fine, but you cannot just jump a guy in the yard.... The guards will see that something is up and they'll start watching us.... [Y]ou start bringing down another guy, and now everyone is involved and it's a mess. So I say, look, talk to the leaders, see if they'll let you take the guy down in a blind spot or in their cell. Keep that shit low-key, right? No need to bring in the cops over some name calling. We can take care of that."[46]

Public acts of violence attract staff attention, which hinders inmates' ability to deal in contraband. Profit-seeking gang leaders have an incentive to control violence. An inmate who served four years described how the inmate rules determine when and where violence is acceptable: "You have the official rules, no going out of bounds and stuff, but there are the rules of the yard and the rules of the cell. We knew when to fight and when not to. You know, there are riots in prison, but those are planned and we know when to let things go. You get confused about all the rules at first, but the longer you are in, the easier it is. At first, I got in a lot of fights cuz some guy would stare me down or say shit to me; then I learned the rules, and I knew when to ignore shit and when to pay attention. The longer you are there, the easier it is. You just have to learn when and where to do your thing."[47]

Gangs create rules to police their own people and to promote market activity, but inmates do fight, stab, and kill each other over disputes. Violence causes trouble for market participants, especially when it occurs in public. After riots, officials put inmates on modified programming, including possibly a complete facility lockdown or a lockdown for particular races. Without access to the mainline population, gang drug-dealers cannot do business and inmates cannot enjoy time outside. A former inmate lamented the ill effects of a lockdown: "Well, we don't fight in a riot and stuff unless we have to, it's too dangerous. We'll go into lockdown which sucks and people get killed and stuff. If I'm locked down, then I'm not working. You can make some serious bank in prison and shot-callers hate it when you're in lockdown."[48] A black inmate explained that shot callers strived to avoid lockdowns, because "the gangs can't sell their stuff, drugs and stuff. They don't want a lockdown, that's true.... Leaders get pissed if there's a lockdown and we don't get yard time, I hated it.... It's best to handle things low-key. No one needs a riot."[49]

When gangs determine that violence is necessary, they orchestrate it to be less disruptive. To settle minor disputes, inmates often fight in a cell. One former inmate explained, "If someone disses me or someone takes my stuff then the leaders tell us to take it to the cell. We slug it out and get things taken care of."[50] Another noted that cell fights allowed inmates to avoid formal reprimands: "We do a lot of cell fights. I may have words with someone, someone may piss me off so we take it to the cell and have a cell fight. No one sees us and we don't get written up."[51] A gang member argued that "the leaders, they control most of the problems and keep the peace. It's not like they show on TV, we don't fight hardly ever. We control the yard and keep the boys in check."[52]

A Hispanic inmate who served a six-year sentence for robbery and assault explained prison gangs' dual nature: "The boys inside, they follow the rules and that means you work with your own boys and do what they say. Look, there is a lot of problems caused by the gangs, no doubt. The thing is, they solve problems too. You want a structure and you want someone to organize the businesses so the gangs have their rules. You don't run up a drug debt, you don't start a fight in the yard and stuff. Gangs are a problem but we took care of business.... The cops split up gangs if there's a big problem so we keep to ourselves and mind our own business."[53] The possibility of earning illicit profits creates incentives for violent criminals to promote order behind bars.

Information and Enforcement Mechanisms

Prison gangs can provide governance effectively because they have clearly defined mechanisms of information transmission and punishment that allow them to enforce rules. There are clear threats that back up the definition of appropriate behavior. These information and enforcement mechanisms facilitate the making and following of rules, and enable prison gangs to monitor and control their own members and the actions of others. Unlike norms, these rules do not rely on decentralized punishment. There are venues for determining the appropriate rules and delegation of the responsibility to monitor and punish infractions.

Gangs create mechanisms to generate and distribute information about people in prison.[54] It is relatively easy for inmates to learn about a new arrival's criminal past. One way is simply to ask the new inmate to see his official paperwork, which will state the offenses for which he was convicted. New inmates violate an important rule by not showing their paperwork, and it often indicates that he has something to hide.[55] Moving to a new facility will not necessarily give an inmate a fresh start either, because inmate correspondence allows people to notify others of the new arrival's status.[56] An inmate can also ask someone on the outside to access an inmate's criminal docket on legal websites like PACER or Westlaw and then mail copies or summarize the findings. In California, contraband cell phones even allow inmates to access the Megan's Law database to find out which inmates are sex offenders.[57] In fact, the simple act of being transferred to a new prison reveals some information about an inmate; it often indicates that he had conflict at his previous prison. One inmate explained his reasoning after he became suspicious that a new arrival (who wouldn't show his paperwork) was a child molester: "He's a transfer, that's a red flag anyway but a transfer without paperwork, yeah he's dirty. So I just tell him okay, that's cool, see ya later. I'm not asking questions, we don't ask questions at that point. I then check with my people, and they say he needs a hit. Three of us take him out in a blind spot."[58] Officials reportedly aid the inmates to some extent in identifying sex offenders, and an inmate claimed, "the COs tell us, they hate these guys, too."[59]

Shot callers educate new inmates on the rules of the prison yard, and they send written communications to collect information. A shot caller will often send a new inmate a note that contains a new-arrival questionnaire. A typical note might have seven questions (called a "seven on seven"). It will ask for the new inmate's name, nickname, date of birth, neighborhood that he's from, when and where he's been incarcerated, charges and offenses, and what rank, if any, he holds in prison and street gangs. These questionnaires tend to be shorter at the county jail level because inmates spend less time there, inmate populations are more transitory, and pre-prison social networks provide more information. At state prisons, gangs use a longer questionnaire and ask about a new inmate's background more extensively. For example, a longer ("forty on forty") questionnaire at San Quentin asked if the inmate's family had ever been in law enforcement, if he was trained in any martial arts, if he had any family members in prison, and if he was willing to work for the gang. When transferring to a new facility, a gang member might smuggle a note from the shot caller at his old prison to the shot caller at the new prison to help establish his reputation in the facility. For instance, the rules governing Northern Hispanic inmates state, "It shall be the responsibility of the lieutenant to inform the captain of the departure of his soldados in order that the familia of the other regiment can be informed."[60] In other words, the shot caller alerts the leader at the new prison that the new arrival is a trustworthy member in good standing.

A similar information-gathering process exists when people leave prison and return to their neighborhoods. A letter sent from a Mexican Mafia member at Pelican Bay State Prison to members of the Florencia 13 street gang outlines the gang's *reglas*, or rules. Rule 3 states:

> We encourage that homies check any paperwork on those who gets out of the joint from the hood. Keep in mind that there are *no exceptions*. … Therefore as a barrio we must make sure all of our homies are who they say they are—by asking for proof and anyone who refuses will be put on a "leva status" [traitor status] until they show proof of their history and who they were with [in prison]. Then we can run a make on them, solid homies will understand the need for this. We ask that all Pres' [gang clique presidents] keep us up-2-date on what's going on in the hood, by keeping in-touch either by themselves or through a home-girl—she is to write to us every now & then or sent to visit…but either way it needs to be done in a round-about way and not straight out!

In a large prison system, a decentralized governance system does a poor job of keeping track of others' behavior. Prison gangs, however, have the incentive and ability to monitor people's reputations. They maintain detailed "enemies lists" of inmates who are deemed "no good." The Nuestra Familia (NF) calls their directory the Bad News List.[61] These lists include the names of "defectors, informants, witnesses, and enemy gang members who are systematically eliminated."[62] Court transcripts indicate, "Every lieutenant in Nuestra Familia was responsible for 'see(ing) to it that something was done about the people on the list.' The higher-ups schooled their subordinates as to the identity of the gang's enemies and a lieutenant could, on his own initiative, order his soldiers to execute a known enemy of the Nuestra Familia."[63]

The gang shot caller checks the list for the names of new prison arrivals. According to the Nuestra Familia's written rules, a member of the gang "shall check all new arrivals who entered his territory against the record books and make a report to his captain"[64] The NF constitution also explains that members "shall question all new familianos assigned to him for information as to unknown enemies of La Nuestra Familia. New information shall go into the record book and whenever one of his *soldados* [soldiers] is transferred to another *pinta* [prison], a copy of the record book shall be sent with the soldado."[65]

Gangs create clear and explicit procedures for obtaining information about an inmate, specifying particular people to collect this information. Gang leaders expect them to perform these tasks and hold them accountable if they do not. By comparison, prior to the 1960s, inmates obtained information in a decentralized fashion. No particular inmate was assigned to collect information about new inmates, there was no list of uncooperative and disruptive people, and there were no explicit channels through which that information was communicated. Reputations were sufficiently well known and populations were small enough that these elaborate information networks were unnecessary and redundant. In today's large prison system, inmates must create explicit protocols and lists to keep track of which inmates are untrustworthy. Gangs govern the social system effectively because they know which inmates are reliable and can exclude and punish opportunistic inmates. Their information collection mechanisms and capacity for violence provide a credible threat that elicits obedience from inmates.

What Rules Do Prison Gangs Enforce?

Like other criminal organizations, many prison gangs have written down the rules of good conduct that they require inmates to follow.[66] Some rules guide behavior between groups. For example, in Illinois, prison gangs agreed on a set of "international rules" for interacting with different racial groups.[67] In California, an officer at San Quentin described how "the inmates have what they call prison politics. And the gangs control all of that. They have, literally, written rules and regulations, and the repercussions for not following those rules are serious."[68] A sergeant in the Investigative Services Unit explained, "All violence in prison is gang related. Especially when you're talking about an assault where weapons were used, where a guy's hurt this badly. It just doesn't happen without being ordered or authorized by the gang.... He [an inmate who was just assaulted] was probably in trouble for one thing or another that he did in his past, violating gang rules."[69] A former inmate noted, "We set up a structure in prison. In fact, in some prisons, like in San Quentin, La Eme has a handbook, you know, like a written book on rules and regulations. The COs spend a lot of time up there confiscating the book. They're such assholes; those books keep us in line. It tells us what to do and what we can't do."[70]

Inmate rules provide a way to secure access to the resources needed on any given day. An inmate explained, "There are so many rules about who goes first in line for meals and who gets the TV first. If you follow all these rules, you end up doing easy time."[71] These rules mitigate the costs that one's actions impose on others. For example, inmates on one occasion assaulted someone who had not showered for a month.[72] Another inmate noted the difficulty that arises when inmates don't know the rules: "I knew prison was hard but I never thought I'd have to know rules about who uses the shower first and who sits with who and who the leaders are. I think that's why there are fights, the dumb guys don't know the code going in and they screw up."[73] These rules help to resolve disputes over conflicts associated with common problems.

The Norteño and Sureño inmate populations are two of the largest and most powerful groups in the California prison system. They are, roughly speaking, Hispanics from north and south of the city of Delano, near Bakersfield.[74] Both gangs have written documents that delineate the characteristics of proper conduct.[75] At the Los Angeles County Jail, Sureño inmates must follow the 28 rules laid out by the shot caller.[76] These rules tell inmates what they may, must, and must not do. The rules govern several types of interactions that arise in the custodial setting. (Parenthetical remarks within the quotes in the following paragraphs are comments and interpretations by law enforcement officials who have examined the rules.)

First, the gang creates rules to govern interactions with non-members. Rule 3 says, "No getting in the *judas'* (correctional officers') face. Stay off the nurse, store clerk, etc. Show respect." As a former member of the Mexican Mafia explains, "It's an understanding that there is no reason to mistreat guards who don't mistreat you."[77] Rule 4 requires that inmates "stay off the *truchas* (inmate workers)." Everyone benefits from having a clean tier, so don't give the inmate workers trouble. Inmates must refrain from doing things that make jail life uncomfortable for others. These include "no yelling down the *tira* (tier)" and "no disrespecting or name calling on the *tira*." Inmates must limit conversations to people in their own cell and neighboring cells, rather than shouting to people in distant cells. The rules require them to "keep the *tira* clean. No trash unless the *tira* is being swept." Since officials may stop visitations for all inmates when they catch someone engaged in prohibited activity, Rule 8 states, "No illegal activity is allowed until the last chain has gone to visiting on visit days."[78] These rules ease inmate interactions.

Second, the gang has rules to govern behavior among Sureños. Some of these rules are straightforward. They prohibit fighting and horseplay. To ensure that Sureños are able to defend themselves against their enemies, the rules require participation in a daily "mandatory workout of your choice, minimum of one hour." The rules remind inmates to "guard your conversation on the phones." Staff can monitor inmate phone calls, so discussing illegal activities can lead to new criminal charges. Even though assaulting correctional officers is discouraged, a Sureño needs to know that others will assist him if he attacks a staff member. Rule 28 requires that "if one of the Homies feels disrespected and takes off (attacks) on the *judas* (correctional officers), all Homies will follow (back him up)."

The gang establishes rules to improve communication. First, "all cell reps are to run down the rules to the new arrivals on their *tira*." Sureños often communicate by passing notes between cells or relaying messages in person. The rules require that "all *wilas* ("kites" or letters), verbals, items being brought from *corte* (court) or just down the *tira* are not to be short stopped." Inmates must not stop or delay communications from reaching their intended recipients. There is a hierarchy of command among Sureño inmates, so when Sureños have trouble with each other, they are required to first discuss it with their "cell rep." Rule 24 explains, "Any issues or complaints are to be taken up with your cell rep. After, and only after, will I accept *wilas* (letters) to settle the matter." These rules facilitate a shot caller's ability to govern Sureño inmates.

An inmate who breaks these rules may be added to the Sureño enemies list—the Green Light List. Landing on the *lista* is the threat that encourages obedience. The list records the names of inmates who others have the go-ahead (green light) to assault. Someone on the list is referred to as "*verde*," Spanish for green. Figure 4.1 shows a Mexican Mafia enemies list found in the gang module at the L.A. County Jail.[79] This Green Light List shows people in three different statuses. "Disciplines" indicate those gangs that inmates have the green light to assault. Anyone in that gang is subject to violence. "Personal HCs" list particular people who the gang wants assaulted.[80] "Passes" records

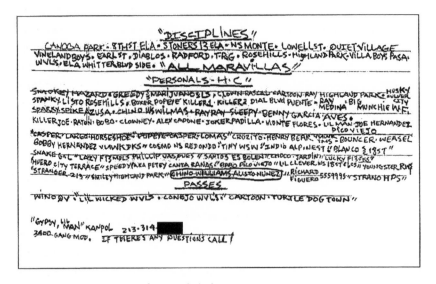

FIGURE 4.1 A Mexican Mafia green light list

those people who the gang previously targeted but who have been forgiven for their transgression.

The gang can put an individual gang member or an entire street gang on the list. If an entire street gang has a green light, any member of that gang (or *varrio*)—regardless of his personal obedience to gang rules—may be attacked. Like the prison environment, street gangs operate in a community responsibility system, so all members of a street gang may be held accountable for one of its member's actions. Rule 21 uses strong language to communicate the need to make use of this enforcement mechanism: "Gang Module Homies (shot-callers) blast (assault) all *verdes, varrios*, and personals (gang or individual green lights). MANDATORY blast unless otherwise stated. Lista *verdes* (green light hit lists) shall be passed every night." Sureños must assault anyone who is on the green light list or whose gang is on the list, and the gang members must update the list on a daily basis. Violence against green-lighted people is not limited to the county jail. Rule 25 requires that "Homies going to court should choose *camaradas* (brothers/partners) and relay *verdes* and personals," meaning to assault people at the court who are on the green light list. One gang member explained, "It's not uncommon for the whole jail to know about greenlight lists. When you get to jail, you get a list of rules and a greenlight list."[81]

Gangs create rules to govern the underground economy. According to a law enforcement official's summary of a rule, "One person per day is responsible for all transactions. There isn't anything in a correctional facility that isn't bartered and all transactions go through a designated person." Drug dealing is especially important, and the shot caller takes a one-third tax on all drugs: "All *clavos* (drugs) are to come to me; I will cut the third." More generally: "All personal transa (transactions) are susceptible to a South Sider [Sureño], and double up when late." A gang expert explained, "A fee or tax is applied by a South Sider to transactions and this fee is doubled when payment is delayed." Of course, secrecy is necessary to conceal this information from officials, so "all South Side business or anything else discussed on the *tira* remains on the *tira*, unless told."

These are the specific rules that Sureños used in a particular jail at a particular time. Examining them doesn't mean that we can generalize about how all gangs provide governance all of the time. However, these rules are informative, for several reasons. First, multiple sources agree that gangs have written rules that provide governance and are enforced. These Sureño rules provide an example. Second, even if we cannot generalize to other inmate groups, these rules govern a very important component of the criminal underworld.

The Los Angeles County Jail system is the largest in the state, and Sureños are arguably the most influential inmate group in the entire state prison system. Third, these rules make sense once one realizes inmates' need for self-governance. It should not be surprising that inmates create rules to reduce conflict with other groups, settle disputes among themselves, and facilitate illicit trade. Doing so is profitable.

Other prison gangs provide similar solutions to the same problems.[82] The Nuestra Familia, for example, has a list of rules called the Fourteen Bonds that Norteños must follow.[83] Like Sureños, the Norteño rules require inmates to get along with each other. Rule 4 demands equal and fair treatment of others: "In order to continue our struggle with far less difficulties, there shall be no tolerance created by internal confrontations, individualism, or homeboy favoritism [favoring those from your own street gang]. No norteño will spread false rumors or negative gossip about a fellow norteño, and at no time will a norteño attempt to take advantage of, or disrespect, a fellow norteño's ruca (girlfriend) or familia. To do so will result in serious repercussions." Rule 7 states, "At no time will a norteño endanger the life of a fellow norteño. There shall be no fighting amongst norteños, nor shall any cowardice dealings with the K-9 [law enforcement] or enemy be tolerated. To do so will be dealt with accordingly." The threat at the end is important to note. These are not requests. These are not norms. These are rules, and if an inmate doesn't follow them, he will be punished.

A Norteño is required to "protect and defend his household to the fullest, no matter the circumstance or consequence. This means standing next to a fellow norteño or the cause both battle or struggle. To abandon such responsibilities will be considered as an act of treason." Like Sureños, inmates must take care of their physical fitness. Rule 8 states, "Be he rank or file, he will have high regard for his physical and mental well-being and will always strive to better himself and become more aware and educated in all aspects relevant to the accomplishments of our set goals."

Norteños use information transmission mechanisms to enforce rules in the inmate social system. New inmates are investigated and interviewed, and "any and all data pertaining to a new arrival shall be reported through its proper channel immediately (see household procedures), especially that which endangers a life or is contrary to the cause." They update Bad News Lists regularly. According to Rule 10, "Every chapter and stronghold of norteños will keep track of all enemy and enemy activities behind enemy lines." All northerners have to learn these rules, and "a norteño should stay abreast of all new laws, policies, and procedures. No portion of this format is to be misinterpreted or abused for personal gain. To do so will be considered as an act of treason."

Inmate groups use written rules to ease tensions among inmates behind bars and to facilitate their illicit businesses. They identify in writing what the acceptable behaviors are and what actions violate the rules. Importantly, unlike norms, these groups have clearly defined mechanisms for making rules, monitoring for rule violations, and communicating these violations to people in authority, and they have methods of punishing infractions. Just like medieval merchants, a community responsibility system helps inmates overcome the challenges of living and trading among untrustworthy strangers.

Predatory or Productive?

Prison gangs provide protection and facilitate the prison drug trade, but there is also no shortage of horrific stories about their victimization of others. What is their net effect on the welfare of inmates? We have already heard much of the inmate's perspective on gangs. They identify ways that gangs make rules, settle disputes, and structure the drug trade. On the other hand, it is obvious that gang members also intimidate and extort some inmates.

Another way to understand the overall effect of prison gangs is to hear what administrators and wardens think they do. In the 1980s, the Department of Justice conducted a national study of prison gangs.[84] They surveyed prison administrators on numerous aspects of prison gang activity. They asked respondents to rate how involved prison gangs are in 19 different criminal acts (1 = very seldom, 2 = seldom, 3 = occasionally, 4 = frequent, 5 = very frequent).[85] Table 4.1 reports the summed scores for each crime. They received responses from 49 jurisdictions, so the maximum number of points possible for any crime was a score of 245. Not surprisingly, gangs are perceived to be engaged in a great deal of predatory behavior, including intimidation, assault, abuse of weak inmates, extortion, theft, strong arm robbery, robbery, rape, murder, and slavery. Intimidation is the most frequent crime reportedly engaged in, although it only receives 60 percent of the possible points. Four of the top five most frequent crimes are of a predatory nature. Clearly, prison gangs do not engage in only benevolent and charitable acts. They are not the Elks Lodge.

However, they do participate in a number of productive and contractual activities, such as selling drugs, protection, prostitution, and sodomy for sale. Although perhaps more scandalous than most people's usual purchases, these are goods and services that many inmates want. The total points for these productive activities are roughly 42 percent of the points assigned to predatory activities.

Table 4.1 Prison Gangs' Involvement in Criminal Acts

Crime	Points	Crime	Points
Intimidation	148	Robbery	89
Drugs	145	Prostitution	88
Assault	134	Rape	83
Abuse of weak inmates	133	Sodomy for sale	83
Extortion	131	Murder	79
Protection	131	Bribery	71
Contraband weapons	128	Arson	61
Theft	117	Slavery	52
Strong arm robbery	99	Explosives	47
Rackets	96		

Source: Camp and Camp 1985, 45

The crime second most frequently engaged in is drugs, just four points shy of being the most frequent. Given that drugs are such an important part of the inmate social system and that inmates have a strong demand for them, this is important to note. Consistent with inmate claims, gangs don't just occasionally deal drugs. It is one of their primary activities.

Several of their activities also have an ambiguous effect on inmates' welfare. For example, participating in the crime of "contraband weapons" receives a high frequency rating, but it is unclear how this influences inmates overall. It might be that gangs use weapons to extort or assault others; on the other hand, inmates may use contraband weapons for protection or to assault correctional officers. Just as a citizen on the street can use a gun to rob someone or to protect his or her home, weapons in prison can be used for good or evil. From an inmate's perspective, the net outcome is not obvious. Other ambiguous crimes on the list include rackets, bribery, arson, and explosives. These crimes are not obviously good or bad for inmates. Bribing an officer might allow a gang member to hurt an innocent person, or it might allow him to smuggle in valuable contraband. Rackets that involve gambling or bootlegging of prison wine (pruno) and alcohol benefit inmates. Of the total points assigned, 60 percent are predatory and 40 percent are productive and contractual or of an ambiguous nature.

This survey provides an indication of the nature of gang influence, but it has several important limitations. First, prison administrators may not fully know what gangs do. Drug dealing, for instance, is something of great importance to inmates, but it is also something that gangs work hard to conceal. Officials are less likely to observe the voluntary interactions that characterize "victimless" crimes than a stabbing or murder, so this measure will tend to underestimate the productive activities. Second, the frequency that a gang engages in some activity isn't the same as its importance. A gang may infrequently murder someone, but that is surely more important than an instance of intimidation. This survey does not account for the importance of the crime, only its perceived frequency. Third, distinguishing between predatory and productive activities from this list is quite subjective. Even assault and intimidation can be good for the inmate community if—as many inmates report—it limits rogue, violent inmates and deters theft. It is commonly believed that governments use the threat of violence to promote peace. In the same way, prison gangs that assault or intimidate others may lead to a more orderly environment.

Recent research has found similar results. A study asked officials at 37 prisons to provide information about the characteristics of prison gang members.[86] Ninety-one percent of respondents believed that the most important reason that inmates join gangs is out of fear of other inmates. Gangs play an important protective role. Moreover, for a majority of inmates, gang membership was desirable because it provided access to contraband, economic benefits, increased status, and a sense of belonging.

Examining the characteristics of gang members and their behavior provides another way to try to understand how predatory or productive prison gangs are. A study of inmates in Nevada found that gang members are more likely to have five or more citations for violating prison rules, be found guilty in disciplinary hearings, and be charged with drugs or fighting.[87] A study by the Ohio Department of Rehabilitation and Correction had similar findings.[88] Past work has shown that, in certain periods, prison gang members committed most prison murders.[89] In Texas, 20 of 25 homicides in 1984 were gang related; 23 of 27 inmate homicides in 1985 were gang related.[90] However, one study found that inmates with the greatest involvement in street and prison gangs were not more likely to engage in prison violence.[91] These studies do not control for other factors or for the selection bias of who joins gangs, so they fail to identify the independent causal effect of gang membership on misconduct and violence. For instance, it might be that the same people who are more likely to be violent are also more likely to join gangs. Without a gang affiliation, they may have caused even more trouble. Officials may also be more likely to cite a gang member for a rule violation. Importantly, from the inmate's perspective, violation of some prison rules enhances welfare if it increases the availability of drugs and other contraband. Moreover, as the qualitative evidence in this chapter suggests, gang-related assaults and murder may improve the overall prison social order. These studies do not provide clear evidence on the overall effect of prison gangs.

A more sophisticated study of prison gang misconduct uses cross-section multivariate regression analysis to compare misconduct by gang and non-gang inmates in federal prisons.[92] The study finds that affiliation with a particular gang "was associated with an increase in the probability of violence for 20 of the 27 gangs and an increase in serious violence for 18 of the 27 gangs."[93] Inmates affiliated with gangs were more likely to be cited for drug and property misconduct (the latter includes theft, damaging property, and gambling). Gang-affiliated inmates were more likely to be written up for being in a prohibited area and disobeying work orders. Inmates with a stronger devotion to their gang engaged in violence more often than those with a looser affiliation. However, violence decreases the longer an inmate is affiliated with a gang. The study found no evidence that gangs are associated with less violence relative to unaffiliated inmates, but "many gangs were no more violent than their unaffiliated peers."[94] This is perhaps the best analysis available to date, but two empirical problems still plague it. First, this study does not show that membership in the gang is the causal factor that makes an inmate more likely to be disruptive. It is likely that inmates who are more likely to break the rules are also more likely to join gangs. Because it is only a cross section, it cannot demonstrate a causal relationship. Second, if gang members use violence to establish order, then these studies are not capturing the true, net effect on violence. By analogy, the average police officer might use force more often than the average citizen, but doing so improves social order. Both cases might tell us there is a specialization in violence, but not what the overall level of violence would be in their absence.

Because of the inability to randomly assign prison gang membership to inmates, all quantitative studies of prison misconduct are correlational or predictive, not causal. Despite the conventional wisdom that prison gangs increase violence, these studies provide no clear empirical link between gang membership and prison violence. A survey of the literature notes, "contrary to popular perception, the relation between inmate characteristics generally, and gang affiliation in particular, and prison violence and disorder, is unknown.... It is remarkable how few quality research studies have been completed on the link between gang/STG [security threat group] membership and prison violence."[95] The authors conclude that "there is simply insufficient scientific evidence from which to draw an accurate profile of those prisoners most likely to engage in various forms of prison violence."[96] The quantitative evidence is inconclusive, and the qualitative evidence suggests that gangs are an important source of governance.

Practical and Theoretical Implications

To correctional officials, prison gangs are a major source of disruption, misconduct, and violence. They promote consumption of controlled substance, gambling, prostitution, and other contraband activities. To staff, this is undesirable. Nonetheless, it would be incorrect to look only at these negative aspects without looking at their productive activities. First, based on both historical and contemporary evidence, prison gangs form and operate to provide protection. Second, gangs adjudicate disputes. Through a community responsibility system, gangs resolve conflicts between rival groups of inmates. In their absence, large-scale impersonal exchange would not be feasible. The option to purchase contraband on credit would be less readily available. From the inmates' perspective, this enhances welfare. Because gangs profit when markets flourish, they have an incentive to promote order. The community responsibility system is not perfect, and no official would have intentionally designed it to operate in this fashion. However, given the demographics of the inmate population and the inability to rely on norms, prison gangs are the low-cost producer of governance in the inmate social system. This does not imply that they are the first-best solution, but relative to a strictly norm-based governance regime, prison gangs improve order.

Understanding the governance mechanisms created by prison gangs has several implications. First, past work on the convict code has characterized its robustness incorrectly. It is neither necessary nor sufficient to provide inmate governance. It is incorrect to claim that the underground economy "can exist only with the protection of the strong inmate culture wherein the inmates generally adhere to the values of the inmate code."[97] Gangs can also provide this governance, so the code is not necessary. Moreover, the convict code is insufficient to support high-volume impersonal trading in large populations, so the cause of the code's decline does not occur only "if the rigor of confinement is mitigated to the point where the sub rosa system is no longer needed."[98] The code also becomes ineffective in the face of certain inmate demographics.

Second, many scholars expected the prison buildup to be characterized by either a rise in disorder and violence or in stricter, totalitarian control of prisons to prevent it. Surprisingly, the best evidence available doesn't show either happening. Bert Useem and Anne Piehl have found that in the United States, from the 1970s to the early 2000s, the rate of riots became less frequent, the homicide and assault rate among inmates declined dramatically, and escapes were less common.[99] At the same time, a slightly smaller proportion of the inmate population was held in protective custody or high-security confinements. Changes in neither architecture nor rehabilitation programs seem to explain the improved social order. With those explanations deemed unsatisfactory, the remaining explanations seem more plausible. They argue, "the data are consistent with the position that political and correctional leadership made prison institutions more effective."[100] It may be true that official governance has improved, but criminal governance has improved as well. Since the study lacks data on the governance created by prison gangs, officials are given credit for all of the resulting social order. Some of the improvement should be attributed to gangs. Gangs' widespread influence in the inmate social system also seems to clash with the claims of improved custodial administration. If officials are so good at what they do, then why must inmates rely on prison gangs for protection?

Third, the increasingly important role that the community responsibility system has played in the last 30 years may mean that official statistics in California are biased. When inmates fight in a cell or a blind spot, official numbers do not capture this violence. Prison gangs orchestrate violence to take place out of officials' watchful eyes. In California, officials lock down inmates on the basis of gang affiliation, race, and ethnicity, rather than confining only those inmates engaged in a particular act of violence, so gangs have greater incentive to discourage rioting and to regulate violence than inmates did in the norm-governed era. Studies of prison social order over time must consider this. Related to this point, it is crucial to distinguish between what Elinor Ostrom calls rules-in-form and rules-in-use.[101] The former are the explicit, *de jure* rules; the latter are the rules that people actually follow and care about. When these diverge substantially, the practices of social life look very different from the way they look on paper. We could say little about prison social order by simply reading Title 15 of the California Code of Regulations or the Department's Operations Manual. Studies of governance institutions based primarily on rules-in-form will often be inaccurate and misleading.

The prison community also provides several important insights into the broader study of self-enforcing exchange. First, past studies of reputation-based governance has failed to distinguish between violent and nonviolent contexts. Unlike in classic studies, for instance, among rural neighbors in Shasta County and Orthodox Jewish diamond traders in New York City, inmates are quite willing to use violence.[102] Boycott alone might be unable to sustain norms in large peaceful communities, but the threat of violence could possibly generate a sufficiently large punishment to deter opportunistic behavior in a large-scale decentralized community. However, what we find in this environment is that even when people are more willing to use violence to support norm-based governance, norms still become ineffective in large populations. They do not scale up.

Second, gangs promote order by adopting racial solidarity and segregation. They do not form gangs simply "to further their racist philosophies," as officials often suggest.[103] In an all-male community where everyone wears the same clothes, race provides a great deal of information about someone very quickly. An inmate can easily observe someone's race, and this facilitates self-policing and community responsibility. While other personal attributes might be more salient and could solidify group identity more strongly, it takes more time for strangers to learn them. For example, inmates could form groups based on a shared religion or set of political beliefs (and some do). The problem is that inmates who don't know each other can't identify as easily whether someone is a Marxist or a Christian, or as quickly, as determining whether the inmate is white or black. When groups coalesce along racial lines, it is easier to identify someone as an enemy or a friend. In addition, an inmate cannot change his race, so racial segregation limits his ability to move from community to community, taking advantage of different groups or falsely claiming membership in a group. Gangs do not form to promote racism; race facilitates criminal governance.

Third, the prison community illustrates a rarely observed outcome. Multiple "protection agencies" occupy the same geographic area. Typically, government or private enforcement agencies do not do this because there are economies of scale in providing protection. Once an organization protects one house, the marginal cost of protecting the next house is much lower. Falling costs lead to a monopoly protection provider in a region.[104] This doesn't happen in prison. One reason for this is that prison gangs provide governance over commerce, and the same economies of scale don't exist in governing trade. There are no large fixed costs to providing governance, so resolving the second commercial or social dispute isn't cheaper than the first.

Fourth, prison gang governance works well, even though it is, in important respects, fully independent of formal governance mechanisms. Past work has debated whether this is possible and whether particular historical examples illustrate robust independent, informal governance mechanisms. For instance, Avner Greif's important early work on the economics of self-enforcing exchange examined the multilateral reputation mechanisms that promoted trade among the Maghribi traders in the Medieval Mediterranean. In a series of papers, Jeremy Edwards and Sheilagh Ogilvie argue that the self-enforcing trading institutions were effective primarily because merchants could use formal courts should informal mechanisms fail.[105] Studying inmate contraband markets avoids this problem—inmates cannot rely on formal mechanisms to adjudicate disputes over illicit goods and services. They are not negotiating in the shadow of the law. They have no recourse to formal institutions, so the illicit market activity in today's prisons supports the contention that self-enforcing exchange can arise fully independent of formal governance mechanisms.

Finally, the development of the inmate governance system informs research on the origin and evolution of government.[106] The transition from small, personal communities to large, impersonal communities requires different governance institutions. The prison social system provides an opportunity to observe how institutional change occurs in a particular context, and it is consistent with claims about when decentralized governance gives way to more centralized power.[107] As economist William Baumol has argued, regarding the similarities between gangs and governments, "there is also much to be learned from a reversal of the comparison, this time not thinking of gangs as quasi-governments, but rather by interpreting most governments in human history as gangster associations."[108] For instance, the study of prison gangs may point to some of the incentives and processes that political elites in early states faced in deciding to adjudicate disputes and to extend political rights. We do not need to assume benevolent motivations on the part of political elites to explain the creation of early states. The ability to benefit from productive economic activity can create the needed incentives. Moreover, the history of prison gangs shows how quasi-governments can emerge through an iterative process rather than from the intentional construction by enlightened political elites.

Theoretical work on self-governance finds that self-enforcing exchange is effective in small, close-knit communities, with good information, populated by people with low time preference who interact indefinitely.[109] In this setting, people have good information about who is trustworthy, they patiently wait to enjoy the benefits of future trades, and they can exclude and ostracize those who act badly. People can make credible threats to punish bad behavior, so people act badly less often. Prisons are different. Inmates can't migrate. They can do little to segregate themselves physically. Prisons are full of a heterogeneous population of untrustworthy people, many of whom are violent. The prison population is large. Nonetheless, inmates participate in a thriving illicit marketplace. Prison gangs provide much of the governance that allows a large number of untrustworthy, heterogeneous traders to engage in large volumes of trade. Inmates, by facing so many impediments to trade, show just how effective and robust self-enforcing exchange can be. The prison contraband trade is not based on the best possible set of trading institutions, and officials do much to undermine it. The fact that it is sometimes more violent than other trading contexts should cause no surprise. Yet despite these shortcomings, drugs, alcohol, sex, cell phones, and a remarkable variety of other contraband are available in jails and prisons. The volume of trade is a testament to the effectiveness of these extralegal governance institutions. Even in this least likely of scenarios, self-enforcing trade can thrive.

Background Check

An Aryan Brother is without a care,
He walks where the weak and the heartless won't dare,
And if by chance he should stumble or lose control,
His brothers are there, to help reach his goal,
For a worthy Brother, no need is too great,
He need not but ask, fulfillments his fate.
For an Aryan Brother death holds no fear,
Vengeance will be his, through his brothers still here,
For the Brotherhood means just what it implies,
A Brother's a Brother,' til that Brother dies,
And if he is loyal, and never lost faith,
In each Brother's heart, will always be a place,
So a Brother am I and will always be,
Even after my life is taken away from me,
I'll lie down content, knowing I stood,
Head held high, walking proud in the Brotherhood.

ARYAN BROTHERHOOD CREED

TYSON WHITE WAS A 38-year-old with a history of drug use and petty crime. In November 2011, police arrested and charged him with aggravated driving under the influence. He pled guilty, and on November 18, he began a two-year sentence in the medium-security Stiner Unit in the Lewis Prison Complex in Arizona. On November 26, White was sitting in the prison yard when an inmate struck him in the back of the head. He ran, but several inmates chased and tackled him. They punched, kicked, and stomped on him until he lay limp on the ground. The assault occurred during an inmate movement period when inmates are allowed to return to their cells, so correctional officers didn't see the assault. As the inmates were walking away from the body, a correctional officer was reentering the yard and noticed White lying on the ground. The officer called for medical attention, and they airlifted him to a nearby hospital. The beating left him permanently brain damaged.

During past prison sentences, White had sought protection by affiliating with the Aryan Brotherhood. When he arrived at the Stiner Unit, he asked other inmates if the Aryan Brotherhood was active on the yard. They were, but because the inmates did not know White, they told him that no one was in charge. Based on inmate interviews from the investigation that followed, White responded by telling inmates that he was now taking charge of the yard on behalf of the Aryan Brotherhood. According to prison officials, White was a "probate." The investigations staff explained, White "began probating while in the county jail. As a probate, they are taught, once you go to a yard, ask to see who is running the yard.... [I]f no one is, then the probate is taught to take over the yard for the Brotherhood. That is what Inmate White did when he got to Stiner Unit." He began conducting Aryan Brotherhood business, including monitoring the drug trade and taking a cut of the profits.

The Aryan Brotherhood member who was actually running the yard didn't care for the intrusion of the unknown inmate. The shot caller began to investigate White and whether he was affiliated with the gang. They wrote letters to Aryan Brotherhood members in other facilities, and they used a contraband cell phone to contact associates on the street. They also sought information from an inmate porter. The porter worked for a correctional officer and had access to a department computer, which held detailed inmate records for everyone incarcerated in the state prison system. As an internal investigation later showed, White's inmate record was accessed four times on November 22, shortly after his arrival. In addition to age, race, and criminal record, an inmate's record reveals if officials have validated him as a member of a prison gang. In White's file, the space in the form where they mark one's prison gang affiliation was blank. The shot caller decided that White was not who he said he was, so he ordered the assault.

Afterwards, an inmate told officials, "The only thing I can say is, once that kid got here he started to say he was some AB big shot. Then they got the call that he wasn't and you know the rest." Another explained, "I'm gonna make it simple. That dude came here and started saying he was somebody come to find out he wasn't nothing." One inmate said, "That dude that got smashed came here and started telling his people that he was somebody and once they found out he wasn't they got him."

Two of the inmates who carried out the assault did so for common reasons. According to the investigative report, the shot caller ordered one inmate to assault White because he had "a drug debt of $2200 to the Mexicans and his participation would zero out the debt." Another one of the assailants wanted to increase his gang standing, and participating in an assault earned him the right to get special gang tattoos. Tattoos play an important role in communicating one's history and gang status to other inmates. The shot caller had also ordered all of the white inmates to go out for yard as a sign of solidarity, and perhaps to make it easier for the attackers to blend into the crowd.

There are conflicting claims about whether White was an Aryan Brotherhood member. The internal investigation concluded that he "wasn't really" a gang member and most of the documentation reiterates this. His lawyer says that he was never an official member and only associated with them for protection. However, the official report does admit he was a probate, and it says, "a short time after the assault occurred, word came down.... Inmate White was who he claimed to be, no one knew because word did not yet reach the other members of Inmate White's probating until it was to late."

Running a large, illicit organization across multiple correctional facilities throughout the state poses important challenges. Gangs must find a way to obtain information about which inmates are members and what rank and authority they hold in the gang. To protect their reputation and profits, they have to prevent people from falsely claiming to be members. In a community responsibility system, each member's actions create obligations on others, and they do not want to be accountable for non-members. A prison gang faces the constant struggle of maintaining secrecy and coordinating members' productive enterprises, and the risk of assaulting one of their own.

5

The Internal Organization
of Prison Gangs

If I go forward, follow me.
If I hesitate, push me.
If I am killed, avenge me.
If I am a traitor, kill me.

LA NUESTRA FAMILIA OATH

Organizational and Strategic Challenges

In developed countries, businesses, nonprofits, and cooperatives can rely on effective institutional environments to capitalize on commercial, charitable, and social opportunities. They have access to fair courts of law. Stock markets and banks are willing and able to provide financing and loanable funds. People can rely on competent accountants, lawyers, marketers, managers, human resources personnel, and consultants to ensure that they run the operation in a profitable manner. These resources aid entrepreneurs in structuring their internal operations, hiring employees, and enticing customers. Any large commercial endeavor must accomplish these tasks, but gangs must do so without the help of mainstream legal institutions.[1]

Gangs create internal structures to address three main organizational challenges. First, they must find ways to recruit high-quality members. They want people who have a credible threat of violence, have street smarts, and are brave and loyal—skilled prison criminals.[2] Low-quality members are lazy, dishonest, disruptive, disloyal, and weak. Gangs with high-quality members have a more credible threat of violence and can more effectively devise and conduct profitable illegal enterprises. A former Mexican Mafia member describes the characteristics that the gang values: "We have our own standards and expectations that govern our behavior. Brutality is lauded. A brother is considered a good man because he has committed acts of violence for the Mexican Mafia. He's not a snitch or a coward. He's a stand-up guy. What the regular world condemns, we praise. Your best friend comes along and brothers vote him out, even though you like the guy, you got to whack him."[3] While most inmates affiliate with a group based on racial, geographic, or gang ties, relatively few inmates take the additional step of becoming a "made" member of a prison gang. Prison gangs need to identify the best potential recruits from within the broader inmate population.

Second, gangs need to limit behavior that imposes costs on other members. If a member doesn't maintain his physical prowess, he diminishes the collective threat the gang poses. If one member acts cowardly, all are shamed. As the Texas Aryan Brotherhood explains, "Each member is a mirror of his Brother. Your actions reflect on all Brothers, and breach of the Brotherhood is a serious matter which will be handled as such."[4] Legally, the Pinkerton Conspiracy doctrine makes each co-conspirator in a gang responsible for reasonably foreseeable crimes committed by all other members. If one gang member is negligent, they all pay.

The third organizational challenge facing prison gangs is the need to monitor members' actions. If gang leaders order someone to do a drug deal or assault someone, they need to have a way to find out if the member did it and did it well. They must build incentives into the structure of the organization that motivate members to follow orders. This requires methods of generating information about what members do and providing that information to people who have an incentive to use it productively. For instance, if a member fails to assault someone as ordered, then this information needs to be communicated to someone who can punish the disobedient member and who has an incentive to do so. Prison gangs that operate across different housing units within a facility or in prisons across the state will find this especially difficult.

Members also need methods of monitoring leaders. Leaders might make bad choices. A leader might extort lower ranking members or needlessly put their life at risk.[5] Employees in a legal business can call the police if their supervisor steals from them or assaults them. Gang members cannot. Members must have a way to remove incompetent people from leadership roles and to select new ones. A gang must also decide which choices it will delegate to individuals and which choices the gang will make collectively. For example, recruiting new members or killing someone may require collective agreement, while how to proceed with a particular drug-dealing scheme is the prerogative of each member.

Gangs must solve this trio of organizational challenges. If not, they will pour resources into inefficient endeavors and break up from within. These problems are interrelated, so improvement in one area can help with the others. If the gang recruits high-quality members, then there is less danger of them imposing costs on others. If they develop effective monitoring methods, then even if members are not of the highest quality, the gang can make them act properly. Successful gangs create internal structures that solve these related problems by generating information for people who have an incentive to use it to enhance the profitability of the gang. Often, gangs write these structures down in a criminal constitution.[6]

Putting the "Con" Into Constitutions

In nearly every type of organization, people find it useful to write down the rules. It helps to lay out clearly what each person in each position is authorized to do and is responsible for doing. New employees often receive manuals that tell them what they may, must, and must not do. These booklets detail what their job entails, who their boss is, and with what resources they will do their job. Employees learn how their supervisor will assess their work, the length of employment, and the consequences of doing a bad job. This is quite common. It happens in private companies, universities, non-profits, militaries, religious groups, and government bodies. It is tremendously helpful to make this information clear and explicit. Therefore, it should not surprise us that prison gangs do the same.

Constitutions define the rules of the game. They create the broad regulations that govern the daily interactions of people living under them. They often dictate the rules for how new rules will be made. They define how the group operates and how to change the rules that structure these activities. Not all constitutions consist of a single written document. In the United Kingdom, for instance, the government relies on a common understanding of the principles derived from a number of documents, treatises, conventions, and legal precedents that constitute the key rules of the game. In the same way, prison gangs use both written and unwritten constitutions. For instance, some gangs reference a commonly understood "code of conduct" rather than a written parchment.

Criminal constitutions become known in several ways. Correctional officers find them during cell searches. One officer noted, "They used to make up these booklets that had rules in them. They'd pass them around and we'd confiscate them and they'd make more. They were very dedicated to making sure that everyone in the gang knows their own rules."[7] Retired correctional and law enforcement officers have written personal accounts that provide and discuss gang constitutions.[8] Researchers and journalists working in and with correctional departments have also gained access to this information, through officials and informants.[9] When an inmate drops out of a gang, he will tell staff about the gang's organization. Law enforcement investigations can also reveal their inner workings. For example, a surveillance camera captured a Mexican Mafia induction meeting in which a member tells the new recruit, "There are certain *reglas* [rules] and guidelines that we go by. When the brother gets a chance, I'm pretty sure he's going to run 'em down to you, man, and we're real serious about it, ya know, real serious about it."[10]

The study of organized crime and mafias often has little to say about their internal governance. It is easier to get evidence about how they interact with non-members. Speculation about the internal organization of organized crime abounds. Economist Stergios Skaperdas writes, "Although precise knowledge of the internal functions of most organized groups is hard to come by, it would be safe to extrapolate from the available information that the great majority of such groups are hierarchically organized, either formally or informally."[11] By looking at prison gangs' constitutions and bylaws, we can go beyond speculation and formulate a clearer understanding of prison gangs' internal organization.[12]

Exit, Voice, and Violence

Economists typically look to two different feedback mechanisms to generate information about inefficiency in a system. The first is "exit." If a restaurant does not provide a quality meal at a reasonable price, people can find alternatives easily. They can exit from their interaction with a particular restaurant. When markets are competitive, people can easily switch to better service providers. The ease of exit means that when a restaurant is not providing what customers want, the restaurant owner learns about it quickly. As fewer people dine, the restaurant owner's profits diminish, and they learn that they need to change something. The market for restaurants operates well. Exit can generate good information and incentives within the system.[13]

However, in some situations, people can't exit easily. For example, it's costly to move to another town or state if one's local government does not provide desired services. It's even more costly to move to another country if one is displeased with the national government. Because exit is costly, the political system does not have the same information and incentives as the restaurant industry. The feedback from fleeing customers doesn't exist. In the absence of exit, "voice" can provide feedback. In political contexts, voicing one's opinion about a local, state, or national government takes place in many ways. Town hall meetings, writing a political representative, protest, petition signing, and voting are all ways that people use voice to communicate disapproval to governments. Voice substitutes for exit as a way to remedy inefficiencies in the system.

Unsurprisingly, inmates face high costs of exit. Prison walls prevent them from physically leaving. Prison gangs also require a lifetime commitment.[14] The Nuestra Familia constitution states, "a Familiano [member] will not be released from his obligations towards the organization because he is being released from prison. But [he] will be expected to work twice as hard to see that a familia is established and work in hand with the organization already established behind the wall's." The constitution further explains that "deserters" will be punished with "an automatic 'death' sentence."

Inmates might violate their oath and quit the gang. When they do, dropouts typically move to protective custody in the Sensitive Needs Yard, a segregated yard designed for inmates who would be in danger in the general population. Dropping out requires going through a debriefing process, in which the inmate tells investigators about the gang's organization, members, and activity. An inmate explained that quitting the gang put his life at risk. He said, "Yeah, if I go to the mainline, or if I go to the streets and someone recognizes me as a gang dropout, they're going to try to hit me, which means kill me, or slice me, or shoot me."[15] A sergeant at Corcoran noted that a gang might also target the dropout's family, so "he has to get his family out of the old neighborhood because they're going to retaliate against his family if they can't get to him."[16]

Gang dropouts generally deride the Sensitive Needs Yard. Inmates who previously had high social status as gang members now live among the most despised members of the community—child molesters, rapists, former law enforcement officers, and informants. A gang dropout at San Quentin expressed his feeling about protective custody (PC): "This is the dirtiest place of all places. If you're PC, then you're going to be amongst the garbage of the system. That's what we are right now. We're the garbage of the system.... If I go to the mainline or get escorted past the mainline, they're going to call me a piece of shit rat because I told certain things to get here."[17] Another inmate expressed his disgust at the community: "I'm in protective custody because I'm a dropout. I get to live with child molesters and rapos and weirdoes and people that are mentally sick. This is what I get for debriefing."[18] Once an inmate goes to protective custody, it is difficult to return to the mainline population. One inmate explained, "I wanted to go to protection, and then I started to think…once they transfer you out it will be on your record that you were in protection…and then you have a bad name, and they make you look like a punk or something."[19] Exit is costly.

If gang members could easily switch between different gangs and there was competition among gangs for gang members, then the possibility of exit would limit gangs' abilities to take advantage of their own members. However, because gang membership is limited by race, ethnicity, and region of origin, competition is limited. The inability to exit easily creates an important need for constitutional constraints. In their absence, potential recruits will fear that once they become committed to a gang, the gang will prey upon them. As a result, the gang will face problems in recruiting high-quality members. A constitutional structure can credibly signal to potential recruits that they can protect themselves and will have a voice to limit opportunism by other gang members. Constitutions benefit gang leaders, members, and potential recruits.

The Challenge of Recruitment

In order to maintain a credible threat of violence and the ability to profit in illicit markets, prison gangs need to recruit high-quality members. However, they often cannot easily identify these attributes simply by looking at an inmate. Gangs rely on several mechanisms to elicit this information. First, gangs frequently require that a member in good standing vouch for a recruit. The recruit's sponsor is someone who has known the recruit for several years, and if he recommends the recruit, then he is responsible for his actions. For example, the fifth rule in the Mexikanemi (a Hispanic prison gang in Texas) constitution requires that "the sponsoring member is totally responsible for the behavior of the new recruit. If the new recruit turns out to be a traitor, it is the sponsoring member's responsibility to eliminate the recruit."[20] This aligns the incentives of people who have information about recruits with the incentives of the organization as a whole.

The Texas Syndicate prison gang conducts a "comprehensive and lengthy recruiting process. Every prospective member must meet the 'homeboy connection' requirement, which means that he is known by one of the active members as a childhood friend. Once this first requirement is met, the prospective member is approached and socialized by that member. In the meantime, a thorough background investigation is conducted by the unit chairman through communicating with other chairmen and their members who may have knowledge of the prospective member."[21] If the investigation finds that the recruit is not acceptable for membership, perhaps because he "served as a police informant or has a questionable sense of loyalty, membership will not be granted to the individual. Instead, the individual will be coerced into paying the gang for protection or be used as a prostitute by the gang."[22]

In California, a Sureño who was incarcerated for robbery explained, "You have to be connected. If you pretend to be a gang member and we find out you're not, you get hurt. We'll punk you out or take you out. We check things; you have to have the right connections, you know what I mean? No posers in the gang. Look, we got the numbers inside we organize and think smart. We give people the rules in writing; our boys learn from us and follow the rules. You won't make it a day if you don't follow our rules."[23] A correctional officer recounted his experience: "Now I worked up north for a while and I know that the Mexican gangs are more inclined to be picky about who they let in. They check references on the outside and make sure you're not lying about where you come from or who you roll with."[24]

Recruits must learn about the gang. An indictment describes the elaborate nature of the Nuestra Familia confirmation process. It explains,

> Usually membership was approved only after a period of indoctrination by Nuestra Familia members in which prospects were schooled and then tested ... about Nuestra Familia criminal activities, including the manufacture of prison weapons, or "shanks," and the commission of murder, robbery and drug dealing inside and outside of prison. Only those who evinced both a knowledge of, and willingness to participate in, these activities were eligible for membership. This perpetration of violence and other crimes was ordinarily a prerequisite to membership in the organization, and membership, once achieved, was for life, as symbolized by the organization's membership phrase, blood in, blood out.[25]

Recruits of the Texas Aryan Brotherhood (ABT) "must serve an unspecified term, wherein he is referred to as a prospect, while his conduct is observed by members.... During this period, the prospect studies and learns the ABT Constitution and the 'prospect schooling guide.'"[26]

Two former members of the Texas Aryan Brotherhood wrote about the recruitment process. During the initial stages, "a prospect after being sponsored to the group by an inmate already a member is put on probation for six months. During this time, the prospect is allowed to get to know the other members and more importantly, the other members get to know the prospect, who could be a future brother."[27] This allows members to learn about his abilities and fit with the gang. During this time, the "prospect is put through a rigorous investigation around the unit to find out if he has had a good character, or if he is something less than admissible. If the prospect has been on another unit in TDC [Texas Department of Corrections], the investigation is expanded to the unit and any AB's who knew someone on that unit would write that person and have them ask around about the prospect."[28] Gang members test a recruit's "basic 'convict sense'" and he is put into situations which would let his brothers know how he could deal with different problems which would be faced as an AB, and if he could do so in such a manner as to keep the Honor, Integrity, and Reputation unsullied and intact."[29] They do not require a recruit to kill an enemy to get in. They write, "a man doesn't have to kill to enter the AB, but he does not leave nor can he terminate his membership except through death. Once in, always in. This holds true even if the member leaves the prison and goes home. He must still contact the organization inside the walls and do as ordered outside."[30] The probation period and information-gathering process provide essential information to the gang about the recruit's quality. If the recruit has proven himself, then "after the complete investigation is through, and nothing has come up to besmirch the integrity of the prospect, and after he has completed his probation/training and has shown he will stand up for his brothers in any situation, he is allowed to put on the patch" of the Texas Aryan Brotherhood.[31]

One puzzling feature of prison gangs is that they require a tremendous upfront commitment from members. The Mexikanemi constitution, for instance, requires a member to be prepared to sacrifice his own life or to take a life for the gang.[32] The Texas Aryan Brotherhood declares that "Those Brothers chosen for the Organization are life term members; death being the only termination of membership."[33] According to a federal indictment, members must sign a Blind Faith Commitment, "in which they agree to do anything directed or requested by their superiors without question."[34] The Nuestra Familia requires, "A familianos will remain a member until death or otherwise discharged from the O [organization]. He will always be subject to put the best interest of the O first and always above everything else, in prison or out."

One explanation for this devotion requirement is that it helps a gang to identify a potential member's unobservable characteristics. An inmate knows more about his loyalty than someone else does. Because gangs cannot tell how loyal a person is just by looking at him, it's useful to impose substantial costs. An inmate who wants the benefits of membership but is tiring of being "in the mix" of prison life will not take on the obligation of a lifetime commitment. On the other hand, the inmate who is truly devoted to the gang's ideals will not consider the lifetime commitment as costly. Because the strict requirements are less costly for the most reliable recruits, they reveal the unobserved information about an inmate's quality and filter the most devoted people into the gang.[35]

After obtaining information about recruits, gang members require a decision-making rule to induct a recruit officially. In the Mexican Mafia, for example, members must vote unanimously for induction. In one instance, a recruit's name was "floated around to all the other Eme members at Folsom, and to any other carnales who could be reached elsewhere. One no vote was an automatic veto of any candidate who was courted for La Eme membership."[36] As former Mexican Mafia member Rene Enriquez explains, "It takes only one veto to deny a member.... A no vote is an automatic veto—no questions, ifs, ands, or buts. This is a vetting process that has proved reliable in the past."[37]

Externalities and Internal Conflict

Gangs have a corporate identity that communicates their credible threat to use violence. In a community responsibility system, gang affiliation also means that each person is accountable for others' actions. If one person engages in behaviors that compromise the gang's reputation, they all suffer to some degree. To prevent this, gangs prohibit certain behaviors. The Mexican Mafia's code of conduct, for instance, forbids members from being a homosexual, an informant, or a coward.[38] Many inmates view homosexuals negatively, so allowing them to join would diminish the reputation of the gang.[39] Allowing known informants into the gang would obviously be a serious risk for the security of the organization. If gangs hire cowards, then they will undermine the credible threat of violence that allows them to operate in illicit markets.

The Nuestra Familia constitution states that the gang intends all members to work together in harmony. It explains, "The primary purpose and goals of this O is for the betterment of its members and the building up of this O on the outside into a strong and self supporting familia. All members will work solely for this objective and will put all personal goals and feelings aside until said fulfillment is accomplished."[40] The Texas Aryan Brotherhood proclaims at the beginning of its constitution, "The Texas Aryan Brothers are solidarity (Brotherhood) among its members. Solidarity is our backbone."[41]

Gangs function less well when members spend time and energy to transfer resources from each other rather than applying those efforts in productive pursuits. For example, gang members may physically assault each other. They may steal from each other. They may try to infringe on each other's money-making activities. The organization would benefit from directing these efforts at productive rather than redistributive activities. Many of the prison gangs in California and Texas have rules to limit such waste. The middle portion of the Mexican Mafia code of conduct requires the following:[42]

4. A member must not raise a hand against another member without sanction.
5. A member must not show disrespect for any member's family, including sex with another member's wife or girlfriend.
6. A member must not steal from another member.
7. A member must not interfere with another member's business activities.
8. A member must not politic against another member or cause dissension within the organization.

An early version of the Nuestra Familia constitution says, "An automatic death sentence will be put on a familianos that turns coward, traitor, or deserter. Under no other circumstances will a brother familiano be responsible for spilling the blood of another familiano. To do so will be considered an act of treason." Later in the constitution, the gang outlines other forbidden conduct:

SECTION IV.   Under no conditions will there be fighting between familianos. To do so will bring on disciplinary action and if blood is spilled, it will result in the expulsion of one or all parties involved (Art II, Sec. V).
SECTION V.   No member of this O shall put material things, whether it be drugs, money, women, or punks (as related to the pinta) before the best interest of La Nuestra Familia or a familianos.
SECTION V(A).   No familiano shall lie about his position in La Nuestra Familiano when discussing familianos business to a superior or a brother member. There shall be no lying or giving false impressions.
SECTION VI.   It is the sacred duty of a familianos guerrero [warrior] to do battle for La Nuestra Familia, and no soldado should feel that because he fought for his O that he is entitled to special privileges. All that matters is that you as a guerrero of La Nuestra Familia are living up to your responsibilities. Remember that a true guerrero does not need to boast of his accomplishments.

The punishment for violating these rules is an automatic death sentence (outlined in Article II, section V).

If a gang's constitution works reasonably well to reduce internal conflict, then we would expect to see people punished for violating it. The evidence suggests that people often are. For instance, one Mexican Mafia member was targeted for death because he acted cowardly. He and two other members went to rob a drug dealer, but when the drug dealer pulled a gun, the member ran away. On another occasion, a gang dropout chased him out of his own neighborhood.[43] The gang agreed to kill another member who had tried to "take over operations" at the county jail and who had put a hit on another member without approval.[44] One member was stabbed because, as Rene Enriquez explained, he was "perceived as a 'nutcase' whose politicking could no longer be tolerated. He became an embarrassment."[45] The Mexican Mafia's constitution has teeth.

Just as gangs desire to punish people for violating the rules, they also respect people who follow the rules. Enriquez describes Ernest "Chuco" Castro as a model Mexican Mafia member. "He was an upstanding carnal. No one ever politicked against Chuco or even said a bad word about him. He was the Mafia golden boy who always did the right mob thing, a killer with influence among younger and older brothers, and an idol. We all looked up to him."[46] Being an upstanding member guarded him against those who violated the rules. The Mafia decided to kill one member, because as Enriquez explains, "Puppet was targeted because of his politicking against Chuco and threats to kill three other Carnales."[47]

The gang's constitution continues to constrain behavior, even when it's least likely to. In one instance, Enriquez's ex-wife (who had a relative in the Mexican Mafia) reportedly wanted to have him killed over their divorce. However, Enriquez and the relative agreed that, in Enriquez's words, "our relationship shouldn't be affected by women. No matter what, we are always carnales first. Eme goes beyond family ties."[48] More generally, Enriquez explained, "There are ever-shifting loyalties in the mob.... It's byzantine. One day I'm friends with a good Mafia member, we do business together in the organization. The next day there is a power shift, and the same brother is my adversary. He won't even say my name. He'll cut me loose, and if there is a vote to kill me, he'll vote yes. That's just how it is."[49] A group of murderers—some of whom might despise each other—follows the gang's code of conduct by voting on the kill rather than acting independently. Far from impulsive when dealing with hated enemies, gang members abide by the constitutional code of conduct.

Checks and Balances

What is the optimal decision and control structure for a prison gang? One option is to have a dictator make all decisions. Centralizing control lowers decision-making cost. On the other hand, a dictator in a large organization may not have access to the most useful information with which to make decisions. Total consensus is an alternative organizational structure to dictatorship. Many gangs require consensus among the shot callers within a facility. However, requiring consensus across all of the gang's members would be tremendously costly. An Aryan Brotherhood member described the problem: "We used to be one man one vote, included damn near everything. I mean, damn near everything. Somebody getting in, whacking somebody... You damn near had to have the whole state's okay... You had to send some kites and runners and lawyers and this and that. It always got tipped off by the time we got back to you and said, 'Yeah, dump the guy.'... You can't have someone in the yard that you want to bump and let them be out there for two or three weeks."[50] Achieving complete consensus is prohibitively costly.

The difficulty of corresponding between prisons makes reaching agreement especially costly. Officials forbid inmates from sending mail to or calling each other. They can use pay phones, but officials often monitor and record these conversations. Many gang members learn obscure languages to obfuscate their discussions, such as the ancient Aztec language Nahuatl. Inmates use "micro writing," letters written smaller than a quarter of inch. They use codes and ciphers, some of which are obviously ciphers, others that appear to be normal letters to friends and loved ones. Gang members include messages in drawings and artwork. They relay lengthy messages via released members and visitors. Officials are not allowed to read legal paperwork, so inmates often write letters that appear to be legal work and slip the messages in with the legitimate documents. Some correctional staff smuggle notes out for gang members. A creative inmate might also write a message in his own urine. After it dries, it becomes invisible, but once the recipient heats the paper, the hidden message returns.[51] Though effective, these forms of communication are costly.

Because of the high cost of communication, even a supreme gang leader who wants to direct all activity at all prisons would find it useful to decentralize command to some degree. The leader cannot make all of the decisions for the gang regiment at each prison, because he lacks the necessary information about what problems they face, the personalities of the people involved, and the state of prison politics. Delegating authority and responsibility to one or more shot callers at a particular facility means that they may make wrong choices, but it is too expensive to control each regiment directly. Local shot callers resolve many different problems that arise with greater speed and effectiveness than could a leader in a distant prison.

While a decentralized structure improves the operation of the gang by reducing communication costs, it also creates an opportunity for laziness and predation. A single, powerful leader in a prison might take advantage of gang members. The leader could steal from a member or require him to participate in dangerous kamikaze-style attacks. The high cost of leaving a gang means that the leader might renegotiate the terms of membership once a recruit joins. The recruit will be hesitant to join out of fear of this, so a gang run by a single shot caller may have trouble recruiting new members. The gang needs a way to credibly commit to potential members that they will not renegotiate. An all-powerful leader cannot do this precisely because he is all-powerful.[52]

Having a single person in charge at a prison can also increase infighting among influential members who each wish to grab the reins of power. For instance, the Mexican Mafia used to run its regiments based on a *llavero* (keyholder) system where "just one camarada had total control to make decisions."[53] As Enriquez explains, they eliminated this system in favor of the *Mesa* (table) system. The Mesa was "a selected group of four or five camaradas, maybe one from each cell block, that made collective decisions on how to run the mainline yards for La Eme. The *Meseros* replaced the *llavero* (keyholder) system.... We eliminated the llavero concept because it was causing conflict on the mainlines. More than one camarada was claiming the right to be the llavero. The Mesa seemed to cut down on abuses of the single boss notion and kept the drugs and other black market activities running smoothly."[54]

The problem of constraining abuse by authorities faces political bodies writ large, and it is an important reason for the adoption of political constitutions. American founder James Madison recognized this in his writings to promote ratification of the U.S. Constitution. In Federalist Paper #51, Madison wrote, "If men were angels, no government would be necessary. If angels were to govern men, neither external nor internal controls on government would be necessary. In framing a government which is to be administered by men over men, the great difficulty lies in this: you must first enable the government to control the governed; and in the next place oblige it to control itself."[55] Assuming angels do not run prison gangs, how can the gang assert authority and at the same time oblige it to control itself? For both Madison and prison gangs, a key solution is the use of constitutions and democratic decision-making processes.

The original Nuestra Familia (NF) constitution outlined a system of checks and balances designed to help the gang to limit shirking by members and predation by leaders.[56] The constitution created incentives for those with the lowest cost of observing opportunism to use that information. It helped them capture the benefits of delegating authority. The gang's original constitution outlined a four-tier hierarchy consisting of a general, captains, lieutenants, and soldiers (Figure 5.1).

The NF constitution, titled the "Supreme Power Structure of La Nuestra Familia," declared, "the Nuestro General (NG) is the supreme power in the organization known as La Nuestra Familia.[57] His power shall have no limit (within Art. I, II, III). Solely he can declare war for the entire O and once in a state of war, peace shall not prevail until the announcement from the NG." The leader has supreme power, but he is also constrained, as it notes, by the limits in articles one through three. There were 10 captains, typically in different prisons, who controlled operations at their respective facilities. Captains, in turn, each had authority over numerous lieutenants and soldiers.

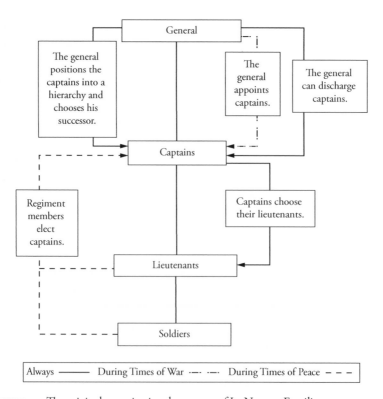

FIGURE 5.1 The original organizational structure of La Nuestra Familia

The gang used several methods to staff these positions. During times of peace, the soldiers and lieutenants elected their own regiment captains. Members typically knew these individuals well, interacted with them on a regular basis, and knew how effective their leadership would be. Captains chose their lieutenants. During times of war, the general could appoint a captain without going through the process of conducting an election among soldiers and lieutenants. Regardless of whether a captain was elected or appointed, the general could always determine where each one ranked among the other captains. The general also had the power to discharge captains at any time.

The constitution aligns the incentive of higher-ranking and lower-ranking members to discourage predation by captains and lieutenants. For instance, both the leaders and the soldiers want the group to be prepared for battle. The leaders want the group to stay in power, and for their own safety, the soldiers want to be prepared when violence occurs. The NF constitution requires lieutenants to provide weapons to each soldier. If the soldiers have no weapons, they know this and have an incentive to report it to a higher ranked member.

The Nuestro General determined how the group operated, and he had the ability to declare war against rival gangs, other inmates, and staff. The general remained in power until he was within one year of finishing his prison sentence, became physically ill or injured, or was impeached. Several checks and balances constrained his power (Figure 5.2). First, the general was limited in his power during times of peace. During times of war he could appoint and discharge captains, but during peace, he could only discharge them. When he did, the members of the regiment elected a replacement captain. The general may have wished to appoint all of the captains, but this would require a constant state of war, which would have reduced the gang's profitability. During wars, members are hurt or killed, transferred to other facilities, and placed in more secure lock-ups. As an Aryan Brotherhood member explained, "We weren't looking to have wars…it would slow business down."[58]

Under unanimous agreement, the captains could impeach the general. The general could challenge the legitimacy of the captains' signatures supporting impeachment. If he did, a solider would verify each signature. Once impeached, the highest-ranked captain became the new acting general. The highest-ranking captain, therefore, had an incentive to monitor the actions of the general. If he could convince the other captains that the general should be removed, then he could rise to power. On the other hand, the general could choose who the highest-ranked captain was, so he would choose someone sympathetic. However, because the regiments elected the captains, the general

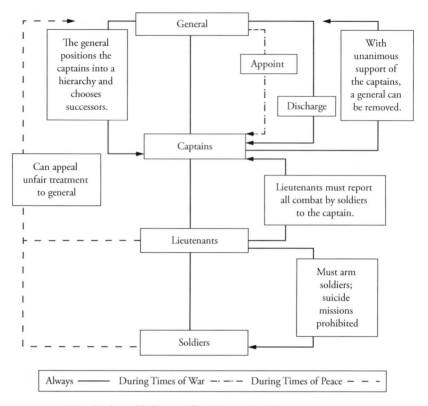

FIGURE 5.2 The checks and balances of La Nuestra Familia

had a limited selection from which to choose. The general could protect himself from impeachment by dismissing a seditious captain, but this did not guarantee that a more compliant captain would be elected in his place.

The general was, in part, protected against *coup d'état* because war was declared immediately if he was assaulted, and he could then appoint whomever he wished. A conspiracy among the captains that failed gave the general freedom to choose their replacements. In addition, the captain who was responsible for protecting the general would "have no power to appoint or replace any or all positions in the high command," and after the war ended, he would be demoted. Since the general could choose who among the captains would be his successor, he could elicit the help of the soon-to-succeed captain to monitor for conspiracies.

In a hierarchical organization, the highest-ranking persons aren't the only group of people who can take advantage of subordinates or shirk in their duties. At each prison facility, an NF captain controlled a regiment of lieutenants and soldiers. The captain directed them in the selling of drugs, extortion, and other endeavors. The captain also determined how to punish disobedient members. The general ranked captains "according to their leadership ability and overall foresight." According to the Federal Bureau of Investigation, a captain moves up in rank by "making good 'hits' [murders] on 'hermits' [enemies of NF]."[59] The prospect of promotion reduced opportunism and shirking.

While the general could only appoint captains during times of war, captains could appoint and discharge their underlings—lieutenants—as they wished. The constitution did not require a specific number of lieutenants to serve under a captain. This flexibility allowed him to adapt to a changing prison environment. However, that same discretion could open up opportunities to do wrong. When the gang was not at war, a discharged lieutenant could appeal to the general if he wished to complain about unfair removal. When complaints were made, the general was required to assign at least three soldiers to gather information about the termination. If the general felt that the dismissal was inappropriate, he could punish the captain and reinstate the discharged lieutenant. In addition to termination, a lieutenant could also appeal punishment to the general (though not during war). The general always had authority to monitor and remove a captain, so he was always accountable to the general. If soldiers and lieutenants made a sufficient number of complaints, or made a compelling case to the general, then they could have the captain removed, and the members would elect a new representative.

The lieutenant was the primary representative to other inmates, and he worked directly with the soldiers. He monitored the actions of members, set a good example for them, and administered discipline at the captain's command. According to the constitution, he was responsible for "schooling and basic needs and conduct." One report explained that "all recruits must master the rules.... The classes are divided between academic discussions of drug rings, armed robberies and the gang's constitution, and workshops, where lieutenants teach how to make bombs from matches, knives from cologne bottles and zip guns from toothpaste tubes."[60] An NF drop out explained, "They drilled us eight hours a day.... It was brainwashing."[61] A former NF member described his role as educator: "I'm in charge of educating other people on the bonds, the format, how to make knives, how to stab people, you know, where to stab people, what would be the best times, exercising, and making sure that everybody is following the guidelines of our game."[62]

These constitutional attempts to control opportunistic behavior proved insufficient. In 1978, the Nuestra Familia had operated successfully for more than a decade and they were earning tens of thousands of dollars of illegal revenue. The general, Robert Sosa, administered these funds to further the gang's interests. However, NF members learned that Sosa had embezzled more than $100,000 from the gang's coffers. According to former NF members, Sosa denied appropriating funds and any other wrongdoings. They impeached him.[63] Sosa refused to go along with the impeachment process, so NF members ordered his murder.[64] Violation of the constitution, especially embezzlement, was unacceptable and warranted punishment by death. Sosa survived the NF's murder attempt. However, he was no longer an NF member and he remained a high-priority enemy on the gang's hit list.

In part as a response to Sosa's malfeasance, the NF transformed the top position of the gang from a single general into an Organizational Governing Body (OGB), a three-member board.[65] The members of this board were elected and received "equal yet limited authority."[66] Their decision-making powers were the same as the general's, but decisions now required two-thirds support of the governing body.[67] The captains could remove members of the OGB with three-fourths of the captains' support. The NF's revised constitution explained that the members of the governing body should "respectfully guide the directives and honor the will of the people." Like the Mexican Mafia, the gang found that having a small group of shot callers struck the right balance between lowering decision-making costs and protecting against abuse. They also dropped the paramilitary names in favor of a category ranking system. Category I members are recruits and those members who are new to the organization. Category II members have proven themselves as loyal to the gang. Category III members take a managerial role and have at least five years in NF.[68]

Former NF member John "Boxer" Mendoza's history of the gang shows that there was a constant struggle to coordinate member's plans, reduce rent seeking, overcome the high cost of communication, and limit opportunism by influential members.[69] Gang members experimented with different constitutional structures to try to solve these problems. The gang often failed. However, it is also clear that members were promoted and demoted, and there was a process for complaining about superiors that used checks and balances and voting procedures. The internal governance rules were often quite effective. Gang members recognized, in theory, the power of constitutional constraints, and these constraints altered behavior in practice. The constitution was more than simply ink on parchment.

The Nature of the Gang

Not all prison gangs have the same internal structure and constitutional rules, and they change as gang members discover what works and what doesn't. In general, prison gangs are worker-owned, and they prohibit a secondary market for membership. They often lack a clear residual claimant and use inclusive voting systems. In these ways, their internal organization resembles a traditional cooperative. Clearly, gangs are not run perfectly. Plenty of internal fighting and violence occurs. Many men who join gangs wish they had not. These facts raise the question of just how effective gangs are at overcoming organizational dilemmas.

On the one hand, gangs are the major participants in prison-based drug dealing. They provide a highly sought-after product. Based on the prevalence of contraband in prisons, gangs seem effective. They also provide protection and governance to the inmate community. Much of the discussion here has focused on the Mexican Mafia and the Nuestra Familia, who, according to federal indictments, are the first and second most powerful prison gangs in California. Similarly, many prison gangs have existed for decades, and some for more than 50 years. They demonstrate a remarkable robustness.

A study of 48 gang dropouts in Texas identifies some of the reasons why people quit prison gangs.[70] These include losing interest in the gang (10 respondents), refusal to hit a non-gang member (9), disagreement with the direction in which the gang was going (7), refusal to hit a gang member (6), violating a gang rule (5), maturing out of it (5), becoming an informant (4), and refusal to engage in gang crime (2).[71] From the gang's perspective, dropouts are evidence of failure. However, the study found that fewer than five percent of prison gang members drop out, and the rate of defection for some gangs was only 1 out of every 100 members.[72] Another report found that roughly three percent of gang members drop out.[73] Given the nature of the business, the number of disaffected members who have quit seems rather low. In addition, gangs do not treat their members badly enough that it discourages others from joining. A sergeant at Corcoran notes, "for every one inmate that debriefs, you have ten in line waiting to get into the gang."[74] Despite their failures, they continue to entice new members.

On the other hand, there is no shortage of complaints about prison gangs. Many of these criticisms come from gang dropouts, who would presumably be the least satisfied with gangs. A Hispanic inmate at Corcoran explained why he dropped out after assaulting another Hispanic inmate: "The guy was weak…weak meaning he couldn't keep up with the exercise. That was the reason. This is how stupid this is. I said 'hey, this guy doesn't deserve this.' And when I did speak up for him, it was placed on me. 'Well since you're speaking up for him, you'll deal with it.' I regret it. I'm sorry for that guy I stabbed. I really am. I regret that I did that to him."[75] A Nuestra Familia dropout described how the constitutional constraints failed: "People would be put in the hat, meaning they would be put on the hit list, for any personal reason. It could be a personal agenda."[76] A lieutenant at Corcoran noted, "An individual can be in good favor with the gang for years, and do their dirty work: smuggle drugs, stab people, beat people, do whatever. But if he says the wrong thing to the wrong person some day, or looks funny at somebody, somebody think they were disrespected by him, he's through. They'll stab him. They'll kill him. They'll toss him away like he's nothing."[77] A former Mexican Mafia member described how the gang turned on him: "I find out I'm on the list. That's a death sentence. My heart broke. I'm going to be honest with you. I'm like 'you gotta be shitting me.' A spotless career and I'm on the list?"[78] A correctional official observed the apparent hypocrisy: "They're told that what they're doing is for the betterment of their race, or their group, or whatever it is. But in reality, what it is, it's all about making money for those guys that are running and controlling the gangs."[79] A former NF member warned, "Don't believe a lot of the ideologies that the so-called gang members have. You know, they're out to use you. I don't care how much work, how much stabbings you put in, how much money you bring into the organization. If you don't meet the creed of that organization, you're going to be used. You're going to get abused. You know, they say, we're trying to uprise our own race, the Mexican race, bring pride to it and what have you. But in actuality, these gangs and these organizations, you know, they bring a disgrace to our race."[80]

MacArthur Park

MACARTHUR PARK IS a landmark in Los Angeles. Surrounded by the asphalt and concrete pavement of the city, the park is lush with green grass, beautiful trees, and a small lake. It is named in honor of the celebrated military leader, General Douglass MacArthur, who never lived in Los Angeles, nor did he have a particularly strong passion for public parks. In fact, the most salient relationship between the World War II general and the park is that it has become a hotly contested battleground. The park separates warring neighborhoods controlled by two of the largest and most powerful street gangs in Southern California: the Mara Salvatrucha and the 18th Street Gang—gangs run by seasoned killers.

On a sunny Saturday afternoon in September 2007, the park and the streets of the Westlake neighborhood surrounding it were alive with bustling shoppers, picnickers, Latino food carts, and unlicensed vendors selling everything from candy and phone cards to clothing and electronics. Amidst this pleasant scene, shots rang out.

A member of the 18th Street gang fired a .22-caliber pistol at a vendor's head from a few feet away. The vendor had refused to pay a $50 gang "tax" for the right to sell his goods in the area. Bullets struck the vendor, including once in the jaw, leaving him seriously injured, but alive. One of the bullets intended for the vendor hit and killed a 23-day-old baby in a nearby stroller. When the gunman learned about the baby's death, he knew he was in trouble—not only from the police, but because he knew the Mexican Mafia was hunting him. The Mexican Mafia wields tremendous influence over Hispanic street gangs in Los Angeles, and their rules forbid killing a child.

The gunman's fellow gang members told him to flee the country for his own safety. Three of his friends drove him to Tijuana. They started drinking. They plied him with alcohol until he passed out. In the dead of night, they poured the inebriated gunman into the front seat of the car and headed to Mexicali. During the trip, they pulled the car over to a remote roadside location. They slipped a rope around the sleeping man's neck, tightened it, and pulled hard against his throat. As he struggled to get free, they shouted at him to die and violently choked the life out of him. When they believed that he was dead, they dragged his lifeless body out of the car and threw it down a steep embankment.

Rules govern the criminal underworld. Not the government's rules, but rules nonetheless. Prison gangs play a surprising and important role in making law for the outlaws, even outside of prison. The fact that gang members are willing to kill one of their own to appease the prison gang offers strong evidence of their ability to proclaim edicts to the criminal underworld. Even if we assume that everyone who operates in the underworld is greedy and violent, there are still powerful economic forces at work that constrain brutality, victimization, and chaos.

How Prison Gangs Govern the Outside

Anybody that thinks a prison gang, such as the Mexican Mafia, can't reach out and touch ya on the street is a fool for thinking that way. Because they can. They can reach out and touch anyone they want.

Sergeant, Corcoran State Prison[1]

The Economics of Extortion

Imagine a horde of roving bandits whose sole desire is to accumulate as much wealth as possible. One day, the bandits are roaming the countryside. In the distance, they see a small community, whose residents enjoy substantial material comfort. They drive nice cars, have expensive electronics, and own beautiful pieces of artwork. The bandits descend on the town. They run amok, beat and terrify the locals into submission, and steal everything of value. The bandits depart with the riches, and the local townspeople are impoverished. At first, there seems to be little hope for the townspeople, for they cannot defend themselves from the deadly brigands. It appears that the bandits are an unmitigated disaster for the townspeople. However, this might not be the case. Imagine that instead of roving bandits, the bandits are stationary. Instead of a never-ending nomadic life, they live just down the road from the community. How does this change their incentive to plunder?

First, the bandits now have an incentive not to take everything from the townspeople. If they took everything of value from them every day, then the townspeople would have no incentive to create anything of value in the first place. Complete theft would leave the bandits with nothing to steal. However, the townspeople may be willing to produce something of value if they can keep a share of it. The total wealth the bandits can steal, therefore, depends on how much they steal and how much the townspeople are willing to produce, given different rates of theft. The bandits earn nothing in two scenarios: (1) if the bandits steal everything that is produced, then the townspeople will stop producing anything; (2) if the bandits steal nothing, they get nothing. Therefore, the bandits maximize their extraction by stealing some, but not all, of the town's wealth. The stationary bandit maximizes its thievery by constraining its theft.[2]

We can extend this logic a step further. If the bandits know that they can steal a portion of the wealth, then they may actually have an incentive to help the townspeople grow even richer. The bandits might not only constrain their theft, but also produce public goods that encourage wealth creation. For instance, they may protect the townspeople from other bandits. They might provide market-enhancing goods, such as roads, police, and venues for resolving disputes. By doing so, they promote wealth creation and increase the amount of wealth that they can steal. If the bandits can steal from everyone in the town, then they can internalize the benefits of producing public goods. Their encompassing interest makes it profitable to produce governance. Despite their ill intentions, a stationary bandit may actually provide the essential governance institutions that make the town richer than it would have been in the bandits' absence.

The logic of the stationary bandit can fail in several ways. If the stationary bandit's time horizon goes from long to short, then he will steal everything. If the bandit isn't going to be around to steal, then he doesn't care if his theft discourages future production. The townspeople also must believe that the stationary bandit has a long time horizon. The bandits must be able to organize themselves effectively. If some of the bandits want to be stationary and some want to be roving, for instance, then costly infighting occurs. Importantly, the bandits have to care about wealth more than anything else. If the bandits enjoy making people suffer and are willing to give up wealth to do so, then they will not produce all possible market-enhancing governance institutions.

Like the stationary bandit, prison gangs provide governance institutions that allow illicit markets to flourish. They adjudicate disputes and protect property rights. They orchestrate violence so that it is relatively less disruptive. They do not do this because they are benevolent dictators. Gangs do it because they profit from doing so. In addition to governing prisons, these gangs are also an important source of governance to the criminal world outside of prison. They wield tremendous power over street gangs, specifically those participating in the drug trade. Because of this power, governance from behind bars helps illicit markets to flourish on the streets.

Drug Dealers Pay Taxes

A defining characteristic of a prison gang is that it operates in prison, but that doesn't mean it only operates in prison. According to some sources, since at least the early 1970s, prison gangs have been active in county jails and on the streets.[3] The county jail system plays an important role in how the criminal underworld functions. It is a crucial link between prison crime and street crime. It allows prison gangs to project their influence beyond prison walls.[4]

Unlike state or federal prisons that hold convicted inmates, county jails typically hold three types of people: people charged with crimes who have not been convicted, people serving less than a year, and people who have been convicted of a crime and are waiting to be transferred to a state prison. The Los Angeles County Jail system is one of the largest in the United States. The county jails serve an area that comprises more than 4,000 square miles and nearly 10 million people. The L.A. District Attorney's office handles more cases each year than any other office in the country.[5] On a typical day, the system holds about 19,000 people. The largest facility in the system, Men's Central Jail, holds about 4,600 inmates.[6] Inmates stay in jail, on average, 60 days. There are few places as important to street gang members as the Los Angeles County Jail.[7]

Many people have dubbed L.A. the "gang capital of the world," so it is a useful place to study to understand the remarkable influence prison gangs can have over street gangs. The Bloods and Crips are perhaps the best-known gangs in popular culture, but in L.A., Hispanic gangs are actually more important in terms of numbers and influence. The most recent data available, from reports by the Los Angeles Police Department, indicate that the city of Los Angeles is home to about 720 street gangs. There are 417 Hispanic gangs, compared to 228 Bloods and Crips gangs. The L.A. Police Department estimates that there are about 22,000 Hispanic gang members and 15,500 Bloods and Crips members. Not all of these gangs sell drugs, but many do. For gangs engaged in the drug trade, it is typically their most important source of revenue.[8]

These drug profits have caught the Mexican Mafia's eye. For many drug-dealing Hispanic street gangs, the Mexican Mafia demands an extortion payment. The gang members refer to these payments as "taxes," "gang taxes," "tribute," "*feria*," and "rent." A street gang typically pays between 10 and 30 percent of its drug revenues to the Mexican Mafia. They pay these taxes on a monthly or weekly basis to three types of Mexican Mafia tax collectors.[9]

First, a non-incarcerated Mexican Mafia member may collect taxes from a gang. If so, it will usually include collecting from a gang with which he has a history of interacting, perhaps as a former member or business partner. Second, the Mexican Mafia may authorize an associate, who is not a full-fledged member, to collect taxes on the prison gang's behalf. It has become increasingly common, for example, for the wives and girlfriends of incarcerated members to have the responsibility of collecting taxes.[10] Third, the Mexican Mafia may delegate the responsibility to collect taxes to a high-ranking and well-known member of the street gang that is being taxed.[11] For instance, the Mexican Mafia allowed a prominent MS-13 member to collect gang taxes from cliques within MS-13. Although they collect the taxes, these representatives know that they are only an intermediary. According to one law enforcement official's summary of a wiretapped phone conversation, two Mexican Mafia members discussed the fact that "the tax collectors who work for the Mexican Mafia know the money they collect was not their property and that they were working on a salary."[12] These collectors also do so because it increases their status in the eyes of the Mexican Mafia and is a route to membership.

Mexican Mafia members control these funds in a variety of ways. Until the mid-2000s, incarcerated prison gang members had inmate bank accounts that officials rarely monitored.[13] They could transfer funds into and out of these accounts with ease. Some inmate accounts held tens of thousands of dollars. According to a former Mexican Mafia member, "It's the perfect method to cleanse money. There is so much money leaving and entering the prison—tens of thousands of dollars moving on and off the books on a regular basis, dirty money that is laundered with the help of the CDC [California Department of Corrections] system."[14] Gang members reportedly invested in U.S. Treasury Bonds, CDs, double-e series U.S. savings bonds, homes, and commercial real estate.[15] In the last 10 years, however, officials have started monitoring these accounts much more closely.

Now a more common way to hold funds is to have them sent to a trusted associate, such as a wife, who can disperse these funds as needed.[16] These women, often referred to as *Señoras*, are "high-level female associates, who often have close personal relationships with Mexican Mafia members. Largely due to their close ties to members, Senoras can have the most authority amongst non-members. That authority, which is given to them by a member, often empowers them to speak on the member's behalf and direct Mexican Mafia business, including ordering murders or assaults. Senoras, like other associates, will also collect 'taxes,' or extortion/protection payments, and distribute drugs."[17]

The prison gang faces two major challenges in monitoring the tax collection process: They must prevent tax collectors from keeping a portion of the money, and they must ensure that imposters do not pose as tax collectors. An obvious solution is to threaten to kill people who break these rules. In March 1994, for example, law enforcement was secretly recording a Mexican Mafia meeting where gang members discussed Ramiro Valerio. According to the 9th Circuit Court Ruling, the gang members believed he was "collecting money from drug dealers by claiming he was a member of the Mexican Mafia. At the videotaped March 27, 1994 meeting, the members present clarified that Valerio was not a member and therefore had no authority to collect money or act on the Mexican Mafia's behalf."[18] The gang members decided to kill Valerio. Later that year, officials listening in on a phone call heard two Mexican Mafia members discussing the operation. The ruling explains, "Castro called Rodriguez to advise him that the police had arrested Valerio and he was in jail, so R. Castro now had the opportunity to kill him. During subsequent conversations, R. Castro devised a plan to kill Valerio while in custody."[19]

The taxpayers themselves also have an incentive to ensure they are paying the right person: they want to get credit for doing so. In one case, a street gang member named Mendoza, who had recently been paroled from Pelican Bay, falsely claimed to be a Mexican Mafia member. While at a dope house, he demanded that the drug dealer give him drugs and money.[20] Several people grew suspicious of his credentials, and one telephoned around to find out if the Mafia had authorized him to collect taxes. A short time later, a Mexican Mafia member tracked Mendoza down at an apartment. According to the appellate ruling, Mendoza "came to the door…but did not respond when defendant asked if he was from the Mexican Mafia. Defendant asked, 'Are you a carnal?' [a Mexican Mafia member] Mendoza said nothing, but began to pull up his shirt as if to show his prison tattoos.… At that moment, defendant fired a gun at Mendoza, who grabbed his chest and said, 'Ah, shit. They shot me.'"[21] To avoid these problems, tax collectors often work with neighborhoods with which they have a relationship. A history provides credible information to taxpayers and assures them they are paying the right person. It is also easier for tax collectors to know about the volume of business the street gang is doing and the personalities of the people involved.

The taxation structure imposed on the Varrio Hawaiian Gardens (VHG) street gang is typical of many Sureño gangs. A shot caller of the street gang collects taxes that he then remits to the Mexican Mafia. According to officials, "At any given time, one or more members of the Mexican Mafia has control over the VHG Gang's territory and is empowered to receive the drug 'taxes' from the VHG Gang and to issue orders and instructions to the VHG Gang. A Mexican Mafia member with authority over the VHG Gang's territory typically enlists the assistance of a VHG Gang member and authorizes that VHG Gang member to act in the name of the Mexican Mafia member.... [He] is empowered to collect drug 'taxes' for that Mexican Mafia member from VHG Gang members and drug traffickers selling drugs in Hawaiian Gardens."[22] The Mexican Mafia member delegates the tax collection responsibility to someone who has the information to carry it out effectively.

The 18th Street gang is one of the most notorious gangs in the world. They have come to dominate much of the L.A. drug trade. The Columbia Little Cycos (CLCS), an 18th Street clique, operates in the areas west of downtown, near MacArthur Park.[23] Despite their power on the street, the Mexican Mafia has taxed them for many years. The CLCS shot caller collected taxes from those selling drugs in its neighborhood and sent them to the incarcerated Mexican Mafia member. His job was to "maintain an accounting of the rent amounts paid to the CLCS Organization by narcotics distributors during each rent collection period, and calculate the percentage of the illicitly obtained proceeds that the CLCS Organization was required to pay to Mexican Mafia Member 1."[24]

The notorious street gang Mara Salvatrucha (MS-13), formed in the mid-1980s in Los Angeles, has since spread to other states and countries.[25] Despite officials' claims that they are one of the "largest and most violent gangs in the world," they too pay gang taxes.[26] As an indictment explains, "each clique contributes a portion of its profits towards a tax paid by MS-13 to the Mexican Mafia. Like all gangs associated with the Mexican Mafia, MS-13 is required to pay a specified sum of money on a regular basis to a member of the Mexican Mafia."[27] The indictment continues, "A single powerful MS-13 member in Los Angeles has been appointed to act as MS-13's representative to the Mexican Mafia."[28]

The Mexican Mafia does not limit its taxation to gang members. They call on the street gangs to look for non-gang drug dealers, and they authorize the street gangs to collect taxes from these people on their behalf. As one indictment explains, "The Mexican Mafia also exercises control of non-gang affiliated narcotics dealers by taxing them, either directly by a Mexican Mafia member...or a gang answering to the Mexican Mafia, such as the Diablos, West Side, Varrio Fallbrook Locos, or Varrio San Marcos gangs. If they pay taxes, drug dealers are permitted to sell illegal drugs in their designated areas. If a drug dealer fails to pay the required tax either directly to a Mexican Mafia member or to a gang collecting tax under the authority of a Mexican Mafia member, the drug dealer may be assaulted or robbed of his/her drugs, money, and/or possessions."[29] The taxation scheme is not optional, and the gang forces compliance. According to one indictment, the defendant explained to a drug dealer, "[You] have to pay taxes.... You're slinging in the city, anyone slinging in the city has to pay taxes...whether you like it or not.... [I]f you get caught lying, you know, or trying to dodge, dodge that kind of shit, you're going to get into some serious shit."[30] Failure to pay taxes results in being assaulted or robbed.

Typically, a single Mexican Mafia member controls taxation in a particular region. For instance, in San Diego, a federal indictment explained, defendant Espudo "is a validated member of the Mexican Mafia who oversees Mexican Mafia activities throughout much of northern San Diego County."[31] He has "the right to sanction the murder and/or assaults of associates of the Mexican Mafia, and others, including Hispanic gang members both in and out of the prison system."[32] Moreover, he is "entitled to receive a portion of 'taxes' collected under the authority of the Mexican Mafia, as well as proceeds from the sale of narcotics within the geographic areas."[33] Because Espudo is now incarcerated, his wife is an important representative for him. According to court documents, "as far as Mexican Mafia associates and facilitators are concerned, [his wife]...speaks for Espudo and her directions are considered as if he were speaking them. [She] collects tax money and drugs on their behalf and passes both information between Espudo and his associates as well as orders Espudo may direct."[34]

There are no data available that systematically track the total amount that street gangs pay the Mexican Mafia, but a few anecdotal examples suggest that it is quite a lucrative amount. Former Mafia member Rene Enriquez regularly earned $40,000 to $60,000 a year while incarcerated.[35] In 2004, institutional gang investigators at Pelican Bay looked into the previously unmonitored inmate accounts and found that some inmates had sizeable holdings. They froze the accounts of 14 Mexican Mafia members, 2 of whom had more than $20,000 in their trust account and 2 others had more than $10,000.[36] Gang experts argue that the Mexican Mafia has laundered "millions of dollars" through their prison trust accounts.[37] Federal prosecutors contend that one member received $40,000 a month in gang taxes while at Pelican Bay.[38] One Mexican Mafia member received $4,000 per week from a single drug dealer.[39] In one instance, Mexican Mafia members kidnapped a drug dealer because he failed to pay the $85,000 in taxes that he owed, which he eventually paid as ransom, along with four kilograms of cocaine.[40] Drug dealers had to pay $15,000 to sell drugs in a two-block area near the Westlake district of downtown L.A.[41] The shot caller overseeing the Lil' Cycos drug operation brought in $250,000 a month in taxes.[42] Rene Enriquez explained that in addition to the money, taxation brought him power: "I know I can say anytime that I need $5,000, a car, or gifts for my family. Boom! It will be done. I need that guy killed. And it was done efficiently."[43]

The Mexican Mafia organization is much smaller than the combined size of the gangs that it taxes. Estimates of Mexican Mafia membership range from 150 to 400. Compared with the estimated 22,000 Hispanic street gang members in L.A., the Mexican Mafia is less than one percent of their size. Despite this, the prison gang is capable of extorting gang taxes from them, and what's more impressive, they are able to do so while many of their members are incarcerated in county, state, and federal facilities. An appellate court ruling on a Mexican Mafia case noted, "Overwhelming evidence in the record shows that Appellants conspired to extort money and firearms from various street gangs."[44] Rene Enriquez claimed that "tens of thousands of gang members adhered to what we said. . . . And it was then that we realized the true potential of the Mexican Mafia . . . because of the finances generated by taxation: taxation, extortion, protection—they all fall under the same umbrella."[45]

The Role of the County Jail System

Cowards and weaklings do not run street gangs. Gangs have often fought wars to win drug territory. They assault, stab, and kill rival gang members. How then can a small group of incarcerated prison gang members force them to pay taxes? The evidence presented here identifies three mechanisms. First, the Mexican Mafia can extort street gangs because they have a credible threat to hurt people in the county jail, and street gang members rationally anticipate spending time there. Second, they can use incarcerated street gang members as hostages to force non-incarcerated gang members to pay. Third, they can encourage street gangs to assault and steal from other, non-taxpaying street gangs.[46]

Regardless of how dangerous a drug dealer is on the street, he is in a fundamentally different position once incarcerated. When a street gang member is arrested, he will typically enter the county jail alone. During the intake process, officials will physically examine and strip-search him, making it difficult to smuggle in weapons. Sometimes a gang member can schedule to turn himself over to jail authorities at a particular time, but incarceration often occurs unexpectedly. For some gang members, entering jail will be a new experience. The routines, requirements, and residents are unknown. He may live in one of several different areas, so even if he has served time in the past, he might not know the layout of the building, the daily schedule, or his privileges as an inmate.

Compared with inmates who have resided there for a longer time, he is at a disadvantage in protecting himself. The experienced inmates know where the blind spots are, if deputies are willing to ignore violence, and when deputies are least likely to observe assaults. They know the other inmates and the current state of prison politics. They have had an opportunity to make weapons. In January 2010, roughly a quarter of the male inmate population was incarcerated for charges of murder, attempted murder, and assault with a deadly weapon.[47] New inmates entering the L.A. County Jail system—even a hardened street gang member—can be at a substantial disadvantage in violent confrontations. As a former L.A. gang member noted about Men's Central Jail, "if you aren't in a gang when you go in, you will be when you get out."[48] The only way to survive is to group up.

While in this vulnerable position, a street gang member may have to intermingle with the Mexican Mafia. Prison gang members often spend time at the county jail because of pending court cases. Commentators have described the L.A. County Jail as the gang's home base and headquarters.[49] Some prison gang members have even intentionally remained in jail to profit from the drug trade. One Aryan Brotherhood shot caller allegedly managed to spend six years at the county jail instead of transferring to a state prison because he was earning $5,000 a week selling drugs.[50] A Mexican Mafia member assaulted and murdered other inmates just to generate new criminal charges so that he could continue selling drugs in the jail.[51] Prison gang members may also represent themselves in court. This gives them the ability to have inmates who are housed in prisons across the state transported to the county jail, under the auspices of testifying in court. In reality, they conduct gang business.[52]

There is a second important reason why the Mexican Mafia has substantial influence within the county jail system. Inmates who either would like to join the Mexican Mafia or who simply want to increase their status in the gang's eyes will follow their orders. One federal indictment describes the relationship between the Avenues street gang and the Mexican Mafia's green light lists. The prison gang can "issue directions and orders, including orders to kill rival gang members, members of law enforcement, and members of the public.... Those orders are to be executed by Avenues gang members and are understood by Avenues gang members as opportunities to gain elevated status with the organization or to potentially become a 'made' member of the organization."[53] In addition, the Mexican Mafia can force inmates who owe them money or drugs to assault others in lieu of payment. Even if a particular Mexican Mafia member in the county jail cannot physically assault another inmate, he can order others to do so—and many inmates will. That means that it only takes a few Mexican Mafia members to control a large portion of the inmate population.

Several additional factors make jail even worse for a drug dealer who is delinquent in paying his taxes. First, inmates in the county jail are segregated by both formal and informal mechanisms. Inmates choose to congregate with members of the same race and ethnicity. For example, a Southern Hispanic inmate would not be welcomed to congregate with black inmates. This makes it difficult to avoid other Hispanics—the people who the Mexican Mafia has the most control over. Officials also frequently segregate inmate housing by race and gang status. This means that they will house a Hispanic drug dealer in the same cells as other Hispanics from Southern California. A street gang member who hasn't paid the Mexican Mafia will be housed among the people he would most like to avoid. Moreover, the Men's Central Jail has specific modules for gang members. Officials may house a delinquent taxpayer in this gang module. As discussed previously, a shot caller is in charge of identifying new inmates and telling them the rules of the tier. In doing so, an inmate's gang affiliation will be discovered. If there's a green light on him or his gang, he's in trouble.

Wire-tapped phone conversations reveal prison gangs' power. Phone intercepts captured a conversation between a non-incarcerated Mexican Mafia member and an associate in the L.A. County Jail. During their talk, they coordinated assaults on street gang members who hadn't paid taxes. A federal indictment explains that the Mexican Mafia member asked another "to contact the A and B rows in the Los Angeles County Jail to determine if there were any prisoners capable of carrying out an assault" against someone who hadn't paid his taxes.[54] On October 25, 1994, a Mexican Mafia member spoke with an associate in the L.A. County Jail, and according to the indictment, "advised the unindicted co-conspirator of the gangs against which the Mexican Mafia had authorized assaults."[55] In a 9th Circuit Court of Appeals ruling, the judges found that "gang members who did not cooperate with the Eme when they were outside could be dealt with if they ever landed in jail—and many of them did. An Eme member or an associate could place an individual or even a whole gang on the 'green light' list, which meant that the individual or gang was targeted for any form of assault up to and including murder."[56]

Drug dealers anticipate spending time in the county lock-up. The California Department of Corrections and Rehabilitation conducted a study to measure recidivism of inmates released from state prisons in 2004. Within three years, approximately 59 percent of inmates were reincarcerated in a state prison. After only one year, nearly 40 percent of inmates were reincarcerated. The study examined 17,139 inmates who had been released after serving time on a drug offense. The two most frequent offenses were possession of a controlled substance and possession of a controlled substance with the intent to sell. After one year, 29 percent of inmates released for possessing a controlled substance with intent to sell and 45 percent for possession of a controlled substance were reincarcerated. After three years, these recidivism rates increased to 46 percent and 66 percent. Only five crimes had higher recidivism rates than those for which people served time for possession of a controlled substance. A national study of recidivism found that after three years, 64.6 percent of Hispanic inmates and 66.7 percent of inmates for whom their most serious offense was drug related were rearrested.[57]

The California recidivism data may also underestimate a street gang member's anticipation of incarceration. First, the study only looks at people who return to a state prison, so it does not account for those street gang members who may spend time in the county jail but never go back to state prison. For example, if a gang member is incarcerated in the county jail for being drunk in public, then he hasn't been counted as having recidivated. Second, these data look at recidivism for all inmates released from the state prison, but gang members have higher recidivism rates than those of non-gang inmates. In Illinois, 75 percent of gang members are rearrested within 750 days of release. The average time from being released from prison and rearrest is less than eight months.[58] The recidivism rate for gang members is six percentage points higher than that for non-gang members.[59] This means that the overall recidivism data, which do not control for gang membership, underestimate the recidivism rates of gang members.

Street gang members recognize the likelihood of arrest. Many of them speak about their first incarceration experience as a badge of honor. It demonstrates one's toughness and machismo. Social networking takes place, and young gang members often enjoy interacting with the "big homies" in the county jail. In fact, serving a relatively short sentence at a young age can be a "career maker" because of the people one meets.[60] Rene Enriquez explained that prison "was kind of like going to college. Once you get there, you're just considered a homeboy who's been to the joint. Homeboys who go to prison are considered *veteranos*. They're well respected in the neighborhood."[61]

On the streets, drug dealers are well armed, organized, and mobile. The county jail system means that any drug dealer, with some probability, will end up in one of only a few county jail facilities. Taylor Morehead, Chief of Custody Operations, describes the filtering of the county jail reception area, noting, "everybody that comes in, comes through the funnel."[62] Sergeant Roger Ross, a gang investigator in the jail, explains, "Los Angeles County Jail is unique in the fact that every gang in Los Angeles County ends up coming here. It doesn't matter if they're a black gang, Asian gang, a Hispanic gang, or a white gang. If they're active in Los Angeles County and they get arrested, they end up coming to the Los Angeles County Jail system."[63] In 2002, an estimated 52 percent of inmates in the L.A. County Jail system had been involved in inmate gangs.

A second way that the Mexican Mafia can extort street gangs is by holding their incarcerated gang members hostage. If the members on the street don't pay taxes, the gang harms their incarcerated members. Officials investigating the Mexican Mafia in the early 1990s described the contents of a monitored telephone conversation in October 1994 in which one member told another "the gangs against which the Mexican Mafia had authorized assaults."[64] Later in November, two members discussed which gangs had a green light due to failure to pay gang taxes, including the Clanton, Hang Out Boys, and Flats street gangs.[65] In one indictment, a Mexican Mafia associate told a street gang member that someone "was going to be assaulted because of a 'green light' on the West Side gang," because "he was still short money for the West Side gang's 'fuckin' two thousand dollar 'tax payment to'" the Mexican Mafia shot caller.[66] The indictment also describes how a Mexican mafia member announced "that all West Side gang members arrested from December 25, 2010 onward would be assaulted for the gang's failure to make a full tax payment on time," and an associate planned to smuggle drugs into the facility to fulfill the gang's tax payment.[67] The green light on the West Side gang was lifted about two weeks later. Two individuals discussed the green light, with one explaining that "they say everything is okay; they send their hello to yourself and the camarada and to send all our love to those from the West Side."[68] The indictment explains that this means "the 'green light' had been lifted from the West Side gang because the gang had fulfilled its Mexican Mafia tax obligation."[69]

A street gang member might try to conceal his gang affiliation so that he can't be held hostage. A problem with this strategy is that a tier's shot caller identifies newly arrived inmates and their gang affiliation. However, even if the shot caller did not conduct an intake interview, inmates can usually identify a street gang member by his tattoos. Gang members usually place tattoos in prominent locations. Given the communal living and showering situation, a gang member cannot conceal his tattoos for his entire jail stay. In fact, often the purpose of getting tattoos is to provide information about one's history and status to strangers. For gang members, tattoos communicate "their membership, rank, specializations, and personal accomplishments....Just as academic vitae announce the prestige of institutional affiliation."[70] Given the importance in the underworld associated with these claims, "information concerning identity can literally be a matter of life and death."[71] Because tattoos are intended to provide important information to strangers, not surprisingly, strangers can often easily see them.

Just as in prison, drug consumers on the street cannot rely on formal governance mechanisms to ensure the quality and safety of the drugs they buy. Consequently, drug dealers in street gangs establish a reputation—both for the quality of their product and their danger to potential thieves. Like prison gangs, street gangs have an advantage in illicit markets and an incentive to invest in long-term reputation mechanisms to provide assurance. This branding only works, however, if consumers can identify which drug dealers are in reputable gangs. This is where tattoos play a crucial role. Precisely because tattoos are permanent and placed in prominent positions, they are a credible signal of gang affiliation.[72] It would be costly for a non-gang member to get a large gang tattoo on his neck because someone in the gang might see it. Gangs maintain their reputation by monitoring who claims to be a member. The reputation of the gang is greatest where the gang is most active. For an imposter to benefit from a gang tattoo, he would have to spend time in the location where he is most likely to be exposed. These costs make it clear that whoever gets a gang tattoo actually is a member of that gang. However, precisely because gang members use these permanent, prominent signals to engage in drug dealing on the street, they cannot easily hide them when in jail. The result is that prison gangs can use these individuals as hostages.

The third way that the Eme controls street gangs is by encouraging street gangs to prey on gangs that don't pay taxes. The Mexican Mafia protects gangs that pay taxes, and they stop protecting those that don't. A defense counsel in court explained, "The Mexican Mafia will issue what is called green lights.... A green light is essentially the okay to assault or kill somebody. That could be in prison, but it can also be on the streets. In the West Myrtle neighborhood, for many years West Myrtle had been the target of green lights. What that meant was that other gangs could come into the neighborhood and commit acts of violence, shootings, assaults, with impunity, without being disciplined by the Mexican Mafia. The Mexican Mafia gave its blessing."[73] One Southern

California gang proudly refused the Mexican Mafia taxation demands and started calling itself "the Green Light Gang." The result was that many of them were murdered in subsequent years.[74] After refusing to pay taxes, members of the Vineland Boys Gang abandoned many of the outward signs of gang membership to avoid detection.[75] They have since become compliant. The street gangs that don't pay taxes are outlaws—literally outside of the law created by the Mexican Mafia in the streets of Southern California.

Criminal Governance for the Drug Trade

The illicit nature of the drug trade means that street gangs cannot rely on the police to protect their property or on courts of law to uphold their agreements with consumers, intermediaries, employees, and suppliers. Conflict can arise for a variety of reasons. There might be a dispute between rival gangs about who can sell drugs in an area. A drug dealer might find himself in conflict with a supplier. Disputes might arise over nonpayment, late payment, receiving poor-quality drugs, late delivery of an item, or disagreement or renegotiation over the price. Conflicts might arise with his customers for the same reasons. A drug dealer's property might not be safe from theft and robbery. In the absence of effective governance institutions, market failures arise and firms must rely on less efficient forms of governance.

In lieu of mainstream governance institutions, criminals often use violence to adjudicate disputes.[76] Evidence suggests that the illegality of the drug trade per se contributes to violence. Historically, the murder rate in the United States has increased when officials increased enforcement of drug and alcohol prohibitions. Greater market prohibition increases reliance on extralegal governance mechanisms like violence. This pushes illicit business into arenas with fewer methods of nonviolent dispute resolution. This result holds even after controlling for other factors that might explain changes in the murder rate, such as the age of the population, incarceration rate, economic conditions, the availability of guns, and the death penalty.[77] If this association is interpreted as being causal, such that enforcement causes an increase in violence, then drug prohibition increases the murder rate between 25 and 75 percent. In a cross-country study of the effect of drug prohibition and gun laws on the murder rate, drug prohibition is also associated with an increase in the murder rate.[78]

A study of a gang's accounting books shows that gang wars adversely affect earnings.[79] Violence drives consumers away because of the possibility of harm amidst inter-gang violence. Wars increase the presence of, and the pressure applied by, law enforcement officials. Residents in the community become less tolerant of the drug trade.[80] Gangs spend money to recruit and arm new members. Of special importance to the Mexican Mafia, gang tribute paid to higher-ranking gang members declines. The prison gang has an incentive to enforce property rights and adjudicate disputes for tax-paying drug dealers. The Mexican Mafia's self-interest leads them to provide governance, which they do in three ways.

First, the Mexican Mafia protects tax-paying Sureños when they are incarcerated. County jails can be dangerous places, and a large number of inmates are from rival gangs. As an L.A. jail official explains, "Almost half of our jail population is street gang members, and they are probably responsible for 70 to 80 percent of the crime that occurs in our jail, and nearly all of our murders have been gang related in one way or another."[81] Gang rivals or other inmate predators might assault a gang member.

The Mexican Mafia might prefer not to protect taxpayers once they arrive, because they have already received the taxes and providing protection takes effort. But for the taxation to persist, the Mexican Mafia must provide protection. Extortion has an unusual feature. To be effective, the extortionist must have monopoly control over violence against the victim. Extortion is only effective when the extortionist can credibly tell the victim that he has the decisive choice to harm him or not. If a taxpayer anticipated being assaulted by other inmates, then there is little benefit to paying in the first place. To incentivize payment, therefore, the Mexican Mafia must both credibly threaten to hurt those who don't pay and effectively protect those who do.[82]

One indictment explains, "the Mexican Mafia provides protection to all MS-13 members incarcerated in county, state, and federal prisons and jails in California."[83] Another reports that by paying taxes, members of the Varrio Hawaiian Gardens gang "assure protection for VHG Gang members once they enter California state or federal penal institutions."[84] In 2011, another indictment noted that members of the 38th Street gang guarantee their protection once entering the penal system by paying taxes.[85] The Mafia provides a similar protective role for the Azusa 13, Eastside Riva, Florencia 13, Lennox 13, 18th Street gang, and many others.[86]

Second, the Mexican Mafia protects drug dealers on the street. One indictment explains how this works: "These tax payments entitle the soldier to conduct illegal activities such as the distribution of drugs under the authority of a given Mexican Mafia member. Having the member's authority protects the soldier from interference from the given member and from other gang members. The soldier who pays the taxes can also rely on the given member—or an associate of the member—for assistance (e.g. collection of outstanding drug debts)."[87] An Eme associate testified about his role in protecting drug dealers, explaining that it was his job to give dealers "a safe haven from other dealers and gangs. It was easier for them to pay than get bothered. We protected them from other thieves."[88] In another instance, a group was shaking down a female drug dealer at a local bar who received protection from the Mexican Mafia. When the Mexican Mafia found out, they sent people to the culprit's house and assaulted and robbed him.[89] Likewise, law enforcement officials report that the "Mexican Mafia ensures that no other gang operates in MS-13's territory or otherwise interferes with the criminal activities of MS-13."[90]

To be an effective deterrent, drug dealers must develop credible signals of their affiliation with the Mexican Mafia. When gangs begin paying taxes to the Mexican Mafia, they often add the number *13* to their gang name. This explains why so many gangs in Southern California have this attribute, including MS-13, Toonerville 13, Puente 13, and Florencia 13.[91] The letter *M* is the thirteenth letter of the alphabet, so it stands for the Mexican Mafia and signals a drug gang's affiliation. Attaching *13* to one's gang name tells potential thieves that if they steal from the gang, the Mexican Mafia will exact retribution.

A third, and perhaps the most important, form of governance that the Mexican Mafia provides is adjudication of disputes between tax-paying gangs.[92] A federal indictment notes that "the criminal activity of the Mexican Mafia also includes the resolution of disputes between the street gangs and the authorization of one street gang to assault members of another street gang."[93] For example, in early 1994, an 18th Street gang member killed a member of the Mara Salvatrucha. On February 5, law enforcement officials reported that a Mexican Mafia member met with "representatives of the 18th Street gang and the Mara Salvatrucha gang to discuss the dispute between the gangs over the murder of Mara Salvatrucha member 'Sal,' by 18th Street member 'Deffer.' "[94] In another instance, on January 19, 1995, one drug dealer complained to the Mexican Mafia that two people were selling drugs from his driveway, and as the indictment summarizes, this was "making it impossible for the unindicted co-conspirator to sell drugs."[95] In response, on January 19, the Mexican Mafia "negotiated a territory dispute between drug dealers."[96] In May 2006, the Mexican Mafia helped resolve disputes among cliques within the 18th Street gang. Law enforcement officials reported that "Mexican Mafia Member 1 would back him up as long as [defendant] paid taxes to Mexican Mafia member 1, and to assemble a meeting of shot callers for the cliques of the 18th Street Gang under Mexican Mafia Member 1's control in order to stop infighting and to unite their efforts on behalf of the 18th Street Gang and the Mexican Mafia."[97] Later that month, the gang member on the street wrote to the incarcerated Mexican Mafia member and assured him that the cliques of the 18th Street gang were "now working in concert."[98] Rather than letting gangs go to war, the Mexican Mafia provides governance. As one appellate court judgment summarizes, the prison gang "actually strove to minimize inter-gang violence so each gang would be more efficient in its drug-selling activities and would pay more taxes to the Eme."[99]

A related type of governance that the Mexican Mafia provides is to constrain negative externalities. In the summer of 1992, Mexican Mafia members began promoting a sort of quasi-peace treaty among Hispanic gangs.[100] The most well-known part of this process occurred when the Mexican Mafia made an announcement—the Eme Edict—that forbade street gangs from doing drive-by shootings and required that all Sureños swear allegiance to La Eme. When a gang does a drive-by shooting, many parties are affected. Innocent victims and neighbors may be killed, if not only frightened. The shootings generate media and police attention that negatively affects the ability of all neighboring gangs to sell drugs.[101] These negative externalities mean that each gang does not bear all of the costs of its actions, so each will do too many drive-by shootings.[102] The Mexican Mafia sought to regulate drive-by shootings by requiring that a person have at least one foot on the ground when shooting at someone, the so-called "one foot policy."[103] In late 1993, a Mexican Mafia member recorded by Federal Bureau of Investigation surveillance reportedly said, "If you gotta down somebody, down 'em. All we're saying is don't drive-by."[104]

Rene Enriquez, who takes credit for helping to devise the edict, began sending notes throughout the prison system and gang neighborhoods to notify people of the ban.[105] One highly respected Mexican Mafia member passed around a document that explained that anyone who violated the rule would be treated "as a child molester, a rat, a rapist, which all means coward."[106] According to one source, there were 20 Mexican Mafia members and associates holding meetings with gangs in public parks to lay out the rules.[107] A note confiscated from a teenage gang member in the county jail (dated November 24, 1993) provides some perspective on how people responded to the edict:

> So the homeboy Johnny got the green light by the Eme. Man, that fool is fuckin' stupid.... They out there blasting on fools or what? That shit makes the varrio look real bad. They're gonna fuck around and throw the varrio on a green light pretty soon.... I say this is what you should

do: talk to a couple of the homeboys and see if you vatos can throw a meeting between the varrio. Talk about what's going on with the Eme and about the "Peace Treaty." Those vatos do mean business. Man, you need to get the homeboys on the right track. It's about making money nowadays, not shooting' your own Raza up. If you guys wanna shoot somebody go shoot up those niggers from Westside 357 or Ghost town. You don't need to blast up your own kind no more. That shit's dead.[108]

In the weeks and months following the Edict, drive-by shootings declined. Hispanic gang-related homicides declined 15 percent in all of Los Angeles County, and it declined by as much as 50 percent in other areas.[109] Al Valdez, former supervisor of the Gang Unit in the Orange County District Attorney's Office writes, "between April and September of 1992, after the edict was announced, there were no drive-by shootings in the East Los Angeles area, a part of L.A. that was traditionally very active with gang violence and notoriously deadly."[110] A study of drive-by gang homicides found a 28 percent decline for all ethnicities between 1992 and 1994, but only a 5 percent decline in gang homicides overall. This suggests that gang members were changing the way that they killed rather than stopping the killing altogether. Los Angeles County Sherriff Sherman Block confirmed that "drive-by shootings have gone down, but street killings have not."[111]

We do not have the data available to measure how much, if any, of the change in drive-by shootings can be attributed directly to the edict.[112] However, the edict itself is well documented and is consistent with our understanding of why and how the prison gang provides governance. According to the *Los Angeles Times*, law enforcement officials say the "Mexican Mafia's true motive was to reduce the publicity caused by death of innocent lives caught in the cross-fire so it could organize with little outside scrutiny."[113] One source suggests that the prison gang believed "the killing of innocents energized law enforcement and politicians to launch extraordinary measures."[114]

In general, the Mexican Mafia imposes rules on drug-dealing street gangs that limit violence, promote order, and stimulate market activity. One indictment explains, "The Mexican Mafia has established rules to govern acts of violence committed by local street gang members, including Avenues gang members. The Mexican Mafia thus requires Avenues gang members to adhere to protocols for the conduct of violent attacks, narcotics trafficking, and murders, including the issuance of 'green light' authorizations for murder. Failure to adhere to Mexican Mafia rules can lead to the issuance of a 'green light,' directing an attack on the offending member, or the requirement that money be paid."[115]

The logic of the incarcerated bandit explains why some drug dealers pay taxes and receive extralegal governance. It also predicts who won't pay taxes to the Mexican Mafia and who won't have access to the benefits of their governance institutions. First, the Mexican Mafia cannot extort taxes from drug dealers who they cannot harm in jail. Members of other races are less susceptible to Mexican Mafia threats behind bars. They are often held in different cells and housing areas. They also rely on their own prison gangs for protection. Second, the Mexican Mafia doesn't extort taxes from people who don't anticipate incarceration. The threat of harming someone when he goes to jail is not salient if the person doesn't expect to go to jail. Moreover, law-abiding citizens can rely on the police to defend themselves from extortion. There is no evidence of the Mexican Mafia extorting legitimate businesses in this systematic, wide-scale fashion. A letter confiscated by officials that was sent from a Mexican Mafia leader in Pelican Bay's Secure Housing Unit to an affiliate on the street explains, "all legit businesses are to be left alone in our district, no taxing—this includes bars, etc."[116]

Furthermore, the Eme cannot extort all criminals with the same ease.[117] Some crimes, by their very nature, are difficult to observe. A skilled thief is unseen. A drug dealer must make his presence known to entice customers. In attracting customers, he must at the same time risk attracting the attention of the Mexican Mafia. Successful drug dealers also have cash on hand. People who commit violent crimes, like murder, aggravated assault, and rape, don't receive money that the prison gang can extort. The nature of the crime is therefore more resistant to extortion. The Mexican Mafia also needs criminals to be relatively immobile. Because rival drug dealers defend their turf with violence, drug dealers cannot easily move to a new region to avoid taxation. In fact, the Mexican Mafia tried to tax prostitutes, but when they did, the prostitutes simply worked elsewhere.[118] Finally, it's easier for an extortionist to tax someone who earns money on a regular basis. If a burglar gets a big score every several months, then the extortionist doesn't know when he can come to collect. A drug dealer who gets paid every day is a more reliable victim.

Finally, the prison gang can only extort drug dealers who live within the jurisdiction that would lead to incarceration in a county jail controlled by the gang. The Mexican Mafia cannot intimidate a Hispanic drug dealer in Northern California by threatening to hurt him if incarcerated in the Los Angeles County Jail. It is unlikely that the drug dealer will be incarcerated in L.A., so it's an empty threat. Consistent with the claim about how jail-based extortion works, these people don't pay drug taxes to La Eme. Moreover, prison gangs in other county jails tax drug dealers on the street, too. Prison gangs engage in jail-based extortion of drug dealers across the country. This provides further confirmation of the underlying logic for how prison gangs control the streets. In short, it is not from the benevolence of the Mexican Mafia that we expect them to govern the drug trade, but from their regard to their own interest.

There are two reasons to expect that the broad picture that these indictments and court documents paint is valid. First, correctional officers, police officers, lawyers, district attorneys, inmates, street gang members, and former prison gang members agree with the general structure described in these legal documents. The specific charges against particular people may be less reliable, but observers agree in the overall depiction that these documents present. Another way to determine the reliability of federal criminal allegations is to look at what relatively neutral observers think about the evidence. For instance, Judges Fletcher, Canby, and Rawlinson, in an appellate court ruling, assessed the weight and magnitude of the evidence used to convict a number of Mexican Mafia members in earlier cases. They found that "any rational trier of fact could have found the essential elements of the crime beyond a reasonable doubt."[119] This includes evidence presented that "the key to the Eme's power was its ability to threaten the members of smaller gangs as well as others with assault and even death if they did not comply with the Eme's demands. In particular, the Eme's power within the prison system gave it leverage even over gang members outside of prison."[120] Several Mexican Mafia members have been indicted in major cases based on multi-year investigations, with evidence coming from "hundreds of taped conversations which corroborated the appellants' efforts to organize and tax the drug distribution of street gangs."[121] The appellate judges wrote, "the evidence at trial clearly established that the drug taxing and drug trafficking conspiracies were undertaken by individuals on behalf of the enterprise, and were in fact an integral part of the conduct of the Eme's affairs."[122]

In the opening statement of a trial involving associates and members of the Mexican Mafia, even the defense lawyer admitted the prison gang's influence: "Well, in California, the California prisons are run by a prison gang known as the Mexican Mafia. You heard this from Mr. Staples [an Assistant U.S. Attorney], and it's well-known. Law enforcement knows it. People who have been to prison know it. They control the prisons through violence. They control the drug trading in prisons, but they also exercise control on the streets by virtue of their control in the prisons. By virtue of their ability to commit acts of violence in the prison, they can control the behavior of people on the streets."[123] What happens behind bars is often of substantial importance in the free world.

Puppet

IsAAC GUILLEN WAS born to a single mother in a poor neighborhood in Riverside, California. He was one of five kids. The Casa Blanca neighborhood where he grew up was a tough place, and at the age of 11, he joined a gang. He broke into houses and stole cars; he served several sentences in the California Youth Authority, including once for aggravated assault with a deadly weapon. By his 20s, he was married with kids, but he was still active in the gang. One night, with his family at home, rival gang members shot up his house. Guillen decided to make a change.

He dropped out of the gang and went to school, first to a local community college and then to the University of California at Berkeley. He excelled. His sociology professor, Martin Sanchez-Jankowski, an expert on street gangs, recalls, "He was excited about ideas. He wasn't a one-dimensional person. He was smarter than that."[1] Guillen wrote a thesis on Latino prison gangs, and he graduated with honors in 1994. He was accepted into the UCLA School of Law, and three years later, he proudly walked across the stage at the commencement ceremony—a remarkable success story.

While in law school, Guillen's criminal record made people hesitant to hire him for an internship. The Los Angeles District Attorney's office turned him down, so he approached the federal public defender's office. They hired him as a law clerk. The office was in the process of handling a major Mexican Mafia case. An 83-page indictment alleged a massive criminal conspiracy by the Avenues street gang, run by infamous gang leader Alex "Pee Wee" Aguirre.[2] Guillen helped with the case, and he ended up getting to know several of the defendants. His hard work and proficiency won him advocates among his senior colleagues.

His criminal record initially prevented him from sitting for the bar exam, but a strong letter of support from his supervisor convinced the State Bar to let him take the test. He passed, and he began practicing law in 1998. Guillen's business prospered, in part, because of his willingness to speak at length with clients who had a background similar to his own. The Mexican Mafia members whom he had worked with in previous years recommended him to their friends and associates. (When he graduated from law school, they sent him a signed card congratulating him.) At this time, Guillen was introduced to an incarcerated Mexican Mafia shot caller named Francisco "Puppet" Martinez, who was serving multiple life sentences for racketeering.

Martinez was housed at a federal prison, the Administrative Maximum security facility (ADX), in Florence, Colorado. ADX Florence is known as the "Alcatraz of the Rockies." It has arguably the most restrictive housing of any facility in the federal or state prison system, and it houses the most dangerous, violent, and high-profile inmates in the country. Inmates spend at least 20 and up to 24 hours a day in their cells.[3] It houses many notorious prisoners, including the Olympic Park bomber Eric Rudolph; Ramzi Yousef, the man who plotted the 1993 World Trade Center attack; Zacarias Moussaoui, a conspirator involved in the 9/11 terrorist attacks; Terry Nichols, who helped plan the Oklahoma City bombing; and "Unabomber" Ted Kaczynski and "Shoe Bomber" Richard Reid. Timothy McVeigh was a resident before his execution in 2001. One of its lesser-known residents, Thomas Silverstein, is a major reason ADX Florence exists. In 1983, Silverstein, an Aryan Brotherhood member, stabbed a guard to death at the federal penitentiary in Marion, Illinois. His ability to murder in a maximum-security federal prison made officials rethink just how restrictive they could be. Silverstein isn't the only prison gang member at ADX. In addition to Francisco "Puppet" Martinez, about a third of the inmates are members and shot callers from the Mexican Mafia, the Nuestra Familia, and the Aryan Brotherhood.[4]

After Guillen and Martinez became acquainted, Martinez started referring customers to him, as well as hiring him for his own legal needs. During a meeting at ADX Florence, Martinez asked Guillen to send a message to one of his other clients, Alberto Pina, to say hello and inquire about his wellbeing. Guillen agreed. It turned out to be the first step down a dangerous road. Guillen later admitted that the nonchalant greeting was probably a coded message. When Pina's sister paid Guillen for his legal services, she gave him an additional $15,000. Martinez had sent him the money to manage on his behalf. Guillen's relationship with Martinez continued to grow closer and more dubious.

A year later, Guillen was defending a member of the Black Angels street gang when the judge called him into his chambers. He told Guillen that his life was in danger. The judge had obtained information that the Mexican Mafia had ordered Guillen's client to kill him. Guillen was alarmed. He contacted Martinez to find out what was going on, and Martinez assured him that he would look into it. He later told Guillen that everything was okay; the Mexican Mafia didn't have a problem with him. But this apparent act of protection came with a price. Guillen later explained in court that Martinez used that favor to manipulate and control him. "He'd use it at times. 'I saved your life.' I felt like I owed him something."[5]

By this time, Guillen was doing lots of work for Martinez. Guillen deposited $500 of Martinez's stashed funds into his inmate account each month. Federal indictments indicate he sent a total of $27,500 to Martinez over the following years. Guillen traveled to Guadalajara to check on a $170,000 investment Martinez had made in a brothel. Guillen reported that the building was in poor shape and that the construction records appeared fraudulent.

Guillen's law practice was flourishing. He bought an expensive home and nice cars and had an affluent office. However, he was increasingly engaged in questionable—and outright illegal—practices. He began sending gang communications under the guise of legal paperwork, including coded messages written on his own letterhead. At ADX Florence, Guillen smuggled drug ledgers to Martinez for review. Guillen and Martinez were also partners in several businesses, including a limousine service, a liquor distributor, and a real estate holding company. He served as intermediary between street gang members and Martinez, meeting to pick up thousands of dollars. An 18th Street gang member even delivered gang taxes to Guillen's law office.[6] On one occasion, he took $50,000 to Martinez's family in Mexico.

However, as the 18th Street gang came under increasing pressure from law enforcement, their legitimate businesses ran into financial trouble.[7] Martinez was not pleased. Around that time, a Mexican Mafia dropout gave investigators a letter. The letter, written by Martinez, complained about Guillen's inability to run the businesses profitably and ordered, "At the end of all this I want Huero [one of Guillen's nicknames] taken out when he goes to TJ [Tijuana], just to set an example."[8] Martinez's orders to kill Guillen did not succeed because the hit man dropped out of the gang. Unfortunately, things still didn't end well for him.

In the summer of 2009, Guillen was indicted, along with 38 members and associates of the Columbia Little Cycos. The indictment listed him second, and reported his street name as "Coach." Initially, he kept quiet and was loyal to Martinez and the Mexican Mafia. However, after officials showed him Martinez's letter ordering his death, Guillen became an informant. He pled guilty to participating in a racketeering conspiracy, a money-laundering conspiracy, and 10 acts of money laundering. He had laundered $1.3 million for the Mexican Mafia, earning $180,000 in the process. In December 2010,

Guillen was disbarred from practicing law in the State of California. In exchange for his testimony, the government relocated his family. He was sentenced to seven years in prison.

It is difficult to imagine a prison setting that is more restrictive than ADX Florence. Nonetheless, prison gang members in the most secure federal facilities in the country can wield tremendous influence in the criminal underworld, even from several states away. They do this partly by manipulating and corrupting people with whom they interact. Their illicit profits help them buy people's compliance. Even with constitutional prohibitions against cruel and unusual punishment, officials are allowed substantial freedom to restrict, segregate, control, and monitor dangerous inmates—and they do. Nonetheless, even these practices have failed to stop ambitious criminals like Francisco "Puppet" Martinez.

7

What Works?

*Thus there are no "solutions"... but only trade-offs that still
leave many desires unfulfilled and much unhappiness in
the world.*

THOMAS SOWELL[1]

The Fundamental Problem of Political Economy

Prison offers a unique context in which to study social orders, but it also relates
to a much broader literature in economics and political science that seeks
to understand institutions, institutional change, and economic performance.[2]
There is substantial evidence that institutional quality explains why some
countries are rich and others are poor.[3] Consequently, a fundamental human
problem is determining how to create or preserve institutions that guide
self-interested behavior to promote the welfare of others.[4] In practice, an effective and robust institutional regime is often comprised of a combination of
both formal and extralegal governance institutions.

The government provides many formal institutions. However, roughly
two billion people—nearly a third of the world's population—live in countries that are on or near the cusp of state collapse.[5] Governments often fail to
provide adequate governance. Moreover, much of the world's economic
activity takes place outside of markets regulated by formal institutions. The
World Bank looked at the shadow economies of 88 developing countries.
They found that the average size of the shadow economy (which official
statistics do not incorporate) was 34 percent of the size of official gross domestic
product, and for some countries it was much higher. In Peru, Panama, and
Bolivia, the value of the shadow economy was 59, 63.9, and 66.9 percent of
official gross domestic product.[6] The total value of economic activity in all
shadow economies combined would comprise the world's second largest
economy.[7] In countries like these, a vast amount of economic activity is taking

place in the informal economy. Because exchange occurs outside of formal institutions and is conducted off the books, the shadow economy requires extralegal governance. To what extent can extralegal institutions promote economic activity and development?

Historical and contemporary cases find that extralegal governance institutions can be remarkably effective. They worked well among the 11th-century Maghribi merchants in the Mediterranean, in the European Champagne Fairs during the early Middle Ages, between Europeans and indigenous communities in precolonial Africa, aboard 17th- and 18th-century pirate ships, and in the early 19th-century mining districts of Mexican California (to offer just a few examples).[8] More recently, self-enforcing contracts govern the diamond trade among Orthodox Jewish merchants in New York, support the international Hawala money transfer system, and support relatively successful economic development in stateless areas of Somalia.[9] These examples provide an indication of the breadth, diversity, and complexity of self-governance institutions studied in the academic literature. One conclusion from this work is that there is no "one size fits all" institutional regime.[10] Rather, by studying a variety of settings, we can understand the general design principles that promote socially beneficial outcomes and those that tend to undermine it. The prison social order contributes several lessons to this broader study of institutions.

First, to understand aggregate economic and social outcomes, we must understand the extent to which people rely on extralegal governance. We would know little about the prison economy or social order if we only studied approved items purchased in the prison commissary or only formal mechanisms of social control. Likewise, to study only the local stock market or national government would ignore much of the economic and political processes in operation, especially in those countries that have the weakest formal institutions. Unsanctioned bazaars, unregistered street vendors, private forms of regulation, and extralegal dispute resolution mechanisms play an important role in many economies.[11] Ignoring the extralegal sphere obscures a crucial part of the story, and this is particularly true for understanding developing economies.

Second, extralegal institutions not only matter, but they may matter even more than formal institutions. In the context of the prison social order, inmates often care much more about what gang politics tells them to do than what officials tell them. Economists Claudia Williamson and Carrie Kerekes looked at the relative importance of formal and informal forms of property rights enforcement.[12] They argue that previous studies that focus on formal institutions might actually be measuring the influence of informal institutions indirectly. To avoid this problem, Williamson and Kerekes looked at data on formal institutions (electoral rules and judicial constraints) and informal cultural institutions (people's trust, feeling of control over one's life, respect for others, and obedience to others). Once they unbundled institutions into formal and informal measures, they found that "the impact of formal constraints is greatly diminished, while informal constraints are highly significant in explaining the security of property."[13] Not just institutions, but informal institutions rule.

The third lesson from studying the prison social order is that cooperation and economic exchange often thrives in the absence of strong, effective governments. The challenge is to identify under what conditions this is possible. We know that extralegal governance is more likely to lead to good outcomes in particular situations. Communities characterized by a high level of social, religious, and cultural homogeneity rely on other-regarding preferences and the threat of ostracism to promote cooperation. Smaller communities leverage reputations to encourage good conduct. Cooperation is easier when people are engaged in simple economic exchanges and in situations where the stakes are low. Self-governance is more feasible when people have high self-control and low discount rates and the benefits of future exchange can discipline opportunistic behavior. Studying the criminal underworld is an attempt to examine a community in which many or all of these beneficial aspects are absent. Given these conditions, can self-governance institutions emerge that effectively guide self-interested individuals into activities that are socially beneficial? The availability of contraband and the violence-constraining activity of today's prison gangs suggest that, even in this worst-case scenario, institutions can help coordinate the actions of self-interested individuals to dovetail with socially desirable needs for exchange and order. The existing economic and social order is not the best that is theoretically possible, but given the actual alternatives and constraints faced, the extralegal governance institutions of the inmate community are quite effective.

Finally, one of the most important implications is that institutions need not be consciously created. Inmates did not intentionally design and implement the convict code or gang-based governance or engineer the change between them. Shot callers are in charge of each gang and racial group, but none of them has the decisive choice to impose racial segregation or gang politics for the inmate social order. The founding members of prison gangs in the 1950s and 1960s didn't intend to create this polycentric governance regime. No one came up with the idea of a community responsibility system and proposed it to the other inmates, after which they approved and adopted it. The social order that exists was not chosen. No one is in charge. There are competing centers of authority that interact with each other in an iterative process. There is no central planner organizing things from the top down. The system has emerged as inmates seek ways to mitigate social conflict and increase access to illicit goods and services. This bottom-up process of institutional emergence was the result of inmate action, but not the execution of any inmate design.[14]

Inmates did not come together, agree on a social contract, and then pull some imaginary lever to implement a community responsibility system based on gang affiliation. In California, it emerged through the interactions of hundreds of thousands of inmates across as many as 30 prisons over more than 60 years. These interactions, and the institutions that emerged from them, resulted from changes in the resources, constraints, and preferences of inmates, officials, and potentially many others, including civil rights activists, lawyers, law enforcement officials, politicians, families, and religious communities. An important implication here is that officials also do not have access to a lever that they can switch back to eliminate prison gangs. The social order that exists is not subject to direct choice or control. It is the outcome of a complex process. At best, officials can alter the conditions that give rise to a gang-governed social order, but for the most part, they have focused on supply-side strategies that attempt to control the social order directly.

How Should Officials Respond?

Given the inmate demographics and the current effectiveness of formal governance mechanisms, gangs improve order in the inmate social system. Inmates benefit from these activities, so gangs are not a problem. In fact, if officials were able to disband gangs—eliminating their information transmission and enforcement mechanisms—then inmates would be worse off, because norms have proven insufficient for providing governance under current conditions. However, what's good for inmates is not necessarily what's good for prison staff. Successfully prohibiting trade in tobacco, drugs, and alcohol harms inmates, but it helps officials. If officials want to reduce prison gangs' influence, they might consider the suggestions that the governance theory of prison gangs has to offer. Primarily, they should remove the inmate needs that create a demand for extralegal governance and thus establish a place for gangs. Current correctional practices, however, are not in line with these ideas and instead focus on controlling the prison gangs directly.

In 2006, three criminologists argued, "It should cause no surprise that some of the most violent and least stable individuals in American society will take it upon themselves to group, form gangs, and divide along racial and ethnic lines in the prison setting. This is a finding that will likely characterize prisons forever."[15] It is certainly true that race-based gangs thrive in today's prisons, but this wasn't always the case. Since gangs did not exist for more than 100 years in California's prison system, there is reason to believe that they won't necessarily always exist. If, as this book has argued, gangs thrive because of a demand for governance, then gangs will be influential only as long as inmates have a need for their services. If racial segregation and violence are primarily means of securing social order, rather than inmates' desired ends, then prisons need not be destined to bigoted brutality.

Academics have not studied how to stem the rise of prison gangs. Prison officials have tried numerous strategies, but as criminologists Mark Fleisher and Scott Decker note, there are "no published research evaluations testing the efficacy of these suppression strategies on curbing prison gang violence and/or other criminal conduct inside correctional institutions."[16] County, state, and federal incarceration facilities do not provide the data on prison gangs and gang membership that are necessary to assess suppression strategies. In California, inmate data are spread across 80 unlinked databases, and there are no longitudinal studies of inmates' experiences.[17] Since we lack access to the data necessary to assess gang control approaches, any discussion of public policy must be speculative. In fact, this suggests that the first step for public policy is to make corrections departments more transparent. Data on inmate demographics and other theoretically relevant variables need to be more widely available.

Although officials have not provided data on gang membership, they have been clear about what tactics they use. Two approaches comprise the California Department of Corrections and Rehabilitation's (CDCR) current gang management strategy. The primary effort is "to identify gang affiliated offenders/parolees, track them, monitor their conduct, take interdiction action, and apply sanctions when they are found to be involved in illicit or unlawful gang activity."[18] One of the most common ways that officials attempt to disrupt prison gangs is to identify their hard-core members and house them in highly restrictive housing areas. Historically, the CDCR "has approached gang identification and management through intervention and suppression strategies.... CDCR has identified the gangs with the greatest propensity for violence and has separated the affiliated offenders from the general offender population by placement into a Security Housing Unit

(SHU) environment."[19] This strategy will only be effective, however, if supply-side factors drive gang activity entirely. If violence serves an end—such as resolving a drug debt or establishing property rights—then removing the people who participate in violence does not remove the underlying dispute that gives rise to violence. The unmet need for governance still exists.

Second, officials discourage gang activity by advising new inmates about the dangers of gangs, showing them a "gang diversion video," and making programs, like Cage Your Rage, available to inmates.[20] This approach is based on the idea that gangs form because people are ignorant or inherently violent. It ignores the fact that gangs arise to address specific problems in the inmate social system. Both of these programs target the supply side of the prison gang problem. Both have failed.

The California Department of Corrections and Rehabilitation is not an outlier in this practice. A survey of 148 correctional facilities in 48 states asked, "What strategies does your facility use to control gangs?"[21] The staff members who responded gave 19 answers. Four of the most popular responses focused on disrupting or intercepting gang communications. These included monitoring phone calls and mail, using informants, and interrupting communications. A second major tactic to combat gangs focuses on limiting members' movement and interactions. Respondents identified six strategies for doing so, including transfers, segregation, lockdown, displacement, and locking up gang leaders. Officials appeared not to use any tactics aimed at reducing demand for extralegal governance.

The fact that gangs have such great influence in California's prisons is evidence that these policies have failed. About two-thirds of the nearly 6,000 inmates in California's Security Housing Unit (SHU) are gang members or gang-affiliated.[22] In some cases, they are locked up for 23 hours a day. Yet, SHUs have not eliminated gangs. In 2007, San Quentin Warden Robert Ayers explained, "The Department of Corrections has pretty much given over control of the general populations to gangs."[23] This is a rather stunning admission of gangs' dominance in California prisons. It's common knowledge, not even an open secret, that gangs are an important part of prison life. In a study conducted by Rebecca Trammell, a correctional officer describes the failure of interdiction efforts, noting, "we try to break them up, we'll move the shot-callers to Pelican Bay, we split up the gangs and they just continue what they're doing in their new prison. The gang problem is big."[24]

Despite transferring the most active gang members to the most secure facilities in the state, gangs continue to rule prison cellblocks and yards. Segregation likely has some marginal deterrent effect, but there's no evidence that it has diminished the power of gangs overall. An important reason for this is that segregation of one gang member simply means there is a new job opening. A former warden with 30 years of corrections experience writes, "If a gang leader is neutralized by transfer or long-term lockup, the group names new leadership; like corrections officials, they are prepared for succession."[25] Likewise, a Department of Justice survey concluded that isolating gang leaders simply leaves a void for new leaders to emerge and fails to eliminate gangs.[26] Breaking up one gang opens the door for another to form or for young members to step into leadership roles. Moreover, shot callers in the SHU can often still give orders to gang members in other prisons and jails and on the street. Disrupting the supply side causes trouble for particular gang members, but it does not put an end to gangs, because the demand for their services still remains.

The governance theory of prison gangs suggests that a better approach for reducing the power of prison gangs is to alter the conditions that give rise to inmates' demand for them and to identify what substitute mechanisms are available. If removing gangs means that inmates have to rely on norms, then prisons will become less orderly. In this scenario, gangs should not be undermined. Alternatively, if officials can provide formal governance institutions that are more effective or reduce inmate's demand for extralegal governance, then removing gangs can improve prison order. There is a limit to this, however, in that officials will presumably not be willing to adjudicate disputes in illicit markets. Given these concerns, three possible solutions to reduce the influence of prison gangs are to (1) make prisons safer and more liberal, (2) incarcerate fewer people, and (3) hire more police.

Improving formal governance mechanisms will reduce inmates' demand for extralegal governance. Mark Kleiman offers a number of proposals to improve prison management.[27] First, a performance-measurement system should be developed that rewards wardens on the basis of inmates' post-release behavior. A warden's compensation would depend on how often inmates from his or her facility relapse into drug and alcohol addictions, incur new criminal charges, miss court and parole meetings, and return to prison. This system would provide feedback about what works and give wardens a stronger incentive to seek out improvements. Related to this, an independent organization should interview released inmates about their experience and prison conditions. Prisons that are safe, calm, and predictable should be rewarded. Second, an evidence-based analysis of correctional architecture is in order. Kleiman suggests, "In the context of ethnic prison gangs, perhaps the optimal size of a prison is much smaller than it used to be. Be prepared to ignore currently accepted standards, where those standards are unsupported by evidence that they improve prisoner physical or psychological health, improve reintegration, or reduce recidivism."[28] Third, prison safety and the security of inmates' property needs to be improved, by installing closed-circuit TV systems in every area of the prison. A surprisingly large number of prisons, especially older ones, lack video surveillance. The more officials can protect an inmate's person and property, the less they will turn to gangs. In addition, some correctional facilities have experimented with attaching small video cameras to each officer's uniform. By creating a record of their actions, it protects officers from false allegations by inmates and documents inmate and staff misconduct. Other policies that might improve prison order include single-person cells instead of double bunking, in-cell cameras, and even roving drones that record inmate activity. Demand for extralegal governance could be reduced by allowing a prison economy and making some contraband, like tobacco, legal. By outlawing all trade, inmates are pushed to find alternative governance mechanisms.

If we designed a prison intended to meet inmates' demand for governance, it would not resemble the ones we currently have. Radical changes, or at least a willingness to question current practices, are in order. Legal scholar Alexander Volokh makes the novel suggestion that we create a "prison voucher" system akin to proposals for school choice, where inmates can choose where to serve their time. As he explains, "vouchers empower the prisoners themselves to reward and punish prisons, creating powerful incentives for prisons to improve in accordance with the prisoners' own standards."[29] Prisons would compete against each other for more inmates by offering better and possibly different incarceration experiences. Prisons could specialize in offering a particular set of amenities, including the availability and types of health care, access to therapeutic and rehabilitative programs, high school and university education, vocational training, the quality of gym and recreation resources, a devout religious lifestyle, better visiting facilities, cheaper phone calls, access to the Internet, and location near family. Inmates will avoid prisons known to be disorderly or to lack desirable programming options. Prisons would then have an incentive to discover what inmates want and to find ways to provide it efficiently. This might include more training for correctional officers, developing a meaningful internal grievance system, or even establishing an independent system of external monitoring with the aid of a third party, such as the Red Cross. Compared with the bureaucratic incentives that guide prison management today, prison vouchers might be able to generate superior information and incentives to improve prison order. Of course, the system would require restrictions on what types of amenities and freedoms inmates could receive. Nevertheless, few people would disapprove of prisons that were more safe, predictable, calm, and rehabilitative, and it seems reasonable that inmates would reward prisons that could provide these.

Another way to reduce the influence of prison gangs would be to reduce the demand for extralegal governance, by reducing the number of people in prison. We live in an era of mass incarceration. Large segments of the population are systematically incarcerated, and prisons are increasingly run in a warehouse-like or waste management–like manner.[30] The sheer scale of incarceration is difficult to comprehend. There are more prisoners in the United States than in any other country in the world—2,240,000 prisoners. This exceeds the reported total prison populations in those 40 countries with the highest incarceration numbers (Figure 7.1). The number of prisoners in the United States exceeds the combined numbers of doctors, lawyers, and clergy in the entire country.[31] If all U.S. prisoners comprised a single city, they would make up the fourth largest city, falling between Chicago and Houston. If they comprised a single state, it would be more populous than New Mexico, Nebraska, West Virginia, and 12 others. If they represented a single country, it would be larger than 97 other countries and larger than the 50 least populous countries combined. The United States holds more than 20 percent of all of the world's prisoners, despite having only about 4 percent of the world's population.

According to data from the International Centre for Prison Studies, the U.S. rate of incarceration in jails and prisons is also the highest in the world,

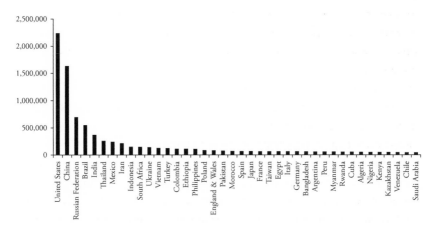

FIGURE 7.1 Prison population by country

Source: International Centre for Prison Studies, Prison Population Totals data

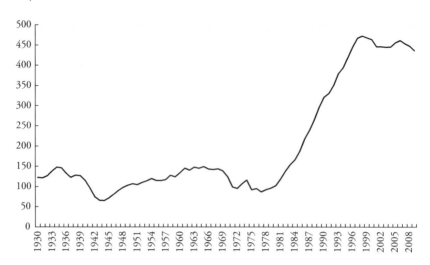

FIGURE 7.2   California incarceration rate per 100,000 residents, 1930–2009.

Source: Data for 1960–1989, from California Department of Corrections 1990 Annual Report, page 74; for 1990–2009, from California Department of Corrections and Rehabilitation, 2009 Annual Report, page 9

716 out of every 100,000 residents.[32] That is four and a half times higher than the average rate of incarceration in Europe (157 out of 100,000 residents). These rates deviate from historical trends as well. For instance, from 1930 to 1975, the incarceration rate in prison in California averaged only 117 out of every 100,000 residents (Figure 7.2). From 2000 to 2009, the incarceration rate averaged 450 people per 100,000. In certain demographics, the incarceration rate is much higher. The state and federal incarceration rate for Hispanics and blacks is 1,200 and 3,161 out of every 100,000 residents.[33] In 1995, one of every three black males between the ages 20 to 29 was under some form of criminal justice supervision.[34] By the end of 2004, about eight percent of black males between the age of 25 and 29 were in prison.[35] For the land of the free, a remarkably large number of Americans are not.

Smaller communities can better rely on norms because they are characterized by personal exchange instead of impersonal exchange. People in the former scenario can adjudicate disputes with decentralized sanctions, while the latter requires the information transmission and enforcement mechanisms that gangs use with expert skill. These mechanisms are costly to create and use, so when norms are effective, inmates choose norms. Additionally, fewer mutually beneficial exchanges exist in smaller communities, so inmates have less demand for the extralegal governance that underlies exchange. To the extent that drug offenders have the greatest demand for extralegal governance, curtailing the drug war may be a particularly effective way of reducing prison gang influence.[36] In 2010, 24 percent of all people entering prison with a new commitment did so for drug offenses. In 2002, 58 percent of drug offenders (about 125,000 inmates) neither had a violent history nor participated in high-level drug activity.[37] Mass incarceration is a major driver of prison gang growth, and revising policing and incarceration practices and policies can help remedy the situation.

A recent change in state corrections provides some evidence on the relationship between prison populations and gangs. In 2009, a U.S. Supreme Court ruling required the state of California to reduce its prison population from 188 percent of the system's designed capacity (previously at 202 percent in 2006) to 137.5 percent of designed capacity by June 2013. Assembly Bill 109, passed in 2011, began diverting nonserious, nonsexual, and nonviolent offenders to county jails. Instead of going to prison, many of these offenders now serve their sentence in county jail. As a result, the state prison population has fallen, which, if this trend continues, will make norms a more feasible alternative to gangs. Inmate populations at county jail, however, have risen substantially. Consistent with the governance theory, as county jail populations have surged, gangs have become a larger, more important part of the social system.

A major concern with reducing the prison population is that it will increase the crime rate. Prisons might reduce crime in several ways. The threat of incarceration deters people from committing crimes. Offenders recognize that they might be apprehended, and the risk of going to prison stops them from committing crime in the first place. Incarceration might rehabilitate a person so that he or she does not commit crime once released. Incarceration also reduces crime simply because inmates cannot commit (as much) crime while behind bars. The fact that they are incapacitated reduces the crime rate. Despite these possible lines of causality linking prisons with crime control, there are several reasons to think that reducing the prison population will lead to few, if any, increases in the crime rate.

Past work finds that the amount of crime reduction that incarceration produces depends on the scale of incarceration.[38] When few people are incarcerated, increasing the rate of people in prison has relatively large effects on reducing crime. The people who commit the most crime are the most likely to be apprehended with the initial enforcement efforts. The newly incarcerated would have engaged in the most crime, so getting them off the street makes a big difference. As more people are incarcerated, prisons fill with people who commit crime less often. For a state with the median state prison population, increasing incarceration by 10 percent reduces the crime rate by only 1 percent. As the scale of incarceration rises, the resulting decline in crime decreases at a faster and faster rate. The payoff in crime reduction gets smaller at an accelerating rate. At higher levels of incarceration, increasing the incarceration rate actually increases the crime rate. More inmates means more crime. Estimates suggest that increasing the incarceration rate leads to more crime when a state's incarceration rate reaches 325 out of every 100,000 residents.[39] With California having passed that rate in 1991 and with an incarceration rate of 436 in 2009, the state has likely surpassed the point of crime reduction. A survey of the empirical literature on the relationship between crime and incarceration concludes that "there is little evidence that increases in the severity of punishment yields strong marginal deterrent effects; further, credible arguments can be advanced that current levels of severity cannot be justified by their social and economic cost and benefits."[40]

This counterproductive effect has a number of possible explanations. A criminal record reduces legitimate employment opportunities, which increases criminal activity and recidivism.[41] Going to prison provides a networking opportunity to offenders. One study finds, after controlling for other factors, that being locked up with more serious offenders and with people serving longer sentences, a person engages in more crime in the future.[42] Incarceration increases future illegal earnings.[43] Meanwhile, family and community ties strain when parents go to jail. This collateral damage weakens the social network of a community, and breaking the law or going to prison can become destigmatized. Crime is a complex social problem, but if these estimates are roughly accurate, then both the prison population and the crime rate can be reduced at the same time.

More broadly, the prison buildup was not simply a response to rising crime rates, which actually plummeted in the 1990s. A variety of factors contributed to prison growth. Political incentives encourage incarceration, often for reasons unrelated to the crime rate. The federal government has become increasingly involved in crime control and provides substantial resources to local, state, and federal law enforcement officials. Moreover, politicians at the local, state, and national levels now all simultaneously legislate on the same criminal justice issues. Well-funded, single-issue special interest groups dominate the state and national legislative arenas. Law enforcement bodies and district attorneys associations have substantial influence, and they often lobby for greater discretion and stricter punishments.[44] The California Correctional Peace Officers Association actively lobbies for tough-on-crime laws and harsher sentences.[45]

Local governments pay for local law enforcement, but not for prisons, so the public elects prosecutors and judges who send criminals to prison rather than collecting more tax dollars to pay for local law enforcement.[46] Evolving legal doctrines during and preceding the buildup gave prosecutors greater discretion to use plea bargains. With nearly 95 percent of all criminal convictions coming from guilty pleas, the prison buildup would be much more costly without the extensive use of plea bargains.[47] Related to this, a major cause of prison growth is that prosecutors have increased the number of felony filings per arrest.[48] The content of the criminal statutes and political priorities became more punitive as well, including the Drug War, mandatory and determinate sentencing guidelines, and a variety of three-strikes laws.[49] Changes in other policies have also led to prison growth. For example, the deinstitutionalization of the mentally ill increased prison populations.[50] Jonathan Simon argues that government has used the public's fear of crime to increase its political power and is part of a more general shift toward "governing through crime."[51]

Finally, incarceration isn't the only way to control crime. Increasing the number of police officers on the streets does the job, too. In examining the crime decline of the 1990s, Steven Levitt found that both increases in incarceration and the number of police officers reduced crime. However, on the margin, a dollar spent on prisons provided about 20 percent less crime reduction than a dollar spent on more police.[52] In other words, it cost between $700 million and $840 million on hiring police officers to reduce the crime rate by 1 percent. For spending on prisons and jails, it cost $1.6 billion to achieve the same.[53] As criminal justice scholar William Stuntz summarizes, "The lesson of the 1990s is that, given our already swollen prison population, the most cost-effective crime-fighting strategy is putting more police boots on violent city ground, not putting more criminals in prison cells."[54] More police deter crime before it happens, so it doesn't require increasing the incarceration rate. There is also greater criminal deterrence from increasing the certainty of crimes rather than the severity of the punishment.[55] This suggests both a reform of three-strike laws and other sentence enhancements and further supports the argument for increasing police numbers. Additionally, to increase the effectiveness of these efforts, police should concentrate on crime hot spots rather than random patrolling, use focused deterrence approaches on the most active and violent individuals engaged in crime, and emphasize reducing crime and disorder rather than the number of arrests.[56]

Focusing on the supply-side factors associated with prison gangs has failed to explain their existence. It has also failed to provide solutions for how to control them. Prison gangs do not form to promote racism and violence or because street gangs exist in the community and import their organizational structures into prison. Violence and racial segregation are means to achieve other ends. To understand the gang situation and to design effective public policy, we must recognize that inmates have a demand for gangs, and gangs do much to improve inmates' welfare. Prison gangs form and operate to provide essential extralegal governance institutions. When prisons are dangerous, inmates form gangs for protection. When mutually beneficial exchanges abound, inmates turn to gangs for assurance. Therefore, to constrain gangs, officials must reduce inmates' demand for their valuable services: lock up fewer people, make prisons safer and more liberal, and deploy more police in the community.

Endnotes

CHAPTER 1

1. DiIluio 1987, 130
2. Klien and Gomez 2012
3. Veblen 1898 [1998], 411
4. Kaminski 2004, 1; also Toch 1992, 64–65
5. The rational choice approach to crime is not new. Caesare Beccaria's work (1764) is a seminal study of crime and punishment. Becker (1968) and Ehrlich (1972) have made important contributions in the modern era. Much of this book follows the tradition laid out in Thomas Schelling's (1967; 1971) superb institutional analysis of organized crime and in important empirical work by Peter Reuter (1983) on American organized crime and Diego Gambetta (1993) on the Sicilian Mafia.
6. Dixit 2009, 5
7. Demsetz 1967
8. Libecap 1994
9. Holcombe 1993, Ch. 2; Friedman 1994; Friedman 2001, 112–27
10. Holcombe 1993, 12
11. For example, Houser and Wooders 2006
12. Munger 2010
13. Benson 1990; 1998
14. Leeson 2005b; Leeson 2006; Leeson 2007c; Stringham 2007; Leeson 2008; Leeson 2009b; Powell and Stringham 2009. On the positive analysis of anarchy, see Boettke (2005).
15. Dixit 2009, 6
16. Gambetta 2009, 3–29
17. On the economic consequences of illegality and underground economic activity, see Reuter (1983, 109–31), Staley (1992, 145–80), Venkatesh (2006), Cook et al (2007), and Meadowcroft (2008).

18. Lahm 2008; Fleisher and Krienert 2009; additional perspectives exist, too (DeLisi et al 2013)
19. Sykes 1958 [2007]
20. Irwin and Cressey 1962
21. Posner 2000, 11–35; Kaminski 2004
22. However, see Williams and Fish (1974) and Kalinich and Stojkovic (1985).
23. Following the literature in political science and economics on institutions and institutional change, this book uses an analytical narrative framework (e.g., Bates et al 1998; Greif 2006b, 3–23, 124–152, 350–376).
24. Neuwirth 2011, 27
25. Leeson and Williamson 2009, 77
26. Williamson 2009; Williamson and Kerekes 2011
27. Edwards and Ogilvie 2012; Greif 2012
28. Lyman 1989, 48
29. Blatchford 2008, 7
30. Buentello, Fong, and Vogel 1991
31. Gangs make exceptions, but it's rare (Morrill 2005, 49).
32. Pyrooz et al 2011, 4, Table 1
33. Camp and Camp 1985, vii
34. American Correctional Association 1993, 9
35. Winterdyk and Ruddell 2010
36. Trulson, Marquart, and Kawucha 2006
37. Petersilia 2006, 35
38. Knox 2000, 434 cited in Volokh 2011, 839
39. MSNBC 2005a
40. Gaes et al 2002, 360
41. Fleisher and Decker 2001, 2
42. Studies have tended to focus on major events, like riots and court cases, rather than the ordinary life of institutions (Simon 2000, 289).
43. Wacquant 2002, 371; see also Wacquant 2001, 109. On the political consequences of incarceration, see Weaver and Lerman (2011) and Page (2011). See Simon (2007) on the rise of political governance through crime.
44. Trammell (2011a) describes gang activity in California, but her goal is not to explain the observed variation in prison gang activity. See also important work by Kruttschnitt and Gartner (2005), Goodman (2008), Crewe (2009), Fleisher and Krienert (2009), and Dolovich (2012).
45. Trulson, Marquart, and Kawucha 2006, 26
46. Pyrooz et al 2011, 15
47. Petersilia 2006, ix
48. Ball 2010
49. Pyrooz et al 2011, 13; see also DiIulio 1987, 51
50. Fleisher and Decker 2001, 3; Fong 1987, iii

51. A rare exception is Levitt and Venkatesh (2000).
52. Fong 1987, iii
53. California Department of Corrections and Rehabilitation 2012d, 15–25
54. Pyrooz et al 2011, 12; Gaes et al 2002, 360
55. I am grateful for permission to use quotes from *Enforcing the Convict Code: Violence and Prison Culture*, by Rebecca Trammell. Copyright © 2011 by Lynne Rienner Publishers, Inc. Used with permission by the publisher.
56. More specifically, I use documents prepared by the state-level corrections authority, which has held several different names. In 1929, the Department of Penology was created. It was renamed the Department of Corrections in the 1940s. In 2005, it became the Department of Corrections and Rehabilitation. For more on this history, see Gilmore (2007).
57. Wacquant 2002, 387

MEN'S CENTRAL JAIL

1. Los Angeles County Witness Statements 2011, 106–10.
2. *Rosas and Goodwin v. Baca* 2012; Los Angeles County Citizens' Commission on Jail Violence 2012

CHAPTER 2

1. Williams and Fish 1974, 12
2. MSNBC 2008c
3. MSNBC 2010b
4. Levin 1996; also Toch 1992, 52–53
5. California Code of Regulations 2009, 178–82
6. California Department of Corrections and Rehabilitation 2012a, 1
7. MSNBC 2006; Kaminski (2004, 6) corroborates the widespread lack of trust.
8. DiIulio 1987, 51
9. Useem and Piehl 2006, 94
10. Useem and Piehl 2008, 96
11. Useem and Piehl 2008, 97
12. Useem and Piehl 2008, 99
13. Useem and Piehl 2008, 101
14. Many studies examine formal governance mechanisms and prison order (e.g., DiIulio 1987; Sparks, Bottoms, and Hay 1996; Bottoms 1999).
15. California Code of Regulation 2009. Officers also use informal mechanisms of social control (Santos et al 2012).
16. Scholars continue to debate how much, if any, architecture matters in creating order (see Useem and Piehl 2006, 109–11).
17. Goffman 1961
18. Kollock 1998

19. Bowker 1980. On routine prison victimization, see O'Donnell and Edgar (1998). Criminals typically display low self-control, making it more difficult to elicit cooperation (Pratt and Cullen 2000).
20. Earley 1992, 68
21. Sykes 1958 [2007], 82
22. Officials also need the assistance of inmates (Parenti 1999; Useem and Piehl 2008, 84; Trammell 2011a, 132).
23. Hobbes 1651 [2009]
24. Toch 1992, 279
25. MSNBC 2007c
26. Fleisher and Krienert 2009, 105
27. Trammell 2011a, 22
28. Kaminski 2003; Kaminski 2004, 145–68; Jacobs 1977, 45
29. Owen 1988
30. Trammell 2011a, 96
31. Toch 1992, 208
32. Earley 1992, 287–88
33. Donald Cressey's introduction to Irwin 1980, vii. Irwin (1980, 125–26) also suggests that some guards are racist, which may remove access to formal governance mechanisms for segments of the prison population.
34. Allen and Bosta 1981; also Crouch and Marquart 1989, Ch. 3
35. Webb and Morris 1985, 205–206; see also Owen 1988, 25–30
36. Dolan 2011
37. *United States v. Michel* 2012
38. Leonard and Faturechi 2012
39. *Rosas and Goodwin v. Baca* 2012
40. Kalinich 1980; Kalinich and Stojkovic 1985. See also the classic article on the emergence and operation of markets in a P.O.W. camp (Radford 1945).
41. California Code of Regulations 2012, Sec 3192
42. California Code of Regulations 2012, Sec 3006
43. Dolan 2011
44. California Council on Science and Technology 2012, 6
45. California Department of Corrections and Rehabilitation 2012b
46. Levin 1996; United States Department of Justice (1991) surveys inmates about contraband.
47. Sykes and Messinger 1962, 97
48. Smith 1763 [1982], 538–39
49. Tullock 1985; Axelrod (1984) provides a classic analysis of these issues.
50. According to the Folk Theorem (Fudenberg and Maskin 1986), there are an infinite number of Nash equilibrium strategies that might arise in repeated games, including "all-defect and a wide variety of other inefficient profile sequences" (Friedman and Oprea 2012). The stability of cooperative outcomes—a strategy's

evolutionary robustness—in these games depends on how robust they are to invasion by noncooperative actors (see Bendor and Swistak 1995).

51. Schelling 1960, Ch. 3

52. Leeson, Coyne, and Boettke 2006

53. Because inmates have some uncertainty about when their interactions will cease because of, for example, prison transfers, complete unraveling may not occur in practice.

54. Telser 1980

55. Tullock 1985; Axelrod 1984, 130; Tullock 1999

56. Glaeser 1998, 3; also Davis 1988; Lee and McCrary 2005; Beraldo, Caruso, and Turati 2013

57. DiIulio 1996, 16

58. Avio 1998, 145

59. Crawford and Ostrom 1995, 587–591

60. Posner 2000, 11–35; Young 1998

61. Crawford and Ostrom 1995, 586

62. Crawford and Ostrom 1995, 586

63. Sykes 1958 [2007]; Irwin and Cressey 1962; Sykes and Messinger 1962; Rudoff 1964; Carroll 1974; Wieder 1974; Williams and Fish 1974; Jacobs 1977; Irwin 1980; Bunker 2000; Koehler 2000; Bronson 2006; Santos 2007; Copes et al 2013. Early work argued that inmates imported norms from outside prison (Schrag 1954; Irwin and Cressey 1962; Irwin 1970 [1990]; Hassine 2007). However, there appears to be agreement that both street culture and the incarceration experience influence prison culture (Akers, Hayner, and Gruninger 1977; Pollock 1997; Winfree, Newbold, and Tubb 2002). There is also a literature that looks at the prison norms of the *vory-v-zakone* (Varese 1998). Anderson (1999) studies the code of the street in Philadelphia.

64. Bowker 1977, 15

65. Clemmer 1940, 152

66. Fleisher and Krienert 2009, 47

67. Clemmer 1940, 152

68. Sykes and Messinger 1962, 92–94; also Rudoff 1964, 77–79; Irwin 1980, 12

69. Sykes and Messinger 1962, 94

70. Williams and Fish 1974, 24, discussing Schrag 1954

71. Williams and Fish 1974, 53

72. Williams and Fish 1974, 41

73. Williams and Fish 1974, 42

74. Sykes and Messinger, 1962, 94

75. Irwin 1980, 13–14

76. Bowker 1977, 26

77. Robertson 1988, 102

78. Bugliosi and Gentry 1994, 489–90

79. McCorkle and Korn 1954, 90
80. Clemmer 1940, 108
81. Davidson 1974, 45–46
82. Reimer 1937; Sykes and Messinger 1962; Irwin 1970, 7–34; Williams and Fish 1974, 17–37; Crewe 2009, 149–300
83. Clemmer 1940, 107
84. Clemmer 1940, 153
85. Bowker 1977, 15
86. Toch 1992, 183
87. Williams and Fish 1974, 6; also Clemmer 1940, 88–98. Fleisher and Krienert (2009, 141–89) provide a lexicon of prison sex slang.
88. MSNBC 2007d
89. Clemmer 1962, 112
90. In contrast to the results of many theoretical studies of social dilemmas, case studies find that graduated rather than extremely harsh punishments facilitate cooperation more effectively (Dixit 2009, 17; Ostrom 1990, 94–100).
91. MSNBC 2007c. Hamill (2011, 74) finds a similar information component within the Irish Republican Army's choice to shoot people in the kneecaps.
92. Irwin 1980, 58
93. Clemmer 1940, 129
94. Clemmer 1962, 113; also Irwin 1980, 58–60
95. Irwin 1980, 58
96. Irwin 1980, 60
97. Clemmer 1940, 141
98. Clemmer 1940, 143
99. Irwin 1970 [1990], vi
100. Irwin 1980, 181
101. Irwin 1980, 192
102. Jacobs 1975, 478
103. Skarbek 2012. On theories of institutions and institutional change, see Knight (1992); March and Olson (1996); Pierson (2000); Greif and Laitin (2004); and Kimbrough and Wilson (2013).
104. North 1987; Ostrom 1990, 188; Ellickson 1991, 177–8; Posner 2000, 16; Dixit 2009, 16
105. Clemmer 1940, 299
106. Rudoff 1964, 81–82
107. Fleisher 1989, 131
108. Landa 1981, 1994; Bernstein 1992, 1996, 2001; Schaeffer 2008. For studies of self-enforcing exchange and extralegal governance more generally, see Friedman (1979); Carr and Landa (1983); Benson (1989); Greif (1989, 1993); Kreps (1990); Clay (1997); Dixit (2004); Leeson (2007c). On the robustness of self-enforcing exchange see Leeson (2005a; 2005b; 2006; 2007c; 2008; 2009b).
109. Irwin 1970 [1990], 56

110. Bunker 2000, 132; see also Irwin 1980, 9
111. Bunker 2000, 145
112. Irwin 1970 [1990], vii; also Irwin 2005, 93
113. Alesina and Spolaore 1997; Easterly and Levine 1997; Alesina, Baqir, and Easterly 1999
114. Ethnic fractionalization (EF) is calculated as $EF = 1 - \sum_{i=1}^{n} s_i^2$, where s_i is the share of the group i in the total population.
115. Age is also a good predictor of prison violence, and younger inmates fight more often than older inmates (Lahm 2008, 122). Gambetta (2009, 91–94) argues that young inmates fight more often because they lack the "violence capital" that older inmates have accumulated that deters violence.
116. Hunt et al 1993, 405
117. Hunt et al 1993, 405
118. Hunt et al 1993, 406
119. Hunt et al 1993, 405
120. Hunt et al 1993, 406
121. Hunt et al 1993, 405
122. California Department of Corrections 1975
123. California Department of Corrections 1975, xii

DEATH ROW

1. California Department of Corrections and Rehabilitation 2012b
2. Castro 2007
3. *People v. McGhee* 2010
4. *People v. McGhee* 2010
5. *People v. McGhee* 2010
6. Keith 2009

CHAPTER 3

1. Falcone 1991, 56
2. Skaperdas 2001, 174. More generally, self-protection plays an important role in influencing the amount and distribution of crime (Cook 1986).
3. Gambetta 1993
4. Bandiera 2003, 221
5. Gambetta 1993; Buonanno et al 2012
6. Skaperdas 2001, 175; Campana 2011. Likewise, Hamill (2011, 42) argues that the Irish Republican Army provides policing services in West Belfast because the rule of law has been contested and formal police services are often prohibitively costly. Drug traffickers provide criminal governance in the form of crime control and dispute resolution in the *favelas* of Rio de Janeiro (Arias 2006; Arias and Rodrigues 2006).

7. Varese 2005; Varese 2011

8. Frye and Zhuravskaya 2002

9. Frye 2002

10. Milhaupt and West 2000, 41; Hill 2003

11. Milhaupt and West 2000, 41

12. Wang 2011

13. Jankowski 1991, 122–23. Thrasher (1927 [2000]) is the seminal study of American street gangs.

14. Melde, Taylor, and Esbensen 2009, 566

15. Sobel and Osoba 2009

16. Reuter 1983, 151–73

17. Skaperdas 2001, 176; Reuter 1983, 151–73

18. Varese 2011; Alexander 1997

19. Varese (2011) provides a superb theory of mafia migration.

20. Page 2011, 16; Simon 2007, 149. Bookspan (1991) and Kruttschnitt and Gartner (2005, 8–38) provide histories of the early years of the California prison system. McGee (1981) writes about his professional experience and correctional philosophy.

21. Rudoff 1964, 8

22. Rudoff 1964, 10

23. Rudoff 1964, 8

24. Rudoff 1964, 8–9

25. Rudoff 1964, 13

26. Rudoff 1964, 14

27. Rudoff 1964, 15

28. Rudoff 1964, 15

29. Rudoff 1964, 10, ff5

30. Rudoff 1964, 17

31. Rudoff 1964, 19

32. Rudoff 1964, 22

33. There is some debate about which was the first validated prison gang (Morrill 2005; Morales 2008, 55). These were not the first organized criminal groups to exist in prison anywhere; the *vory-v-zakone* in Russia and the Neapolitan Camorra are two examples (Varese 1998).

34. Rudoff 1964, 151

35. Blatchford 2008, 4

36. Morrill 2005, 46

37. Camp and Camp 1985, 93; Morrill 2005, 47

38. Morrill 2005, 60

39. Morrill 2005, 70

40. Fuentes 2006, xv–xvi. Nina Fuentes is the pen name of former Nuestra Familia member-turned-informant Robert Gratton.

41. Morrill 2005, 30, 47; also Camp and Camp 1985, 93
42. Fuentes 2006, xvi
43. Camp and Camp 1985, 93
44. Mendoza 2005, 16
45. Camp and Camp 1985, 93
46. Mendoza 2005, 17
47. Camp and Camp 1985, 93
48. Mendoza 2005, 17
49. Gambetta 1993, 40–46
50. The organization has also been referred to as the Black Hand, the Mob, and, for a short time, The Family.
51. Mendoza 2005, 19–20; Fuentes 2006, xvii
52. Morrill 2005, 47
53. Mendoza 2005, 16
54. Mendoza 2005, 22–23
55. Federal Bureau of Investigation 2012d, 30; see also Federal Bureau of Investigation 2012e
56. Mendoza 2005, 23
57. Fuentes 2006, xvi
58. Fuentes 2006, 3; Morales 2008, 6
59. Irwin 1980, 190; Federal Bureau of Investigation 2012c, 7
60. Fuentes 2006, 1; Mendoza 2005, 23. Mendoza (2012, 172–73) explains that a less formal group had already been emerging.
61. Camp and Camp 1985, 93
62. Camp and Camp (1985, 93) explain how the gang's name evolved. They "called themselves first the 'Blooming Flower,' then 'La Familia,' then 'La Familia Mexicana,' and finally 'La Nuestra Familia.'"
63. Fuentes 2006, 1
64. Fuentes 2006, 2
65. Fuentes 2006, 3
66. Fuentes 2006, 11
67. Fuentes 2006, 5
68. Fuentes 2006, 37
69. Morrill 2005, 69
70. Federal Bureau of Investigation 2012a, 7
71. Venable 2007, 6; also, Fleisher and Decker 2001, 4
72. Rudoff 1964, 146
73. Buentello et al 1991, 5; also Camp and Camp 1985, 106; Crouch and Marquart 1989, 205
74. Fuentes 2006, xvii
75. Porter 1982, 14
76. Porter 1982, 14. Similarly, Berman and Laitin (2008) and Berman (2009) identify how club goods in terrorist groups facilitate internal cooperation and reduce defection.

77. *United States v. Rubalcaba et al* 2001, 2
78. Koehler 2000, 174
79. Fong, Vogel, and Buentello 1993, 46
80. Federal Bureau of Investigation 2012b, 5; Morales 2008, 142, 155, 169, 175; Blatchford 2008, 302; Pelz, Marquart, and Pelz 1991
81. MSNBC 2005b
82. Camp and Camp 1985, 45
83. Morales 2008, 6
84. Federal Bureau of Investigation 2012d, 6; also Federal Bureau of Investigation 2012a, 143.
85. National Center on Addiction and Substance Abuse at Columbia University, 2002, i
86. Petersilia 2006, xi, 4
87. National Center on Addiction and Substance Abuse at Columbia University, 2002, ii
88. MSNBC 2007a
89. MSNBC 2007a
90. Blatchford 2008, 97
91. Morrill 2005, 63; Blatchford 2008, 97
92. Morrill 2005, 63; Jacobs 1977, 184–85
93. Fong 1990, 42; also Crouch and Marquart 1989, 158–59; Bruton 2004; *United States v. White et al* 2013
94. Crouch and Marquart 1989, 191
95. MSNBC 2009a
96. For example, Federal Bureau of Investigation 2012a, 27–32
97. Crouch and Marquart 1989, 209
98. Crouch and Marquart 1989, 209
99. Federal Bureau of Investigation 2012a, 9–10
100. More generally, see Klein and Leffler 1981
101. Morrill 2005, 63
102. Mendoza 2005, 20; Morrill 2005, 64
103. Irwin 1980, 211
104. Morrill 2005, 69
105. Fuentes 2006, xvii
106. Davidson 1974, 96; also Moore 1978, 178
107. Toch 1992, 234
108. Davidson 1974, 96–97
109. Davidson 1974, 97
110. Davidson 1974, 119, 118–25. The Chicano Pinto Research Project (1970) criticizes some aspects of Davidson's research, but his key findings are consistent with other research.
111. Porter 1982, 18
112. Davidson 1974, 124, 83
113. Hunt et al 1993, 400

114. Camp and Camp 1985, 44–45, 52–53
115. Camp and Camp 1985, 52
116. Koehler 2000, 170–71
117. MSNBC 2009a
118. DiIulio 1987, 130
119. This theory relates to a class of arguments that focus on how rather than why prison gangs form. See Knox and Tromanhauser (1991, 16) on importation, indigenous formation, and social imitation theories of gang origins.
120. Jacobs 1977
121. Buentello et al 1991, 4
122. Winterdyk and Ruddell 2010
123. Camp and Camp 1985, 215
124. Rafael 2007, 241; Blatchford 2008, 85; Howell and Moore 2010, 10
125. Jacobs 1977, 9
126. Bleich 1989, 1149–50; Schlanger 1999, 2000
127. Bleich 1989, 1150
128. Schlanger 1999, 1995
129. Jacobs 1977, 9
130. Bleich 1989, 1151
131. Crouch and Marquart 1989, 1
132. Crouch and Marquart 1989, 1
133. Jacobs 1977, 26; Irwin 1980, 98–106
134. Jacobs 1977, 106
135. Crouch and Marquart 1989
136. Fong 1990, 36; Crouch and Marquart 1989, 185
137. United States Department of Justice 1979
138. Another problem is that court interventions are correlated with other factors that might explain gang formation. If these other factors are not controlled for, then we cannot accurately identify the independent effect of judicial intervention.
139. Boylan and Mocan 2013, 6–7
140. Kaminski and Gibbons (1994) and Gambetta (2009) discuss the substitutability of formal and informal governance mechanisms in the prison context. Anderson (1999, 34) argues that the code of the street arises where police influence is weak. More generally, Fukuyama (2013) notes the notoriously poor state of empirical measures of governance.
141. Reuters 2012
142. Skarbek 2010b
143. Crewe 2009, 105; Phillips 2012b, 134–43. Contraband markets are "limited" in U.K. prisons (Crewe 2009, 367).
144. Phillips 2012a. On U.K. prison gangs, see also Wood and Adler (2001); Wood (2006); Wood, Moir, and James (2009); Wood, Williams, and James (2010).
145. Irwin 1980, 41
146. California Department of Corrections 1975

147. Irwin 1970 [1990], 65
148. Trammell 2011a; Owen 1998, 137, 158–59
149. Trammell 2011a, 55; also Kruttschnitt and Gartner 2005, 91
150. Trammell 2011a, 56
151. Owen 1998, 153; also Kruttschnitt and Gartner 2005, 107–108, Table 5–4 on 116
152. Trammell 2011a, 34
153. Trammell 2011a, 97
154. Owen 1998, 64
155. Buentello et al 1991
156. Trammell 2011b, 307
157. Trammell 2011b, 307
158. Dolovich 2012, 1002
159. Wells et al 2002, 16
160. Dolovich 2012, 1046–47
161. Dolovich 2012, 1025–55
162. Dolovich 2012, 1019
163. Carlson 2001, 12
164. Pinker 2011, 464–73
165. California Department of Corrections and Rehabilitation 2012d, 2
166. California Department of Corrections and Rehabilitation 2012d, 5; Beard 2013
167. Useem and Piehl 2008, 81–115
168. Fleisher and Decker 2001, 3
169. Fong, Vogel, and Buentello 1993, 47
170. Venable 2007
171. California Department of Corrections 1975, 49
172. California Department of Corrections 1975, 67
173. California Department of Corrections, 1975, 67. An inmate's disciplinary history was the best predictor of whether he would be a stabber (California Department of Corrections 1975, 65). This measures the average number of 115 Rule Violations an inmate received each month. Major rule infractions that fall under this code currently include serious offenses, such as harming staff and inmates, and less serious offenses, such as possessing alcohol, being drunk, receiving a tattoo, refusal to work, participation in a strike, refusal to take a drug test, possessing contraband, and gambling (California Code of Regulations 2011, 134–35).

MY BROTHER'S KEEPER

1. Furillo 2010
2. Furillo 2010
3. Inmate groups sometimes act as liaisons between inmates and officials (Marquez and Thompson 2006).

4. Furillo 2011b
5. Furillo 2011a
6. Furillo 2010
7. Furillo 2011c

CHAPTER 4

1. Sykes 1958 [2007], 13
2. MSNBC 2005b
3. Fearon and Laitin 1996; Greif 2004; Greif 2006a; Greif 2006b, 309–49
4. Valentine 2000; Axelrod 1984, 139–41
5. California Department of Corrections and Rehabilitation 2012d, 12–13
6. Dolovich 2012, 994, ff123; see also Irwin 2005, 93–98
7. Some inmates affiliate with "churchgoers" in the prison community (Colwell 2007, 451).
8. *Johnson v. California* 2005
9. MSNBC 2009a
10. MSNBC 2007b; also Dolovich 2012, 997
11. Goodman 2008, 746
12. MSNBC 2005c
13. MSNBC 2009a. Kalyvas (2006) examines how people's sense of identity and affiliation can be endogenous in the context of civil wars, a situation which, in many ways, resembles the prison community. See also Blattman and Miguel (2010).
14. MSNBC 2005c
15. MSNBC 2008a; also Dolovich 2011, 52; Dolovich 2012, 1000
16. MSNBC 2008a; also Dolovich 2011, 52; Dolovich 2012, 1000
17. Morales 2013, 7
18. Trammell 2011a, 49; also Dolovich 2011, 52
19. Trammell 2011a, 47
20. MSNBC 2008a; also Dolovich 2012, 998
21. Goodman 2008, 758
22. Trammell 2011a, 27
23. Trammell 2011a, 29. Inmates and officers have reached a "negotiated settlement" to ensure racial segregation in housing (Goodman 2008).
24. Goodman 2008, 749
25. Goodman 2008, 747
26. Trammell 2011a, 28
27. Goodman 2008, 756
28. MSNBC 2009a; also Dolovich 2012, 992–97. Langohr's (2013) quasi-biographical account of prison life in California describes many of the issues discussed in this chapter.
29. MSNBC 2007c
30. MSNBC 2005b

31. Colwell 2007, 455
32. MSNBC 2007c
33. Trammell 2011a, 90. Dispute resolution among criminals is not a new phenomenon, as, for example, the *vory-v-zakone* developed informal inmate courts (Varese 1998).
34. Trammell 2009, 759; also, Colwell 2007, 449
35. Trammell 2009, 762–63; also Dolovich 2012, 1019–20
36. MSNBC 2009b
37. Trammell 2009, 764
38. Trammell 2009, 766; see also Dolovich 2012, 1019
39. Colwell 2007, 455
40. Colwell 2007, 449
41. Trammell 2009, 760
42. Colwell 2007, 449–50
43. Trammell 2009, 763–64; Also Santos 2007, 119–20. On the history and causes of prison riots, see Useem (1985), Useem and Kimball (1987); Useem, Camp, and Camp (1996); and Goldstone and Useem (1999).
44. Trammell 2011a, 28
45. Trammell 2011a, 92
46. Trammell 2011a, 29; see also Dolovich 2012, 1019, ff236
47. Trammell 2011a, 23
48. Trammell 2009, 762
49. Trammell 2009, 763
50. Trammell 2009, 760–61
51. Trammell 2009, 761
52. Trammell 2009, 760; also Goodman 2008, 755
53. Trammell 2009, 755
54. Mendoza 2012, 116, 241, 275
55. Trammell and Chenault 2009, 342; Kiriakou 2013
56. Robertson 1988, 106
57. Burge 2011
58. Trammell and Chenault 2009, 341–42. Prison gangs also often require official paperwork to document when their members become informants before they will authorize killing a member (Rafael 2007, 115; Diaz 2009, 123; Mendoza 2012).
59. Trammell and Chenault 2009, 342
60. Fuentes 2006, 9
61. Mendoza 2012, 148
62. Camp and Camp 1985, 107
63. People v Garnica 1981; also Mendoza 2012
64. Fuentes 2006, 9
65. Fuentes 2006, 9
66. Leeson 2007a; 2009a; 2010

67. Jacobs 1977, 155
68. MSNBC 2007c
69. MSNBC 2007c
70. Trammell 2011a, 26
71. Trammell 2009, 756; also Dolovich 2012, 998–99
72. Trammell 2011a, 91
73. Trammell 2009, 756
74. Morales 2008, 48
75. Rafael 2007, 44
76. Sureño Report 2008. Black inmates at Stateville also distributed rules to black inmates upon arrival (Jacobs 1977, 149–50).
77. Blatchford 2008, 77
78. Inmates rarely get violent in the visiting areas (Wacquant 2002, 376), and gang rules about racial segregation do not apply there.
79. Courtesy of Robert Morrill.
80. HC stands for "hard candy," jailhouse humor referring to the fact that a shank that was held in an inmate's bowels, once retrieved, may resemble a chocolate candy bar.
81. Rafael 2007, 309
82. These types of governance institutions operate in youth facilities as well (Rayman 2012).
83. Fuentes 2006, 38–40; Morales 2008, 22; Mendoza 2012, 87–91
84. Camp and Camp 1985
85. Camp and Camp 1985, 45
86. Winterdyk and Ruddell 2010
87. Shelden 1991, 55
88. Ohio Department of Rehabilitation and Correction 1998; also Sorensen and Pilgrim 2000; Cunningham and Sorensen 2007
89. Fong et al 1992; see also De Lisi 2003; Huebner 2003; Cunningham and Sorensen 2006; Griffin and Hepburn 2006; Schenk and Fremouw 2012; Sorensen and Cunningham 2010; Worrall and Morris 2012
90. Fong 1990, 37
91. DeLisi, Berg, and Hochstetler 2004, 376
92. Gaes et al 2002
93. Gaes et al 2002, 370
94. Gaes et al 2002, 370
95. Byrne and Hummer 2007, 538
96. Byrne and Hummer 2007, 539; see also Schenk and Fremouw 2012, 431
97. Williams and Fish 1974, 42
98. Williams and Fish 1974, 42
99. Useem and Piehl 2006; 2008, 81–115
100. Useem and Piehl 2006, 87; also Useem and Piehl 2012

101. Ostrom 1990
102. Ellickson 1991; Bernstein 1992; Richman 2006. Knight (1992) and Sutter (1995) model power relationships and institutional formation in anarchy.
103. Carlson 2001, 12
104. Nozick 1974; Buchanan 1975
105. Edwards and Ogilvie 2012; Greif 2012
106. Oppenheimer 1914; Lane [1942] 1966, 1958; Carneiro 1970; Tilly 1985; Knight 1992; Skaperdas and Syropoulos 1995; Bates 2001; Bates et al 2002; Wantchekon 2004; Acemoglu and Robinson 2006; Levi 2006; Bates 2008; North, Wallis, and Weingast 2009; MacLean 2010; Pinker 2011; Acemoglu and Robinson 2012; Konrad and Skaperdas 2012
107. North 1987
108. Baumol 1995, 83
109. Axelrod 1984; Boettke 2005; Powell and Stringham 2009

CHAPTER 5

1. Reuter (1983, 109–31) provides an important analysis of the industrial organization of criminal organizations.
2. Fortune 2003 discusses the characteristics of prison leaders.
3. Blatchford 2008, 53
4. Buentello et al 1991, 10; see also *United States v. Blake et al* 2012
5. Fong 1987, 79–80
6. Leeson and Skarbek 2010; Skarbek 2010a
7. Trammell 2009, 758
8. Morrill 2005; Morales 2008
9. For a number of constitutions and gang documents, see Knox and Robinson 2004 and Knox 2006.
10. Blatchford 2008, 165
11. Skaperdas 2001, 184
12. The same difficulties exist in the study of street gangs (Decker, Katz, and Webb 2008).
13. Hirschman 1970
14. Some of the new Sensitive Needs Yard gangs do not require a lifetime commitment.
15. MSNBC 2007c
16. MSNBC 2005b
17. MSNBC 2007c; also Santos 2007, 83–83
18. MSNBC 2007c; also Toch 1992, 267–88
19. Toch 1992, 62, also Fleisher and Krienert 2009, 100
20. Fong 1990, 40
21. Fong 1990, 41

22. Fong 1990, 41
23. Trammell 2011a, 26
24. Trammell 2009, 758
25. *United States v. Rubalcaba et al* 2001, 2
26. *United States v. Johnston et al* 2010, 4; *United States v. Blake et al* 2012
27. Crouch and Marquart 1989, 207
28. Crouch and Marquart 1989, 207
29. Crouch and Marquart 1989, 207–208
30. Crouch and Marquart 1989, 208
31. Crouch and Marquart 1989, 208
32. Fong 1990, 40
33. Buentello et al 1991, 10
34. *United States v. Johnston et al* 2010, 3
35. Iannaccone 1992; Berman 2000; Hamill 2011, 48
36. Blatchford 2008, 43
37. Blatchford 2008, 165
38. *United States v. Aguirre et al* 1994, 7
39. Davidson 1974, 75. Fleisher and Krienert (2009) offer an important and nuanced analysis of prison sexual culture.
40. Mendoza 2012, 142
41. Buentello et al 1991, 10
42. Blatchford 2008, 44; *United States v. Aguirre et al* 1994, 7; *United States v. Shryock et al* 2003, A; *United States v. Fernandez et al* 2004; *United States v. Colabella* 2010; Rafael 2007, 135–36
43. Blatchford 2008, 63
44. Blatchford 2008, 75–76
45. Blatchford 2008, 196. For additional examples of what appears to be constitutional enforcement, see *United States v. Shryock et al* (2003, B.1, B.2, B.4. B.11, B.13).
46. Blatchford 2008, 186
47. Blatchford 2008, 194. However, Mr. Castro did eventually became a government witness (*United States v. Shryock et al* 2003).
48. Blatchford 2008, 130
49. Blatchford 2008, 81
50. Grann 2004; also Federal Bureau of Investigation 2012a, 144
51. Geniella 2001
52. Gang members recognize that recruits think about future interactions (Blatchford 2008, 133).
53. Blatchford 2008, 22
54. Blatchford 2008, 22
55. Madison 1788; also Weingast 1995; Leeson 2007a
56. Lewis 1980; Fuentes 2006, 3–11
57. Fuentes 2006, 3; also Lewis 1980

58. Gangland 2007
59. Federal Bureau of Investigation 2012c, 7
60. Sandza and Shannon 1982
61. Sandza and Shannon 1982
62. MSNBC 2009a
63. Fuentes 2006, 28; Mendoza 2012, 177–81
64. Fuentes 2006, 28
65. Fuentes 2006, 29
66. Fuentes 2006, 29
67. Mendoza 2012, 142
68. Mendoza 2012, 178–79
69. Mendoza 2012. Reynolds (2008) discusses a recent reorganization of NF.
70. Fong, Vogel, and Buentello 1993
71. Fong, Vogel, and Buentello 1993, 48
72. Fong, Vogel, and Buentello 1993, 47. The dropouts were also not gang leaders. Thirty-one of the dropouts in the study never ranked higher than the entry-level position.
73. Wells et al 2002, 19
74. MSNBC 2005b
75. MSNBC 2005b
76. MSNBC 2009a; Mendoza 2012
77. MSNBC 2005b
78. MSNBC 2010a
79. MSNBC 2005b
80. MSNBC 2009a

CHAPTER 6

1. MSNBC 2005b
2. Olson 1993; McGuire and Olson 1996; Olson 2000
3. Camp and Camp 1985, 94; Morrill 2005, 78; Federal Bureau of Investigation 2012d, 7, 45
4. Wacquant (2001) provides a sociological interpretation of the changing relationship between the prison and the ghetto.
5. Rafael 2007, 66
6. These numbers obviously fluctuate; these particular figures come from a jail population report from late 2009.
7. Tapia (2013) discusses gangs and urban jails.
8. *United States v. Alfaro et al.* 2008, 7; *United States v. Pantoja et al* 2007, 7. Valdez (2011) provides an informative history of the rise of Los Angeles gangs, with special emphasis on 18th Street, MS-13, and the Mexican Mafia.
9. See Mendoza 2005, 308; Blatchford 2008, 123; *United States v. Pantoja et al* 2007, 6–7; *United States v. Alfaro et al* 2008, 8; *United States v. Flores et al* 2008, 9; *United States v. Aguirre et al* 2009, 11; *United States v. Eastside Rivas* 2010, 18–20.

10. *United States v. Roman et al* 2012, 10

11. Blatchford 2008, 123

12. *United States v. Aguirre et al* 1994, 35

13. Blatchford 2008, 263–64; *People v. Torres* 2009

14. Blatchford 2008, 264

15. Blatchford 2008, 264

16. *United States v. Espudo et al* 2012, 7

17. *United States v. Colabella et al* 2010, 4

18. *United States v. Shryock et al* 2003, 10

19. *United States v. Shryock et al* 2003, 10; also Rafael 2007, 80

20. *People v. Torres* 2009

21. *People v. Torres* 2009

22. *United States v. Flores et al* 2008, 15–17; also *United States v. Barajas et al* 2008; *United States v. Henley et al* 2008; *United States v. Sotelo et al* 2008.

23. *United States v. Pantoja et al* 2007, 8

24. *United States v. Pantoja et al* 2007, 81

25. *United States v. Alfaro et al* 2008, 4

26. *United States v. Alfaro et al* 2008, 5

27. *United States v. Alfaro et al* 2008, 8

28. *United States v. Alfaro et al* 2008, 8

29. *United States v. Espudo et al* 2012, 6

30. *United States v. Espudo et al* 2012, 64

31. *United States v. Espudo et al* 2012, 9

32. *United States v. Espudo et al* 2012, 9

33. *United States v. Espudo et al* 2012, 9–10

34. *United States v. Espudo et al* 2012, 10

35. Blatchford 2008, 154

36. Furillo 2004

37. Blatchford 2008, 291

38. Furillo 2004

39. Rafael 2007, 141

40. *United States v. Aguirre et al* 1994, 44

41. *United States v. Aguirre et al* 1994, 46–47

42. Diaz 2009, 133

43. Blatchford 2008, 154

44. *United States v. Shryock et al* 2003, 11

45. American Public Media 2008

46. Skarbek 2011

47. Provided by the Los Angeles County Sherriff's Department database on January 19, 2010

48. On gangs in jail, see Ruddell et al (2006) and Dolovich (2012).

49. Blatchford 2008, 110–11; Rafael 2007, 33

50. Blatchford 2008, 95

51. Blatchford 2008, 76

52. Federal Bureau of Investigation 2012a, 75

53. *United States v. Aguirre et al* 2009, 14

54. *United States v. Aguirre et al* 1994, 32

55. *United States v. Aguirre et al* 1994, 32–33

56. *United States v. Fernandez et al* 2004

57. Langan and Levin 2002

58. Olson, Dooley, and Kane 2004

59. Dooley, Seals, and Skarbek 2012

60. Rafael 2007, 79

61. Blatchford 2008, 32; also Blajos 1996, 88–92

62. MSNBC 2009c

63. MSNBC 2009c

64. *United States v. Aguirre et al* 1994, 32

65. *United States v. Aguirre et al* 1994, 34

66. *United States v. Espudo et al* 2012, 20

67. *United States v. Espudo* et al 2012, 21

68. *United States v. Espudo et al* 2012, 21

69. *United States v. Espudo et al* 2012, 22

70. Phelan and Hunt 1998, 280, 285

71. Phelan and Hunt 1998, 292

72. Gambetta 2009

73. *United States v. Ojeda et al* 2011, 4–5

74. Blatchford 2008, 193

75. *United States v. Yepiz et al* 2006, 6

76. Jacobs and Wright 2006; Anderson 1999, 118–20

77. Miron 1999

78. Miron 2001. Owens (2011) questions the generality of this finding.

79. Levitt and Venkatesh 2000

80. Akerlof and Yellen 1994

81. MSNBC 2008b

82. Schelling 1967, 116; Schelling 1971, 76

83. *United States v. Alfaro et al* 2008, 8; also *United States v. Pantoja et al* 2007, 14, 20; *United States v Eastside Rivas* 2010, 18–20

84. *United States v. Flores et al* 2008, 16

85. *United States v. Orozco et al* 2011, 8

86. *United States v. Pantoja et al* 2007, 5; *United States v. Vasquez et al* 2007, 3; *United States v. Eastside Riva* 2010, 19; *United States v. Estrada et al* 2010, 5–6; *United States v. Rios et al* 2011, 11

87. *United States v. Colabella et al* 2010, 5

88. Rafael 2007, 340

89. Blatchford 2008, 155

90. *United States v. Alfaro et al* 2008, 8–9

91. Some Mara Salvatrucha gang members, especially those outside of Los Angeles, reject the Mexican Mafia's authority, so they do not adopt the MS-13 appendage, opting instead for simply MS.

92. *United States v. Alfaro et al* 2008, 8–9; *United States v. Hernandez et al* 2009, 6. See Brantingham et al (2012) and Smith et al (2012) on the ecology of territorial gang disputes in Los Angeles.

93. *United States v. Aguirre et al* 1994, 5–6

94. *United States v. Aguirre et al* 1994, 27

95. *United States v. Aguirre et al* 1994, 50

96. *United States v. Aguirre et al* 1994, 50

97. *United States v. Pantoja et al* 2007, 25–26

98. *United States v. Pantoja et al* 2007, 26–27

99. *United States v. Fernandez et al* 2004

100. Blatchford 2008, 121; also Rafael 2007, 34–40

101. Rafael 2007, 37

102. Buchanan 1973; Schelling 1967, 118

103. Diaz 2009, 131

104. Rafael 2007, 37

105. Blatchford 2008, 122

106. Blatchford 2008, 122

107. Blatchford 2008, 123

108. Blatchford 2008, 124

109. Blatchford 2008, 124

110. Valdez 2011, 29

111. Lopez 1995

112. For instance, the data are very noisy or may be biased, and we do not have a model or baseline trend to compare them to. It might simply be reversion to the mean.

113. Lopez 1995

114. Rafael 2007, 37; also Morrill 2005, 204

115. *United States v. Aguirre et al* 2009, 14

116. Skeens 2013

117. Schelling 1971

118. Rafael 2007, 160; Reportedly, a way to gauge gang influence in a neighborhood is the presence of prostitutes. When gangs are powerful, prostitutes move to other areas to avoid taxation.

119. *United States v. Fernandez et al* 2004

120. *United States v. Fernandez et al* 2004

121. *United States v. Fernandez et al* 2004

122. *United States v. Fernandez et al* 2004

123. *United States v. Ojeda et al* 2011, 4

PUPPET

1. This quote and many of the facts in the vignette come from Kim (2012).
2. *United States v. Aguirre et al* 1994
3. *Bacote v. Federal Bureau of Prisons et al* 2012
4. Santos 2007, 47
5. Kim 2012
6. *United States v. Pantoja et al* 2007, 29–30
7. For an overview of some of these activities, see Diaz (2009, 57–157).
8. Kim 2012

CHAPTER 7

1. Sowell 1996, 113
2. North 1990; Ostrom 2005
3. Boettke 1994; Rodrik, Subramanian, and Trebbi 2004
4. Munger 2000, 3; Munger 2010, 264
5. Leeson and Williamson 2009, 77
6. Schneider, Buehn, and Montenegro 2010, 18–19
7. Neuwirth 2011, 27–28
8. Greif 1989; 1993, Milgrom, North, and Weingast 1990; Clay 1997; Leeson 2005a, 2005b, 2007a, 2007c, 2008, 2009a
9. Bernstein 1992; Richman 2006; Leeson 2007b; Powell et al 2008; Schaeffer 2008
10. Munger 2010, 267
11. Neuwirth 2011
12. Williamson and Kerekes 2011
13. Williamson and Kerekes 2011, 537
14. Hayek 1973; Schelling 1978; Knight 1992
15. Trulson et al 2006, 30
16. Fleisher and Decker 2001, 7. For anecdotal and survey evidence, see National Institute of Corrections (1991); Gransky and Patterson (1999); Carlson (2001); Wells et al (2002, 21); Forsythe (2006); and Winterdyk and Ruddell (2010). In general, it is no small challenge to collect and analyze data to assess prison policy (Martinson 1974).
17. Petersilia 2006, ix
18. California Department of Corrections and Rehabilitation 2012d, 25
19. California Department of Corrections and Rehabilitation 2012d, 2; also California Department of Corrections and Rehabilitation 2012c
20. California Department of Corrections and Rehabilitation 2012d, 25
21. Knox 2012
22. Shalev 2009, 71
23. MSNBC 2007c
24. Trammell 2009, 759
25. Carlson 2001, 20

26. American Correctional Association 1993, 2
27. Kleiman 2009, 179
28. Kleiman 2009, 179
29. Volokh 2011, 790
30. Irwin 2005; Simon 2012
31. Useem and Piehl 2008, 2
32. International Centre for Prison Studies 2013. These data come from official sources, so numbers from countries like Cuba and North Korea may be incomplete, nonexistent, or false.
33. Sabol, West, and Cooper 2009
34. Mauer 2006, 137
35. Useem and Piehl 2008, 2
36. Stuntz 2011, 267–74
37. King and Mauer 2002
38. Liedka, Piehl, and Useem 2006. Durlauf and Nagin (2011) survey the literature on incarceration and deterrence.
39. Liedka, Piehl, and Useem 2006, 262
40. Durlauf and Nagin 2011
41. Rose and Clear 1998; Western, Kling, and Weiman 2001
42. Bayer et al 2009. However, an experimental design implemented to test the same mechanism did not find significant results (Camp and Gaes 2005). Drago and Galbiati (2011) find evidence suggesting that harsh prison conditions increase post-release criminal activity.
43. Hutcherson 2012
44. Miller (2008) provides a thorough analysis of how federalization affects crime control policy.
45. Page 2011
46. Stuntz 2011, 254–55; Ball 2012
47. Stuntz 2011, 257–60. Most, but not all, of the guilty pleas are the result of plea bargains.
48. Pfaff 2011; also Pfaff 2007
49. Shalev 2009, 29; Irwin 2005, 8
50. Raphael and Stoll 2013
51. Simon 2007. See also Useem and Piehl (2008, Ch. 2) and Irwin (2005, Ch. 8). To explain the variation in imprisonment across democracies, Lacey (2008) emphasizes the role of relatively fluid labor markets in neoliberal democracies as reducing the cost of incarcerating large segments of the population.
52. Levitt 2004, 179
53. See also Levitt 1996; Levitt 1998; Donohue and Levitt 2001; Katz, Levitt, and Shustorovich 2003; Klick and Tabarrok 2005; MacDonald, Klick, and Grunwald 2012; Chalfin and McCrary 2013
54. Stuntz 2011, 278–79. See also Zimring (2008) on determinants of crime.
55. Kleiman 2009; Durlauf and Nagin 2011
56. Kleiman 2009; Telep and Weisburd 2012

References

Acemoglu, Daron, and James A. Robinson. 2006. *Economic Origins of Dictatorship and Democracy*. New York: Cambridge University Press.

Acemoglu, Daron, and James A. Robinson. 2012. *Why Nations Fail: The Origins of Power, Prosperity, and Poverty*. New York: Crown Business.

Akerlof, George A., and Janet Yellen. 1994. "Gang Behavior, Law Enforcement, and Community Values." In *Values and Public Policy*, edited by Henry J. Aaron, Thomas E. Mann, and Timothy Taylor. Washington, DC: Brookings Institution.

Akers, Ronald L., Norman S. Hayner, and Werner Gruninger. 1977. "Prisonization in Five Countries: Type of Prison and Inmate Characteristics." *Criminology* 14(4): 527–54.

Alesina, Alberto, Reza Baqir, and William Easterly. 1999. "Public Goods and Ethnic Divisions." *Quarterly Journal of Economics* 114(4): 1243–84.

Alesina, Alberto, and Enrico Spolaore. 1997. "On the Number and Size of Nations." *Quarterly Journal of Economics* 112(4): 1027–56.

Alexander, Barbara. 1997. "The Rational Racketeer: Pasta Protection in Depression Era Chicago." *Journal of Law & Economics* 40(1): 175–202.

Allen, Bud, and Diana Bosta. 1981. *Games Prisoners Play: How You Can Profit By Knowing Them*. Roseville, CA: Rae John Publishers.

American Correctional Association. 1993. *Gangs in Correctional Facilities: A National Assessment*. Washington, DC: U.S. Department of Justice.

American Public Media. 2008. "Transcript." Gangster Confidential. American Radio Works.

Anderson, Elijah. 1999. *Code of the Street: Decency, Violence, and the Moral Life of the Inner City*. New York: W. W. Norton.

Arias, Enrique Desmond. 2006. "The Dynamics of Criminal Governance: Networks and Social Order in Rio de Janeiro." *Journal of Latin American Studies* 38(2): 293–325.

Arias, Enrique Desmond, and Corinne Davis Rodrigues. 2006. "The Myth of Personal Security: Criminal Gangs, Dispute Resolutions, and Identity in Rio de Janeiro's Favelas." *Latin American Politics and Society* 48(4): 53–81.

Avio, Kenneth L. 1998. "The Economics of Prisons." *European Journal of Law and Economics* 6(2): 143–75.

Axelrod, Robert. 1984. *The Evolution of Cooperation*. New York: Penguin Books.

Bacote v. Federal Bureau of Prisons et al. 2012. Complaint. United States District Court for the District of Colorado. 1:12-cv-01570-RPM.

Ball, W. David. 2010. "E Pluribus Unum: Data and Operations Integration in the California Criminal Justice System." *Stanford Law and Policy Review* 21:277–309.

Ball, W. David. 2012. "Tough on Crime (on the State's Dime): How Violent Crime Does Not Drive California Counties' Incarceration Rates—and Why It Should" *Georgia State University Law Review* 28: 987–1084.

Bandiera, Oriana. 2003. "Land Reform, the Market for Protection, and the Origins of the Sicilian Mafia: Theory and Evidence." *Journal of Law, Economics, & Organization* 19(1): 218–44.

Bates, Robert H. 2001. *Prosperity & Violence: The Political Economy of Development*. New York: W. W. Norton.

Bates, Robert H. 2008. *When Things Fell Apart: State Failure in Late-Century Africa*. New York: Cambridge University Press.

Bates, Robert H., Avner Greif, Margaret Levi, Jean-Laurent Rosenthal, and Barry R. Weingast. 1998. *Analytical Narratives*. Princeton, NJ: Princeton University Press.

Bates, Robert H., Avner Greif, and Smita Singh. 2002. "Organizing Violence." *Journal of Conflict Resolution* 46(5): 599–628.

Baumol, William J. 1995. "Discussion." In *The Economics of Organised Crime*, edited by Gianluca Fiorentini and Sam Peltzman. New York: Cambridge University Press.

Bayer, Patrick, Randi Hjalmarsson, and David Pozen. 2009. "Building Criminal Capital Behind Bars: Peer Effects in Juvenile Corrections." *Quarterly Journal of Economics* 124(1): 105–47.

Beard, Jeffrey. 2013. "Hunger Strike in California Prisons Is a Gang Power Play" *Los Angeles Times*, August 6.

Beccaria, Caesare. 1764 [1995]. *Beccaria: On Crimes and Punishments and Other Writings*. Cambridge, UK: Cambridge University Press.

Becker, Gary S. 1968. "Crime and Punishment: An Economic Approach." *Journal of Political Economy* 76(2): 169–217.

Bendor, Jonathan, and Piotr Swistak. 1995. "Types of Evolutionary Stability and the Problem of Cooperation." *Proceedings of the National Academy of Sciences of the United States of America* 92(8): 3596–3600.

Benson, Bruce. 1989. "The Spontaneous Evolution of Commercial Law" *Southern Economics Journal* 55(3): 644–61.

Benson, Bruce. 1990. *The Enterprise of Law: Justice without the State*. San Francisco: Pacific Research Institute.

Benson, Bruce. 1998. *To Serve and Protect: Privatization and Community in Criminal Justice*. New York: New York University Press.

Beraldo, Sergio, Raul Caruso, and Gilberto Turati. 2013. "Life Is Now! Time Preferences and Crime: Aggregate Evidence from the Italian Regions." *Journal of Socio-Economics* 47: 73–81.

Berman, Eli. 2000. "Sect, Subsidy, and Sacrifice: An Economist's View of Ultra-Orthodox Jews." *Quarterly Journal of Economics* 115(3): 905–53.

Berman, Eli. 2009. *Radical, Religious, and Violent: The New Economics of Terrorism.* Cambridge, MA: MIT Press.

Berman, Eli, and David Laitin. 2008. "Religion, Terrorism, and Public Goods: Testing the Club Model." *Journal of Public Economics* 92(10-11): 1942–67.

Bernstein, Lisa. 1992. "Opting Out of the Legal System: Extralegal Contractual Relations in the Diamond Industry." *Journal of Legal Studies* 21(1): 115–57.

Bernstein, Lisa. 1996. "Merchant Law in a Merchant Court: Rethinking the Code's Search for Immanent Business Norms." *University of Pennsylvania Law Review* 144(5): 1765–1821.

Bernstein, Lisa. 2001. "Private Commercial Law in the Cotton Industry: Creating Cooperation through Norms, Rules, and Institutions." *Michigan Law Review* 99(7): 1724–88.

Blajos, Art. 1996. *Blood In, Blood Out.* Wilmington, DE: Harvest Press.

Blatchford, Chris. 2008. *The Black Hand: The Bloody Rise and Redemption of "Boxer" Enriquez.* New York: William Morrow Paperbacks.

Blattman, Christopher, and Edward Miguel. 2010. "Civil War." *Journal of Economic Literature* 48(1): 3–57.

Bleich, Jeff. 1989. "The Politics of Prison Overcrowding." *California Law Review* 77(5): 1125–80.

Boettke, Peter J. 1994. "The Political Infrastructure of Economic Development." *Human Systems Management* 13: 89–100.

Boettke, Peter J. 2005. "Anarchism as a Progressive Research Program in Political Economy." In *Anarchy, State, and Public Choice*, edited by Edward Stringham. Northampton, MA: Edward Elgar Publishing.

Bookspan, Shelley. 1991. *A Germ of Goodness: The California State Prison System, 1851–1944.* Lincoln: University of Nebraska Press.

Bottoms, Anthony E. 1999. "Interpersonal Violence and Social Orders in Prison." *Crime & Justice* 26: 205–81.

Bowker, Lee H. 1977. *Prisoner Subcultures.* Lexington, MA: Lexington Books.

Bowker, Lee H. 1980. *Prison Victimization.* New York: Elsevier Science.

Boylan, Richard T., and Naci Mocan. 2013. "Intended and Unintended Consequences of Prison Reform." *Journal of Law, Economics & Organization.* doi: 10.1093/jleo/ewt006.

Brantingham, P. Jeffrey, George Tita, Martin Short, and Shannon Reid. 2012. "The Ecology of Territorial Gang Boundaries." *Criminology* 50(3): 851–85.

Bronson, Eric F. 2006. "Medium Security Prisons and Inmate Subcultures: The 'Normal Prison.'" *Southwest Journal of Criminal Justice* 3(2): 61–85.

Bruton, James H. 2004. *The Big House: Life Inside a Supermax Security Prison.* Stillwater, MN: Voyageur Press.

Buchanan, James M. 1973. "A Defense of Organized Crime?" In *The Economics of Crime and Punishment,* edited by Simon Rottenberg. Washington, DC: American Enterprise Institute for Public Policy Research.

Buchanan, James M. 1975. *The Limits of Liberty: Between Anarchy and Leviathan.* Chicago: University of Chicago Press.

Buentello, Salvador, Robert S. Fong, and Ronald E. Vogel. 1991. "Prison Gang Development: A Theoretical Model." *The Prison Journal* 71(2): 3–14.

Bugliosi, Vincent, and Curt Gentry. 1994. *Helter Skelter: The True Story of the Manson Murders.* New York: W. W. Norton.

Bunker, Edward. 2000. *Education of a Felon: A Memoir.* New York: St. Martin's Griffin.

Buonanno, Paolo, Ruben Durante, Giovanni Prarolo, and Paolo Vanin. 2012. "On the Historical and Geographic Origins of the Sicilian Mafia." Working Paper.

Burge, Sarah. 2011. "Jails Call on Cellphone-Sniffing Dogs." *The Press Enterprise,* December 26.

Byrne, James, and Don Hummer. 2007. "In Search of the 'Tossed Salad Man' (and Others Involved in Prison Violence): New Strategies for Predicting and Controlling Violence in Prison." *Aggression and Violent Behavior* 12(5): 531–41.

California Code of Regulations. 2009. "CDC Classification Score Sheet." Title 15, Division 3. Section 3375.3.

California Code of Regulations. 2011. "Contraband." Title 15, Division 3, Chapter 1, Article 1, Section 3006.

California Code of Regulations. 2012. "Contraband." Title 15, Division 3, Chapter 1, Article 1, Section 3006.

California Council on Science and Technology. 2012. "The Efficacy of Managed Access Systems to Intercept Calls from Contraband Cell Phones in California Prisons." http://www.ccst.us/publications/2012/2012cell.pdf

California Department of Corrections. 1975. "Prison Violence in California: Issues and Alternatives." State of California, Department of Finance, Program Evaluation Unit.

California Department of Corrections and Rehabilitation. 2012a. "Average Daily Prison Population." Offender Information Services Branch, Data Analysis Unit. July.

California Department of Corrections and Rehabilitation. 2012b. "CDCR Awards System-wide Telephone Contract That Will Restrict Cellular Phones in Prisons." Press Release, April 16.

California Department of Corrections and Rehabilitation. 2012c. *Operations Manual.*

California Department of Corrections and Rehabilitation. 2012d. "Security Threat Group Prevention, Identification and Management Strategy." March 1.

Camp, George M., and Camille Camp. 1985. *Prison Gangs: Their Extent, Nature, and Impact on Prisons.* Washington, DC: U.S. Department of Justice, Federal Justice Research Program.

Camp, Scott D., and Gerald G. Gaes. 2005. "Criminogenic Effects of the Prison Environment on Inmate Behavior: Some Experimental Evidence." *Crime & Delinquency* 51(3): 425–42.

Campana, Paolo. 2011. "Eavesdropping on the Mob: The Functional Diversification of Mafia Activities Across Territories." *European Journal of Criminology* 8(3): 213–28.

Carlson, Peter M. 2001. "Prison Interventions: Evolving Strategies to Control Security Threat Groups." *Corrections Management Quarterly* 5(1): 10–22.

Carneiro, Robert L. 1970. "Theory of the Origin of the State." *Science* 169(3947): 733–38.

Carr, Jack L., and Janet T. Landa. 1983. "The Economics of Symbols, Clan Names, and Religion." *Journal of Legal Studies* 12(1): 135–56.

Carroll, Leo. 1974. *Hacks, Blacks, and Cons: Race Relations in a Maximum Security Prison.* Lexington, MA: D.C. Heath and Company.

Castro, Tony. 2007. "Words May Hurt, After All Gangser's Rap Lyrics are Seen as Evidence." *Daily News*, May 14.

Chalfin, Aaron, and Justin McCrary. 2013. "The Effect of Police on Crime: New Evidence from U.S. Cities, 1960–2010." NBER Working Paper #18815.

Chicano Pinto Research Project. 1970. "The Los Angeles Pinto: Background Papers and Advance Report of the Chicano Pinto Research Project." Los Angeles: Chicano Pinto Research Project.

Clay, Karen. 1997. "Trade Without Law: Private-Order Institutions in Mexican California." *Journal of Law, Economics, & Organization* 13(1): 202–31.

Clemmer, Donald. 1940. *The Prison Community.* Boston: Christopher Publishing.

Clemmer, Donald. 1962. "Informal Inmate Groups." In *The Sociology of Punishment and Correction*, edited by Norman Johnston, Leonard Savitz, and Marvin E. Wolfgang. New York : John Wiley and Sons.

Colwell, Brian. 2007. "Deference or Respect? Status Management Practices Among Prison Inmates." *Social Psychology Quarterly* 70(4): 442–60.

Conrad, Kai A., and Stergios Skaperdas. 2012. "The Market for Protection and the Origin of the State." *Economic Theory* 50(2): 417–43.

Cook, Philip J. 1986. "The Demand and Supply of Criminal Opportunities." *Crime and Justice* 7: 1–27.

Cook, Philip J., Jens Ludwig, Sudhir Venkatesh, and Anthony A. Braga. 2007. "Underground Gun Markets." *Economic Journal* 117(524): 588–618.

Copes, Heith, Fiona Brookman, and Anastasia Brown. 2013. "Accounting for Violations of the Convict Code." *Deviant Behavior* 34(10): 841–58.

Crawford, Sue, and Elinor Ostrom. 1995. "A Grammar of Institutions." *American Political Science Review* 89(3): 582–600.

Crewe, Ben. 2009. *The Prisoner Society: Power, Adaptation, and Social Life in an English Prison.* Oxford, UK: Oxford University Press.

Crouch, Ben M., and James W. Marquart. 1989. *An Appeal to Justice: Litigated Reform of Texas Prisons.* Austin: University of Texas Press.

Cunningham, Mark D., and Jon R. Sorensen. 2006. "Actuarial Models for Assessing Prison Violence Risk: Revisions and Extensions of the Risk Assessment Scale for Prison (RASP)." *Assessment* 13(3): 253–265.

Cunningham, Mark D., and Jon R. Sorensen. 2007. "Predictive Factors for Violent Misconduct in Close Custody." *The Prison Journal* 87(2): 241–53.

Davidson, R. Theodore. 1974. *Chicano Prisoners: The Key to San Quentin*. Prospect Heights, IL: Waveland Press.

Davis, Michael L. 1988. "Time and Punishment: An Intertemporal Model of Crime." *Journal of Political Economy* 96(2): 383–390.

Decker, Scott H., Charles M. Katz, and Vincent J. Webb. 2008. "Understanding the Black Box of Gang Organization: Implications for Involvement in Violent Crime, Drug Sales, and Violent Victimization." *Crime & Delinquency* 54(1): 153–72.

DeLisi, Matt. 2003. "Criminal Careers Behind Bars." *Behavioral Sciences and the Law* 21(5): 653–69.

DeLisi, Matt, Mark T. Berg, and Andy Hochstetler. 2004. "Gang Members Career Criminals and Prison Violence: Further Specification of the Importation Model of Inmate Behavior." *Criminal Justice Studies* 17(4): 369–83.

DeLisi, Matt, James O. Spruill, David J. Peters, Jonathan W. Caudill, and Chad R. Trulson. 2013. "'Half In, Half Out:' Gang Families, Gang Affiliation, and Gang Misconduct." *American Journal of Criminal Justice* 38(4): 602–15.

Demsetz, Harold. 1967. "Toward a Theory of Property Rights." *American Economic Review* 57(2): 347–59.

Diaz, Tom. 2009. *No Boundaries: Transnational Latino Gangs and American Law Enforcement*. Ann Arbor: University of Michigan Press.

DiIulio, John J. 1987. *Governing Prisons: A Comparative Study of Correctional Management*. New York: The Free Press.

DiIulio, John J. 1996. "Help Wanted: Economists, Crime, and Public Policy." *Journal of Economic Perspectives* 10(1): 3–24.

Dixit, Avinash. 2004. *Lawlessness and Economics: Alternatives Modes of Governance*. Princeton, NJ: Princeton University Press.

Dixit, Avinash. 2009. "Governance Institutions and Economic Activity." *American Economic Review* 99(1): 5–24.

Dolan, Jack. 2011. "California Prison Guards Union Called Main Obstacle to Keeping Cellphones Away from Inmates." *Los Angeles Times*, February 4.

Dolovich, Sharon. 2011. "Strategic Segregation in the Modern Prison" *American Criminal Law Review* 48(1): 1–110.

Dolovich, Sharon. 2012. "Two Models of the Prison: Accidental Humanity and Hypermasculinity in the L.A. County Jail." *Journal of Criminal Law & Criminology* 102(4): 965–1118.

Donohue, John J., and Steven D. Levitt. 2001. "The Impact of Legalized Abortion on Crime." *Quarterly Journal of Economics* 119(1): 407–23.

Dooley, Brendan, Alan Seals, and David Skarbek. 2012. "The Effect of Prison Gang Membership on Recidivism." Mimeograph.

Drago, Francesco, and Roberto Galbiati. 2011. "Prison Conditions and Recidivism." *American Law and Economics Review* 13(1): 103–30.

Durlauf, Steven N., and Daniel S. Nagin. 2011. "The Deterrent Effect of Imprisonment." In *Controlling Crime: Strategies and Tradeoffs*, edited by Philip J. Cook, Jens Ludwig, and Justin McCrary. Cambridge, MA: National Bureau of Economic Research.

Earley, Pete. 1992. *The Hot House: Life Inside Leavenworth Prison*. New York: Bantam Books.

Easterly, William, and R. Levine. 1997. "Africa's Growth Tragedy: Politics and Ethnic Divisions." *Quarterly Journal of Economics* 112(4): 1203–50.

Edwards, Jeremy, and Sheilagh Ogilvie. 2012. "Contract Enforcement, Institutions, and Social Capital: The Maghribi Traders Reappraised." *Economic History Review* 65(2): 421–44.

Ehrlich, Isaac. 1972. "The Deterrent Effect of Criminal Law." *Journal of Legal Studies* 1(2): 259–76.

Ellickson, Robert. 1991. *Order Without Law: How Neighbors Settle Disputes*. Cambridge, MA: Harvard University Press.

Falcone, Giovanni. 1991. *Men of Honour: The Truth about the Mafia*. London: Fourth Estate.

Fearon, James D., and David D. Laitin. 1996. "Explaining Interethnic Cooperation." *American Political Science Review* 90(4): 715–35.

Federal Bureau of Investigation. 2012a. "Aryan Brotherhood." Freedom of Information and Privacy Acts. File No. 183–7396.

Federal Bureau of Investigation. 2012b. "Aryan Circle." Freedom of Information and Privacy Acts. File No. 100A-HO-44640 SUB 4.

Federal Bureau of Investigation. 2012c. "La Nuestra Familia." Freedom of Information and Privacy Acts. File No. 183-HQ-1030.

Federal Bureau of Investigation. 2012d. "Mexican Mafia: File 1." Freedom of Information and Privacy Acts.

Federal Bureau of Investigation. 2012e. "Mexican Mafia: File 2." Freedom of Information and Privacy Acts.

Fleisher, Mark. 1989. *Warehousing Violence*. Newbury Park, CA: Sage Publications.

Fleisher, Mark, and Scott Decker. 2001. "An Overview of the Challenge of Prison Gangs." *Corrections Management Quarterly* 5(1): 1–9.

Fleisher, Mark, and Jessie Krienert. 2009. *The Myth of Prison Rape: Sexual Culture in American Prisons*. Lanham: Rowman and Littlefied.

Fong, Robert S. 1987. "Comparative Study of the Organizational Aspect of Two Texas Prison Gangs: Texas Syndicate and Mexican Mafia." Dissertation. Sam Houston University.

Fong, Robert S. 1990. "The Organizational Structure of Prison Gangs: A Texas Case Study." *Federal Probation* 54(March): 36–43.

Fong, Robert S., Ronald E. Vogel, and Salvador Buentello. 1992. "Prison Gang Dynamics: A Look Inside the Texas Department of Corrections." In *Corrections: Dilemmas and Directions*, edited by Peter J. Benekos and Alida V. Merlo. Cincinnati, OH: Anderson.

Fong, Robert S., Ronald E. Vogel, and Salvador Buentello. 1993. "Blood In, Blood Out: The Rationale of Defecting from Prison Gangs." *Journal of Gang Research* 2(4): 45–51.

Forsythe, Davis. 2006. "Gangs in California Prison System: What Can Be Done?" Reforming California Corrections. California Sentencing & Corrections Policy Series, Stanford Criminal Justice Center Working Papers. January 27.

Fortune, Sandra H. 2003. "Inmate and Prison Gang Leadership." Dissertation. East Tennessee State University.

Friedman, Daniel, and Ryan Oprea. 2012. "A Continuous Dilemma." *American Economic Review* 102(1): 337–63.

Friedman, David. 1979. "Private Creation and Enforcement of Law—A Historical Case." *Journal of Legal Studies* 8(2): 399–415.

Friedman, David. 1994. "A Positive Account of Property Rights." *Social Philosophy and Policy* 11(2): 1–16.

Friedman, David. 2001. *Law's Order: What Economics Has to Do With Law and Why It Matters*. Princeton, NJ: Princeton University Press.

Frye, Timothy. 2002. "Private Protection in Russia and Poland." *American Journal of Political Science* 46(3): 572–84.

Frye, Timothy, and Ekaterina Zhuravskaya. 2002. "Rackets, Regulation, and the Rule of Law." *Journal of Law, Economics & Organization* 16(2): 478–502.

Fudenberg, Drew, and Eric Maskin. 1986. "The Folk Theorem in Repeated Games with Discounting or with Incomplete Information." *Econometrica* 54(3): 533–54.

Fuentes, Nina. 2006. *The Rise and Fall of the Nuestra Familia*. Jefferson, WI: Know Gangs Publishing.

Fukuyama, Francis. 2013. "What Is Governance?" *Governance: An International Journal of Policy, Administration, and Institutions* 26(3): 347–68.

Furillo, Andy, 2004. "Prison Gang's Pockets Deep: Mexican Mafia Uses Pelican Bay Inmate Trust Accounts to Launder Money, Officials Charge." *Sacramento Bee*, October 17.

Furillo, Andy. 2010. "A Killing in Call 3–216." *Sacramento Bee,* September 26.

Furillo, Andy. 2011a. "In Cross-Examination, Folsom Inmate Canchola Says He Didn't Kill Victim." *Sacramento Bee*, September 15.

Furillo, Andy. 2011b. "Jury Hears Defendant, Prison Officer Testify in Cellmate's Death." *Sacramento Bee*, September 14.

Furillo, Andy. 2011c. "Man Gets 45 Years to Life for Killing Brother's Murderer." *Modesto Bee*, December 10.

Gaes, Gerald G., Susan Wallace, Evan Gilman, Jody Klein-Saffran, and Sharon Suppa. 2002. "The Influence of Prison Gang Affiliation on Violence and Other Prison Misconduct." *The Prison Journal* 82(3): 359–85.

Gambetta, Diego. 1993. *The Sicilian Mafia: The Business of Private Protection*. Cambridge, MA: Harvard University Press.

Gambetta, Diego. 2009. *Codes of the Underworld: How Criminals Communicate*. Princeton, NJ: Princeton University Press.

Gangland. 2007. Aryan Brotherhood. Airdate: June 24.

Geniella, Mike. 2001. "Inside Pelican Bay." *The Press Democrat*, April 22.

Gilmore, Ruth Wilson. 2007. *Golden Gulag: Prisons, Surplus, Crisis, and Opposition in Globalizing California*. Berkeley: University of California Press.

Glaeser, Edward L. 1998. "Economic Approach to Crime and Punishment." In *New Palgrave Dictionary of Economics and the Law*, edited by Peter Newman. London: MacMillan.

Goffman, Erving. 1961. *Asylum: Essays on the Social Situation of Mental Patients and Other Inmates*. New York: Random House.

Goldstone, Jack A., and Bert Useem. 1999. "Prison Riots as Microrevolutions: An Extension of State-Centered Theories." *American Journal of Sociology* 104(4): 985–1029.

Goodman, Philip. 2008. "'It's Just Black, White, or Hispanic': An Observational Study of Racializing Moves in California's Segregated Prison Reception Centers." *Law & Society Review* 42(4): 735–70.

Grann, David. 2004. "The Brand: How the Aryan Brotherhood Became the Most Murderous Prison Gang in America." *The New Yorker*, February 16.

Gransky, Laura A., and Marisa E. Patterson. 1999. "A Discussion of Illinois' 'Gang-Free' Prison: Evaluation Results." *Corrections Management Quarterly* 3(4): 30–42.

Greif, Avner. 1989. "Reputation and Coalitions in Medieval Trade: Evidence on the Maghribi Traders." *Journal of Economic History* 49(4): 857–82.

Greif, Avner. 1993. "Contract Enforceability and Economic Institutions in Early Trade: The Maghribi Traders' Coalition." *American Economic Review* 83(3): 525–48.

Greif, Avner. 2004. "Impersonal Exchange Without Impartial Law: The Community Responsibility System" *Chicago Journal of International Law* 5: 109–38.

Greif, Avner. 2006a. "The Birth of Impersonal Exchange: The Community Responsibility System and Impartial Justice." *Journal of Economic Perspectives* 20(2): 221–36.

Greif, Avner. 2006b. *Institutions and the Path to the Modern Economy: Lessons from Medieval Trade*. Cambridge, UK: Cambridge University Press.

Greif, Avner. 2012. "The Maghribi Traders: A Reappraisal?" *Economic History Review* 65(2): 445–69.

Greif, Avner, and David D. Laitin. 2004. "A Theory of Endogenous Institutional Change." *American Political Science Review* 98(4): 633–52.

Griffin, Marie L., and John R. Hepburn. 2006. "The Effect of Gang Affiliation on Violent Misconduct Among Inmates During the Early Years of Confinement." *Criminal Justice and Behavior* 33(4): 419–48.

Habyarimana, James, Macartan Humphreys, Daniel Posner, and Jeremy Weinstein. 2007. "Why Does Ethnic Diversity Undermine Public Goods Provision?" *American Political Science Review* 101(4): 709–25.

Hamill, Heather. 2011. *The Hoods: Crime and Punishment in Belfast.* Princeton, NJ: Princeton University Press.

Hassine, Victor. 2007. *Life Without Parole: Living in Prison Today.* Edited by Robert Johnson and Ania Dobrzanska. New York: Oxford University Press.

Hayek, Friedrich A. 1973. *Law, Legislation and Liberty, Volume 1: Rules and Order.* Chicago: University of Chicago Press.

Hill, Peter B. E. 2003. *The Japanese Mafia: Yakuza, Law, and the State.* Oxford, UK: Oxford University Press.

Hirschman, Albert O. 1970. *Exit, Voice, and Loyalty: Responses to Declines in Firms, Organizations, and States.* Cambridge, MA: Harvard University Press.

Hobbes, Thomas. 1651 [2009]. *Leviathan.* Oxford, UK: Oxford World's Classic.

Holcombe, Randall. 1993. *The Economic Foundations of Government.* New York: New York University Press.

Houser, Daniel, and John Wooders. 2006. "Reputations in Auctions: Theory and Evidence from eBay." *Journal of Economics & Management Strategy* 15(2): 353–69.

Howell, James C., and John P. Moore. 2010. "History of Street Gangs in the United States." *National Gang Center Bulletin* 4(May): 1–25.

Huebner, Beth M. 2003. "Administrative Determinants of Inmate Violence: A Multilevel Analysis." *Journal of Criminal Justice* 31(2): 107–17.

Hunt, Geoffrey, Stephanie Riegel, Tomas Morales, and Dan Waldorf. 1993. "Changes in Prison Culture: Prison Gangs and the Case of the 'Pepsi Generation.'" *Social Problems* 40(3): 398–409.

Hutcherson, Donald T. 2012. "Crime Pays: The Connection Between Time in Prison and Future Criminal Earnings." *The Prison Journal* 92(3): 315–35.

Iannaccone, Laurence R. 1992. "Sacrifice and Stigma: Reducing Free-riding in Cults, Communes, and Other Collectives." *Journal of Political Economy* 100(2): 271–91.

International Centre for Prison Studies. 2013. World Prison Brief: United States of America. http://www.prisonstudies.org/info/worldbrief/wpb_country. php?country=190.

Irwin, John. 1970 [1990]. *The Felon.* Berkeley: University of California Press.

Irwin, John. 1980. *Prisons in Turmoil.* Boston: Little, Brown, & Co.

Irwin, John. 2005. *The Warehouse Prison: Disposal of the New Dangerous Class.* Los Angeles: Roxbury.

Irwin, John, and Donald Cressey. 1962. "Thieves, Convicts, and the Inmate Culture." *Social Problems* 10(2): 142–55.

Jacobs, Bruce A., and Richard Wright. 2006. *Street Justice: Retaliation in the Criminal Underworld.* New York: Cambridge University Press.

Jacobs, James B. 1975. "Stratification and Conflict Among Prison Inmates." *Criminology* 66(4): 476–82.

Jacobs, James B. 1977. *Stateville: The Penitentiary in Mass Society.* Chicago: University of Chicago Press.

Jankowski, Martin. 1991. *Islands in the Street: Gangs and American Urban Society*. Berkeley: University of California Press.

Johnson v. California. 2005. 543 U.S. 499.

Kalinich, David B. 1980. *Power, Stability, and Contraband: The Inmate Economy*. Lake Zurich, IL: Waveland Press.

Kalinich, David B., and Stan Stojkovic. 1985. "Contraband: The Basis for Legitimate Power in a Prison Social System." *Criminal Justice and Behavior* 12(4): 435–51.

Kalyvas, Stathis N. 2006. *The Logic of Violence in Civil War*. Cambridge, UK: Cambridge University Press.

Kaminski, Marek. 2003. "Games Prisoners Play: Allocation of Social Roles in a Total Institution." *Rationality and Society* 15(2): 188–21

Kaminski, Marek. 2004. *Games Prisoners Play: The Tragicomic Worlds of Polish Prisons*. Princeton, NJ: Princeton University Press.

Kaminski, Marek, and Don Gibbons. 1994. "Prisoner Subculture in Poland." *Crime & Delinquency* 40(1): 105–19.

Katz, Lawrence, Steve D. Levitt, and Ellen Shustorovich. 2003. "Prison Conditions, Capital Punishment, and Deterrence." *American Law and Economics Review* 5(2): 318–43.

Keith, Terri. 2009. "Northeast Gang Leader Sentenced to Die." *City News Service*. January 15.

Kim, Victoria. 2012. "A Hard Fall for Lawyer Who Struggled to Escape Gang Life." *Los Angeles Times*, June 5.

Kimbrough, Erik O., and Bart J. Wilson. 2013. "Insiders, Outsiders, and the Adaptability of Informal Rules to Ecological Shocks." *Ecological Economics* 90: 29–40.

King, Ryan S., and Marc Mauer. 2002. "Distorted Priorities: Drug Offenders in State Prisons." The Sentencing Project.

Kiriakou, John. 2013. "Letter from Loretto."

Kleiman, Mark. 2009. *When Brute Force Fails: How to Have Less Crime and Less Punishment*. Princeton, NJ: Princeton University Press.

Klein, Benjamin, and Keith B. Leffler. 1981. "The Role of Market Forces in Assuring Contractual Performance." *Journal of Political Economy* 89(4): 615–41.

Klick, Jonathan, and Alexander Tabarrok. 2005. "Using Terror Alert Levels to Estimate the Effect of Police on Crime." *Journal of Law & Economics* 48(1): 267–79.

Klien, Gary, and Mark Gomez. 2012. "San Jose Murderer Who Killed Inmates Says He Was Avenging Children." *San Jose Mercury News*, April 6.

Knight, Jack. 1992. *Institutions and Social Conflict*. Cambridge, UK: Cambridge University Press.

Knox, George W. 2000. *An Introduction to Gangs*, 5th edition. Peotone, IL: New Chicago School Press

Knox, George W. 2006. *An Introduction to Gangs*, 6th edition. Peotone, IL: New Chicago School Press.

Knox, George W. 2012. "The Problem of Gangs and Security Threat Groups (STG's) in American Prisons and Jails Today: Recent Findings from the 2012 NGCRC National Gang/STG Survey." National Gang Research Center.

Knox, George W., and Curtis Robinson (eds.). 2004. *Gang Profiles: An Anthology*. Peotone, IL: National Gang Crime Research Center.

Knox, George W., and Edward D. Tromanhauser. 1991. "Gangs and Their Control in Adult Correctional Institutions." *The Prison Journal* 71(2): 15–22.

Koehler, Robert. 2000. "The Organizational Structure and Function of La Nuestra Familia Within Colorado State Correctional Facilities." *Deviant Behavior* 21(2): 155–79.

Kollock, Peter. 1998. "Social Dilemmas: The Anatomy of Cooperation." *Annual Review of Sociology* 24: 183–214.

Konrad, Kai A., and Stergops Skaperdas. 2012. "The Market for Protection and the Origin of the State." *Journal of Economic Theory* 50(2): 417–43.

Kreps, David. 1990. "Corporate Culture and Economic Theory." In *Perspectives on Positive Political Economy*, edited by James E. Alt and Kenneth A. Shepsle. Cambridge, UK: Cambridge University Press.

Kruttschnitt, Candace, and Rosemary Gartner. 2005. *Marking Time in the Golden State: Women's Imprisonment in California*. New York: Cambridge University Press.

Lacey, Nicola. 2008. *The Prisoners' Dilemma: Political Economy and Punishment in Contemporary Democracies*. New York: Cambridge University Press.

Lahm, Karen F. 2008. "Inmate-on-Inmate Assault: A Multilevel Examination of Prison Violence." *Criminal Justice and Behavior* 35(1): 120–37.

Landa, Janet. 1981. "A Theory of Ethnically Homogenous Middleman Group: An Institutional Alternative to Contract Law." *Journal of Legal Studies* 10(2): 349–62.

Landa, Janet. 1994. *Trust, Ethnicity, and Identity*. Ann Arbor: University of Michigan Press.

Lane, Frederic. 1958. "Economic Consequences of Organized Violence." *Journal of Economic History* 18(4): 401–17.

Lane, Frederic. [1942] 1966. "The Economic Meaning of War and Protection." In *Venice and History: The Collected Papers of Frederic C. Lane*. Baltimore: Johns Hopkins University Press.

Langan, Patrick A., and David J. Levin. 2002. "Recidivism of Prisoners Released in 1994." Bureau of Justice Statistics Special Report.

Langohr, Glenn. 2013. *The Art of War: A Memoir of Life in Prison with Mafia, Serial Killers and Sex Offenders Who Get Stabbed*. Lockdown Publishing.

Lee, David S., and Justin McCrary. 2005. "Crime, Punishment, and Myopia." NBER Working Paper #11491 Washington, DC: National Bureau of Economic Research.

Leeson, Peter T. 2005a. "Endogenizing Fractionalization." *Journal of Institutional Economics* 1(1): 75–98.

Leeson, Peter T. 2005b. "Self-Enforcing Arrangements in African Political Economy." *Journal of Economic Behavior and Organization* 57(2): 241–44.

Leeson, Peter T. 2006. "Cooperation and Conflict: Evidence on Self-Enforcing Arrangements and Heterogeneous Groups." *American Journal of Economics and Sociology* 65(4): 891–907.

Leeson, Peter T. 2007a. "An-arrgh-chy: The Law and Economics of Pirate Organization." *Journal of Political Economy* 115(6): 1049–94.

Leeson, Peter T. 2007b. "Better off Stateless: Somalia Before and After Government Collapse." *Journal of Comparative Economics* 35(4): 689–710.

Leeson, Peter T. 2007c. "Trading with Bandits." *Journal of Law and Economics* 50(2): 303–21.

Leeson, Peter T. 2008. "Social Distance and Self-Enforcing Exchange." *Journal of Legal Studies* 37(1): 161–88.

Leeson, Peter T. 2009a. *The Invisible Hook: The Hidden Economics of Pirates*. Princeton, NJ: Princeton University Press.

Leeson, Peter T. 2009b. "The Laws of Lawlessness." *Journal of Legal Studies* 38(2): 471–503.

Leeson, Peter T. 2010. "Pirational Choice: The Economics of Infamous Pirate Practices." *Journal of Economic Behavior and Organization* 76(3): 497–510.

Leeson, Peter T., Christopher J. Coyne, and Peter J. Boettke. 2006. "Converting Social Conflict: Focal Points and the Evolution of Coordination." *Review of Austrian Economics* 19(2–3): 137–47.

Leeson, Peter T., and David Skarbek. 2010. "Criminal Constitutions." *Global Crime* 11(3): 279–98.

Leeson, Peter T., and Claudia Williamson. 2009. "Anarchy and Development: An Application of the Theory of Second Best." *Law and Development Review* 2(1): 76–96.

Leonard, Jack, and Robert Faturechi. 2012. " 'Burrito' Deputy Flunked Out of Academy on Reality TV Show." *Los Angeles Times*, January 13.

Levi, Margaret. 2006. "Why We Need a New Theory of Government." *Perspectives on Politics* 4(1): 5–19.

Levin, Marc. 1996. "The Prisoners of the War on Drugs." Home Box Office Documentary. Release Date: January 8.

Levitt, Steven D. 1996. "The Effect of Prison Population Size on Crime Rates: Evidence from Prison Overcrowding Litigation." *Quarterly Journal of Economics* 111(2): 319–51.

Levitt, Steven D. 1998. "Juvenile Crime and Punishment." *Journal of Political Economy* 106(6): 1156–85.

Levitt, Steven D. 2004. "Understanding Why Crime Fell in the 1990s: Four Factors That Explain the Decline and Six That Do Not." *Journal of Economic Perspectives* 18(1): 163–90.

Levitt, Steven D., and Sudhir A. Venkatesh. 2000. "An Economic Analysis of a Drug-Selling Gang's Finances." *Quarterly Journal of Economics* 115(3): 755–89.

Lewis, George H. 1980. "Social Groupings in Organized Crime: The Case of La Nuestra Familia." *Deviant Behavior* 1(2): 129–43.

Libecap, Gary. 1994. *Contracting for Property Rights*. New York: Cambridge University Press.

Liedka, Raymond V., Anne Morrison Piehl, and Bert Useem. 2006. "The Crime-Control Effect of Incarceration: Does Scale Matter?" *Criminology & Criminal Policy* 5(2): 245–76.

Lopez, Robert J. 1995. "U.S. Indicts 22 in Probe of Mexican Mafia." *Los Angeles Times*, May 2.

Los Angeles County Citizens' Commission on Jail Violence. 2012. "Meeting Transcript." May 14.

Los Angeles County Witness Statements. 2011. "Declaration of Civilian Witnesses."

Lyman, M. D. 1989. *Gangland*. Springfield, IL: Charles C. Thomas.

MacDonald, John, Jonathan Klick, and Ben Grunwald. 2012. "The Effect of Privately Provided Police Services on Crime." University of Pennsylvania, Institute for Law & Economics Research Paper No. 12–36.

MacLean, Lauren M. 2010. *Informal Institutions and Citizenship in Rural Africa: Risk and Reciprocity in Ghana and Côte d'Ivoire*. New York: Cambridge University Press.

Madison, James. 1788. "The Structure of the Government Must Furnish the Proper Checks and Balances Between the Different Departments." Federalist Paper #51.

March, James G., and Johan P. Olson. 1996. "Institutional Perspectives on Political Institutions." *Governance: An International Journal of Policy, Administration, and Institutions* 9(3): 247–64.

Marquez, Jeremiah, and Don Thompson. 2006. "Probes Target State's Use of Prisoners to Maintain Order." *Associated Press*, January 23.

Martinson, Robert. 1974. "What Works—Questions and Answers about Prison Reform." *Public Interest* 35(22): 22–54.

Mauer, Marc. 2006. *Race to Incarcerate*. New York: The New Press.

McCorkle, Lloyd W., and Richard Korn. 1954. "Resocialization Within Walls." *Annals of the American Academy of Political and Social Science* 293: 88–98.

McGee, Richard A. 1981. *Prisons and Politics*. Lexington, MA: Lexington Books.

McGuire, Martin C., and Mancur Olson. 1996. "The Economics of Autocracy and Majority Rule: The Invisible Hand and the Use of Force." *Journal of Economic Literature* 34(1): 72–96.

Meadowcroft, John. (ed.) 2008. *Prohibitions*. London: Institute for Economic Affairs.

Melde, Chris, Terrance J. Taylor, and Finn-Aage Esbensen. 2009. " 'I Got Your Back': An Examination of the Protective Function of Gang Membership in Adolescence." *Criminology* 47(2): 565–94.

Mendoza, John. 2012. *Nuestra Familia: A Broken Paradigm*. North Charleston, SC: CreateSpace Publishers.

Mendoza, Ramon A. 2005. *Mexican Mafia: From Alter Boy to Hitman*. Corona, CA: Ken Whitley and Associates.

Milgrom, Paul R., Douglass C. North, and Barry R. Weingast. 1990. "The Role of Institutions in the Revival of Trade: The Law Merchant, Private Judges, and the Champagne Fairs." *Economics & Politics* 2(1): 1–23.

Milhaupt, Curtis J., and Mark D. West. 2000. "The Dark Side of Private Ordering: An Institutional and Empirical Analysis of Organized Crime." *University of Chicago Law Review* 67(1): 41–98.

Miller, Lisa L. 2008. *The Perils of Federalism: Race, Poverty, and the Politics of Crime Control.* New York: Oxford University Press.

Miron, Jeffrey A. 1999. "Violence and the U.S. Prohibitions of Drugs and Alcohol." *American Law and Economics Review* 22(2): 315–39.

Miron, Jeffrey A. 2001. "Violence, Guns, and Drugs: A Cross-Country Analysis." *Journal of Law and Economics* 44(2): 615–33.

Moore, Joan W. 1978. *Homeboys: Gangs, Drugs, and Prison in the Barrios of Los Angeles.* Philadelphia: Temple University Press.

Morales, Gabriel C. 2008. *La Familia—The Family: Prison Gangs in America.* San Antonio, TX: Mungia Printers.

Morales, Jose. 2013. Court Document A132816. Court of Appeals of the State of California, First Appellate District, Division Three, January 23.

Morrill, Robert. 2005. *The Mexican Mafia: The Story.* Denver, CO: Security Threat Intelligence Network Group.

MSNBC. 2005a. "Inside Wabash." *Lockup.* Airdate: December 3.

MSNBC. 2005b. "Return to Corcoran." *Lockup.* Airdate: November 26.

MSNBC. 2005c. "Return to Pelican Bay." *Lockup.* Airdate: November 19.

MSNBC. 2006. "Inside Kern Valley." *Lockup.* Airdate: July 24.

MSNBC. 2007a. "San Quentin: Extended Stay, Conjugal Visit." *Lockup.* Airdate: September 21.

MSNBC. 2007b. "San Quentin: Extended Stay, Slamming in the Slammer." *Lockup.* Airdate: October 12.

MSNBC. 2007c. "San Quentin: Extended Stay, The Gang's All Here." *Lockup.* Airdate: September 7.

MSNBC. 2007d. "San Quentin: Extended Stay, Weapons 101." *Lockup.* Airdate: October 5.

MSNBC. 2008a. "The Convict Code." *Lockup Raw.* Airdate: February 25.

MSNBC 2008b. "America's Toughest Jails." *Lockup Raw.* Airdate: October 25.

MSNBC. 2008c. "Ever Present Danger." *Lockup Raw:* Airdate: July 5.

MSNBC. 2009a. "Ganging Up." *Lockup Raw.* Airdate: May 16.

MSNBC. 2009b. "Inside Folsom." *Lockup.* Airdate: May 9.

MSNBC. 2009c. "Inside L.A. County." *Lockup.* Airdate: May 2.

MSNBC. 2010a. "Predatory Behavior." *Lockup Raw.* Airdate: March 6.

MSNBC. 2010b. "Dues and Don'ts." *Lockup Raw.* Airdate: April 24.

Munger, Michael C. 2000. "Five Questions: An Integrated Research Agenda for Public Choice." *Public Choice* 103(1/2): 1–12.

Munger, Michael C. 2010. "Endless Forms Most Beautiful and Most Wonderful: Elinor Ostrom and the Diversity of Institutions." *Public Choice* 143(3–4): 263–68.

National Center on Addiction and Substance Abuse at Columbia University. 2002. "Trends in Substance Abuse and Treatment Needs Among Inmates, Final Report." NCJ 197073. Washington, DC: U.S. Department of Justice, National Institute of Justice.

National Institute of Corrections. 1991. "Management Strategies in Disturbances and with Gangs/Disruptive Groups." Washington, DC: U.S. Department of Justice.

Neuwirth, Robert. 2011. *Stealth of Nations: The Global Rise of the Informal Economy*. New York: Pantheon.

North, Douglass. 1987. "Institutions, Transaction Costs, and Economic Growth." *Economic Inquiry* 25(3): 419–28.

North, Douglass. 1990. *Institutions, Institutional Change, and Economic Performance*. New York: Cambridge University Press.

North, Douglass, John Wallis, and Barry Weingast. 2009. *Violence and Social Orders: A Conceptual Framework for Interpreting Recorded Human History*. New York: Cambridge University Press.

Nozick, Robert. 1974. *Anarchy, State, and Utopia*. New York: Basic Books.

O'Donnell, Ian, and Kimmett Edgar. 1998. "Routine Victimisation in Prison." *The Howard Journal* 37(3): 266–79.

Ohio Department of Rehabilitation and Correction. 1998. "Gang Membership as an Indicator of Prison Misbehavior." Paper presented at the American Society of Criminology Meetings, Washington, DC., November 11–14.

Olson, David, Brendan Dooley, and Candice Kane. 2004. "Research Bulletin: The Relationship Between Gang Membership and Inmate Recidivism." *Criminal Justice Information Authority* 2(12): 1–12.

Olson, Mancur. 1993. "Dictatorship, Democracy, and Development." *American Political Science Review* 87(3): 567–76.

Olson, Mancur. 2000. *Power and Prosperity: Outgrowing Communist and Capitalist Dictatorships*. New York: Basic Books.

Oppenheimer, Franz. 1914. The *State: Its History and Development Viewed Sociologically*. Indianapolis: Bobbs-Merrill.

Ostrom, Elinor. 1990. *Governing the Commons: The Evolution of Institutions for Collective Action*. Cambridge, UK: Cambridge University Press.

Ostrom, Elinor. 2005. *Understanding Institutional Diversity*. Princeton, NJ: Princeton University Press.

Owen, Barbara. 1988. *The Reproduction of Social Control: A Study of Prison Workers at San Quentin*. New York: Praeger Publishers.

Owen, Barbara. 1998. *In the Mix: Struggle and Survival in Women's Prison*. Albany, NY: State University of New York Press.

Owens, Emily. 2011. "Are Underground Markets Really More Violent? Evidence from Early 20th Century America." *American Law and Economic Review* 13(1): 1–44.

Page, Joshua. 2011. *The Toughest Beat: Politics, Punishment, and the Prison Officers Union in California*. New York: Oxford University Press.

Parenti, Christian. 1999. *Lockdown America: Police and Prisons in the Age of Crisis*. London: Verso.

Pelz, Mary E., James W. Marquart, and Terry Pelz. 1991. "Right-Wing Extremism in the Texas Prisons: The Rise and Fall of the Aryan Brotherhood of Texas." *The Prison Journal* 71(2): 23–37.

People v. Garnica. 1981. Ruling. Court of Appeal, Fifth District, California.

People v. McGhee. 2010. Ruling. Court of Appeal, Second District, California.

People v. Torres. 2009. Ruling. Court of Appeal, Second District, California.

Petersilia, Joan. 2006. "Understanding California Corrections." California Policy Research Center. Berkeley: University of California.

Pfaff, John M. 2007. "The Growth of Prisons: Toward a Second Generation Approach." Fordham Law Legal Studies Research Paper #976373.

Pfaff, John M. 2011. "The Causes of Growth in Prison Admissions and Populations" Fordham University School of Law Working Paper.

Phelan, Michael P., and Scott A. Hunt. 1998. "Prison Gang Members' Tattoos as Identity Work: The Visual Communication of Moral Careers." *Symbolic Interaction* 21(3): 277–98.

Phillips, Coretta. 2012a. "'It Ain't Nothing Like America with the Bloods and the Crips': Gang Narratives in Two English Prisons." *Punishment & Society* 14(1): 51–68.

Phillips, Coretta. 2012b. *The Multicultural Prison: Ethnicity, Masculinity, and Social Relations Among Prisoners.* New York: Oxford University Press.

Pierson, Paul. 2000. "The Limits of Design: Explaining Institutional Origins and Change." *Governance: An International Journal of Policy, Administration, and Institutions* 13(4): 475–99.

Pinker, Steven. 2011. *The Better Angels of Our Nature: Why Violence Has Declined.* New York: Penguin Books.

Pollock, Joycelyn M. 1997. *Prison: Today and Tomorrow.* Gaithersburg, MD: Aspen Press.

Porter, Bruce. 1982. "California Prison Gangs: The Price of Control." *Corrections Magazine* 8(6): 6–19.

Posner, Eric A. 2000. *Law and Social Norms.* Cambridge, MA: Harvard University Press.

Powell, Benjamin, Ryan Ford, and Alex Nowrasteh. 2008. "Somalia After State Collapse: Chaos or Improvement?" *Journal of Economic Behavior & Organization* 67(3): 657–70.

Powell, Benjamin, and Edward Stringham. 2009. "Public Choice and the Economic Analysis of Anarchy: A Survey." *Public Choice* 140(3–4): 503–38.

Pratt, Travis C., and Francis T. Cullen. 2000. "The Empirical Status of Gottfredson and Hirschi's General Theory of Crime: A Meta-Analysis." *Criminology* 38(3): 931–64.

Pyrooz, David C., Scott H. Decker, and Mark Fleisher. 2011. "From the Street to the Prison, From the Prison to the Street: Understanding and Responding to Prison Gangs." *Journal of Aggression, Conflict, and Peace Research* 3(1): 12–24.

Radford, R. A. 1945. "The Economic Organisation of a P.O.W. Camp." *Economica* 12(48): 189–201.

Rafael, Tony. 2007. *The Mexican Mafia.* New York: Encounter Books.

Raphael, Steven, and Michael A. Stoll. 2013. "Assessing the Contribution of the Deinstitutionalization of the Mentally Ill to Growth in the U.S. Incarceration Rate." *Journal of Legal Studies* 42(1): 187–222.

Rayman, Graham. 2012. "Riker's Violence: Out of Control." *Village Voice,* May 9.

Reimer, Hans. 1937. "Socialization in the Prison Community." *Proceedings of the Sixty-Seventh Annual Congress of Correction*. New York: American Prison Association, pp. 151–55.

Reuter, Peter. 1983. *Disorganized Crime: The Economics of the Visible Hand*. Cambridge, MA: MIT Press.

Reuters. 2012. "Six in Ten Prisons 'Self-governed' by Gangs." *The Telegraph*, September 25.

Reynolds, Julie. 2008. "New Leadership, Constitution for Nuestra Familia." *The Monterey Herald*, February 24.

Richman, Barak. 2006. "How Community Institutions Create Economic Advantage: Jewish Diamond Merchants in New York." *Law and Social Inquiry* 21(2): 383–420.

Robertson, James E. 1988. "The Constitution in Protective Custody: An Analysis of the Rights of Protective Custody Inmates." *Cincinnati Law Review* 56(1): 91–143.

Rodrik, Dani, Arvin Subramanian, and Frencesco Trebbi. 2004. "Institutions Rule: The Primacy of Institutions Over Geography and Integration in Economic Development." *Journal of Economic Growth* 9(2): 131–65.

Rosas and Goodwin v. Baca. 2012. Complaint for Injunctive Relief Class Action. United States District Court, Central District of California. ACLU Foundation of Southern California.

Rose, Dina R., and Todd R. Clear. 1998. "Incarceration, Social Capital, and Crime: Implications for Social Disorganization Theory." *Criminology* 36(3): 441–79.

Ruddell, Rick, Scott H. Decker, and Arlen Egley Jr. 2006. "Gang Interventions in Jails: A National Analysis." *Criminal Justice Review* 31(1): 33–46.

Rudoff, Alvin. 1964. *Prison Inmates: An Involuntary Association*. Dissertation. University of California, Berkeley.

Sabol, William J., Heather C. West, and Matthey Cooper. 2009. "Prisoners in 2008." Bureau of Justice Statistics.

Sandza, Richard, and Elaine Shannon. 1982. "California's Prison Gang." *Newsweek*, February 1.

Santos, Michael. 2007. *Inside: Life Behind Bars*. New York: St. Martin's Griffin.

Santos, Saskia D., Jodi Lane, and Angela R. Gover. 2012. "Former Prison and Jail Inmates' Perceptions of Informal Methods of Control Utilized by Correctional Officers." *American Journal of Criminal Justice* 37(4): 485–504.

Schaeffer, Emily C. 2008. "Remittances and Reputations in Hawala Money-Transfer Systems: Self-Enforcing Exchange on an International Scale." *Journal of Private Enterprise* 24(1): 95–117.

Schelling, Thomas C. 1960. *The Strategy of Conflict*. Cambridge, MA: Harvard University Press.

Schelling, Thomas C. 1967. "Economic Analysis and Organized Crime." *Task Force Report on Organized Crime*. President's Commission on Law Enforcement and Administration of Justice. U.S. Department of Justice.

Schelling, Thomas C. 1971. "What is the Business of Organized Crime?" *Journal of Public Law* 20(71): 71–84.

Schelling, Thomas C. 1978. *Micromotives and Macrobehavior*. New York: W. W. Norton.

Schenk, Allison, and William J. Fremouw. 2012. "Individual Characteristics Related to Prison Violence: A Critical Review of the Literature." *Aggression and Violent Behavior* 17(5): 430–42.

Schlanger, Margo. 1999. "Beyond the Hero Judge: Institutional Reform Litigation as Litigation." *Michigan Law Review* 97(6): 1994–2036.

Schneider, Friedrich, Andreas Buehn, and Claudio E. Montenegro. 2010. "Shadow Economies All over the World: New Estimates for 162 Countries from 1999 to 2007." World Bank Policy Research Working Paper 5356.

Schrag, Clarence. 1954. "Leadership Among Prison Inmates." *American Sociological Review* 19(1): 37–42.

Shalev, Sharon. 2009. *Supermax: Controlling Risk Through Solitary Confinement*. Portland, OR: Willan Publishing.

Shelden, Randall G. 1991. "A Comparison of Gang Members and Non-Gang Members in a Prison Setting." *The Prison Journal* 71(2): 50–60.

Simon, Jonathan. 2000. "The 'Society of Captives' in the Era of Hyper-Incarceration." *Theoretical Criminology* 4(3): 285–308.

Simon, Jonathan. 2007. *Governing Through Crime: How the War on Crime Transformed American Democracy and Created a Culture of Fear*. New York: Oxford University Press.

Simon, Jonathan. 2012. "Mass Incarceration: From Social Policy to Social Problem." In *The Oxford Handbook of Sentencing and Corrections*, edited by Joan Petersilia and Kevin R. Reitz. New York: Oxford University Press.

Skaperdas, Stergios. 2001. "The Political Economy of Organized Crime: Providing Protection When the State Does Not." *Economics of Governance* 2(3): 173–202.

Skaperdas, Stergios, and Constantinos Syropoulos. 1995. "Gangs as Primitive States." In *The Economics of Organised Crime*, edited by Gianluca Fiorentini and Sam Peltzman. Cambridge, UK: Cambridge University Press.

Skarbek, David B. 2010a. "Putting the 'Con' into Constitutions: The Economics of Prison Gangs." *Journal of Law, Economics, & Organization* 26(2): 183–211.

Skarbek, David B. 2010b. "Self-Governance in San Pedro Prison." *The Independent Review* 14(4): 569–85.

Skarbek, David B. 2011. "Governance and Prison Gangs." *American Political Science Review* 105(4): 702–16.

Skarbek, David B. 2012. "Prison Gangs, Norms, and Organizations." *Journal of Economic Behavior and Organization* 82(1): 96–109.

Skeens, Anthony. 2013. "Inside the SHU Part 2: Prison Gangs." *Del Norte Triplicate*. June 25.

Smith, Adam. 1763 [1982]. *Lectures on Jurisprudence*, edited by R. L. Meek, D. D. Raphael, and P. G. Stein, Vol. V of the *Glasgow Edition of the Works and Correspondence of Adam Smith*. Indianapolis: Liberty Fund.

Smith, Laura M., Andrea L. Bertozzi, P. Jeffery Brantingham, George E. Tita, and Matthew Valasik. 2012. "Adaptation of an Ecological Territorial Model to Street Gang Spatial Patterns in Los Angeles." *Discrete and Continuous Dynamical Systems* 32(9): 3223–44.

Sobel, Russell, and Brian Osoba. 2009. "Youth Gangs as Pseudo-Governments: Implications for Violent Crime." *Southern Economics Journal* 75(4): 996–1018.

Sorensen, Jon, and Mark D. Cunningham. 2010. "Conviction Offense and Prison Violence: A Comparative Study of Murderers and Other Offenders." *Crime & Delinquency* 56(1): 103–25.

Sorensen, Jonathan R., and Rocky L. Pilgrim. 2000. "An Actuarial Risk Assessment of Violence Posed by Capital Murder Defendants." *Journal of Criminal Law & Criminology* 90(4): 1251–70.

Sowell, Thomas. 1996. *The Vision of the Anointed: Self-Congratulation as a Basis for Social Policy*. New York: Basic Books.

Sparks, Richard, Anthony Bottoms, and Will Hay. 1996. *Prisons and the Problem of Order*. New York: Oxford University Press.

Staley, Sam. 1992. *Drug Policy and the Decline of American Cities*. New Brunswick, NJ: Transaction Publishers.

Stringham, Edward P. (ed.). 2007. *Anarchy and the Law: The Political Economy of Choice*. New Brunswick, NJ: Transaction Publishers.

Stuntz, William J. 2011. *The Collapse of American Criminal Justice*. Cambridge, MA: Harvard University Press.

Sureños Report. 2008. Special Report. Rocky Mountain Information Network.

Sutter, Daniel. 1995. "Asymmetric Power Relation and Cooperation in Anarchy." *Southern Economic Journal* 61(3): 602–13.

Sykes, Gresham. 1958 [2007]. *The Society of Captives: A Study of a Maximum Security Prison*. Princeton, NJ: Princeton University Press.

Sykes, Gresham, and Sheldon L. Messinger. 1962. "The Inmate Social Code and Its Functions." In *The Sociology of Punishment and Correction*, edited by Norman Johnston, Leonard Savitz, and Marvin E. Wolfgang. New York: John Wiley and Sons.

Tapia, Michael. 2013. "Texas Latino Gangs and Large Urban Jails: Intergenerational Conflicts and Issues in Management." *Journal of Crime and Justice*. DOI: 10.1080/0735648X.2013.768179.

Telep, Cody W., and David Weisburd. 2012. "What is Known about the Effectiveness of Police Practices in Reducing Crime and Disorder?" *Police Quarterly* 15(4): 331–57.

Telser, L. G. 1980. "A Theory of Self-Enforcing Agreements." *Journal of Business* 53(1): 27–44.

Thrasher, Frederic. 1927 [2000]. *The Gang: A Study of 1,313 Gangs in Chicago*. Chicago: New Chicago Press.

Tilly, Charles. 1985. "War Making and State Making as Organized Crime." In *Bringing the State Back In*, edited by Peter Evans, Dietrich Rueschemeyer, and Theda Skocpol. New York: Cambridge University Press.

Toch, Hans. 1992. *Living in Prison: The Ecology of Survival*. Washington, DC: American Psychological Association.

Trammell, Rebecca. 2009. "Values, Rules, and Keeping the Peace: How Men Describe Order and the Inmate Code in California Prisons." *Deviant Behavior* 30(8): 746–71.

Trammell, Rebecca. 2011a. *Enforcing the Convict Code: Violence and Prison Culture*. Boulder, CO: Lynne Rienner Publishers.

Trammell, Rebecca. 2011b. "Symbolic Violence and Prison Wives: Gender Roles and Protective Pairings in Men's Prisons." *The Prison Journal* 91(3): 305–24.

Trammell, Rebecca, and Scott Chenault. 2009. " 'We Have to Take These Guys Out': Motivations for Assaulting Incarcerated Child Molesters." *Symbolic Interaction* 32(4): 334–50.

Trulson, Chad R., James W. Marquart, and Soraya K. Kawucha. 2006. "Gang Suppression and Correctional Control." *Corrections Today*, April.

Tullock, Gordon. 1985. "Adam Smith and the Prisoners' Dilemma." *Quarterly Journal of Economics* 100: 1073–81.

Tullock, Gordon. 1999. "Non-Prisoner's Dilemma." *Journal of Economic Behavior & Organization* 39(4): 455–58.

United States Department of Justice. 1979. "Prisoners in State and Federal Institutions on December 31." Advanced Report.

United States Department of Justice. 1991. Office of Justice Programs. Bureau of Justice Statistics. "Survey of Inmates of State Correctional Facilities."

United States v. Aguirre et al. 1994. Indictment, Federal District Court, Central District of California, June.

United States v. Aguirre et al. 2009. Indictment, Federal District Court, Central District of California, June.

United States v. Alfaro et al. 2008. Indictment, Federal District Court, Central District of California, October.

United States v. Barajas et al. 2008. Indictment, Federal District Court, Central District of California, June.

United States v. Blake et al. 2012. Indictment, Federal District Court, Southern District of Texas, October.

United States v. Colabella et al. 2010. Indictment. Federal District Court, Southern District of California, July.

United States v. Eastside Riva. 2010. Affidavit. Federal Bureau of Investigation.

United States v. Espudo et al. 2012. Indictment. Federal District Court, Central District of California, July.

United States v. Estrada et al. 2010. Indictment. Federal District Court, Central District of California, June.

United States v. Fernandez et al. 2004. 388 F. 3d 1199. Court of Appeals, 9th Circuit.

United States v. Flores et al. 2008. Indictment. Federal District Court, Central District of California, June.

United States v. Henley et al. 2008. Indictment. Federal District Court, Central District of California, June.

United States v. Hernandez et al. 2009. Indictment. Federal District Court, Central District of California, February.

United States v. Johnston et al. 2010. Indictment. Federal District Court, Southern District of Texas, September.

United States v. Michel. 2012. "Statement of Stipulated Factual Basis" Case 2:12-cr-00039-UA.

United States v. Ojeda et al. 2011. Indictment. Federal District Court, Southern District of California, September.

United States v. Orozco et al. 2011. Indictment. Federal District Court, Central District of California, September.

United States v. Pantoja et al. 2007. Indictment. Federal District Court, Central District of California, June.

United States v. Rios et al. 2011. Indictment. Federal District Court, Central District of California, February.

United States v. Roman et al. 2012. Indictment. Federal District Court, Central District of California, February.

United States v. Rubalcaba et al. 2001. Indictment. Federal District Court, Northern District of California. April.

United States v. Shryock et al. 2003. 342 F. 3d 948, Court of Appeals, 9th Circuit.

United States v. Sotelo et al. 2008. Indictment. Federal District Court, Central District of California, June.

United States v. Vasquez et al. 2007. Indictment. Federal District Court, Central District of California, February.

United States v. White et al. 2013. Indictment. Federal District Court, District of Maryland, April.

United States v. Yepiz et al. 2006. Indictment. Federal District Court, Central District of California, June.

Useem, Bert. 1985. "Disorganization and the New Mexico Prison Riot of 1980." *American Sociological Review* 50(5): 677–88.

Useem, Bert, Camille Camp, and George M. Camp. 1996. *Resolution of Prison Riots: Strategies and Policies.* New York: Oxford University Press.

Useem, Bert, and Peter A. Kimball. 1987. "A Theory of Prison Riots." *Theory and Society* 16(1): 87–115.

Useem, Bert, and Anne M. Piehl. 2006. "Prison Buildup and Disorder." *Punishment and Society* 8(1): 87–115.

Useem, Bert, and Anne M. Piehl. 2008. *Prison State: The Challenge of Mass Incarceration.* New York: Cambridge University Press.

Useem, Bert, and Anne M. Piehl. 2012. "Prison Governance: Correctional Leadership in the Current Era." In *The Oxford Handbook of Sentencing and Corrections*, edited by Joan Petersilia and Kevin Reitz. New York: Oxford University Press.

Valdez, Al. 2011. "The Origins of Southern California Latino Gangs." In *Maras: Gang Violence and Security in Central America,* edited by Thomas Bruneau, Lucia Dammert, and Elizabeth Skinner. Austin: University of Texas Press.

Valentine, Bill. 2000. *Gangs and Their Tattoos: Identifying Gangbangers on the Street and in Prison.* Boulder, CO: Paladin Press.

Varese, Federico. 1998. "The Society of Vory-v-zakone, 1930s–1950s." *Cahiers du Monde Russe* 39(4): 515–38.

Varese, Federico. 2005. *The Russian Mafia: Private Protection in a New Market Economy.* New York: Oxford University Press.

Varese, Federico. 2011. *Mafias on the Move: How Organized Crime Conquers New Territories.* Princeton, NJ: Princeton University Press.

Veblen, Thorstein. 1898 [1998]. "Why Is Economics Not an Evolutionary Science?" *Cambridge Journal of Economics* 22: 403–14.

Venable, Kenneth. 2007. *What Factors Predict White Male Prisoners to Join the Aryan Brotherhood?* Dissertation, Capella University.

Venkatesh, Sudhir. 2006. *Off the Books: The Underground Economy of the Urban Poor.* Cambridge, MA: Harvard University Press.

Volokh, Alexander. 2011. "Prison Vouchers." *University of Pennsylvania Law Review* 160(3): 779–864.

Wacquant, Loïc. 2001. "Deadly Symbiosis: When Ghetto and Prison Meet and Mesh." *Punishment & Society* 3(1): 95–134.

Wacquant, Loïc. 2002. "The Curious Eclipse of Prison Ethnography in the Age of Mass Incarceration." *Ethnography* 3(4): 371–97.

Wang, Peng. 2011. "The Chinese Mafia: Private Protection in a Socialist Economy." *Global Crime* 12(4): 290–311.

Wantchekon, Leonard. 2004. "The Paradox of 'Warlord' Democracy: A Theoretical Investigation." *American Political Science Review* 98(1): 17–33.

Weaver, Vesla, and Amy Lerman. 2011. "The Political Consequences of the Carceral State." *American Political Science Review* 104(4): 817–33.

Webb, G. L., and David G. Morris. 1985. "Prison Guards." In *Correctional Institutions,* edited by Robert M. Carter, Daniel Glaeser, and Leslie T. Wilkins. New York: Harper and Row.

Weingast, Barry R. 1995. "The Economic Role of Political Institutions: Market-Preserving Federalism and Economic Development." *Journal of Law, Economics, & Organization* 11(1): 1–31.

Wells, James B., Kevin Minor, Earl Angel, Lisa Carter, and Morgan Cox. 2002. "A Study of Gangs and Security Threat Groups in America's Adult Prisons and Jail." National Major Gang Task Force.

Western, Bruce, Jeffrey R. Kling, and David F. Weiman. 2001. "The Labor Market Consequences of Incarceration." *Crime & Delinquency* 47(3): 410–27.

Wieder, D. Lawrence. 1974. *Language and Social Reality: The Case of Telling the Convict Code.* The Hague: Mouton & Co. N.V., Publishers.

Williams, Vergil L., and Mary Fish. 1974. *Convicts, Codes, and Contraband: The Prison Life of Men and Women.* Cambridge, MA: Ballinger Publishing Company.

Williamson, Claudia. 2009. "Informal Institutions Rule: Institutional Arrangements and Economic Performance." *Public Choice* 139(3): 371–87.

Williamson, Claudia, and Carrie B. Kerekes. 2011. "Securing Private Property: Formal versus Informal Institutions." *Journal of Law & Economics* 54(3): 537–72.

Winfree, Tom, Greg Newbold, and Huston Tubb. 2002. "Prisoner Perspectives on Inmate Culture in New Mexico and New Zealand." *The Prison Journal* 82(2): 213–33.

Winterdyk, John, and Rick Ruddell. 2010. "Managing Prison Gangs: Results from a Survey of U.S. Prisons." *Journal of Criminal Justice* 38(4): 730–36.

Wood, Jane. 2006. "Gang Activity in English Prisons: The Prisoners' Perspective." *Psychology, Crime & Law* 12(6): 605–17.

Wood, Jane, and Joanna Adler. 2001. "Gang Activity in English Prisons: The Staff Perspective." *Psychology, Crime & Law* 7(1–4): 167–92.

Wood, Jane, Alice Moir, and Mark James. 2009. "Prisoners' Gang-Related Activity: The Importance of Bullying and Moral Disengagement." *Psychology, Crime & Law* 15(6): 569–81.

Wood, Jane, Graham Ross Williams, and Mark James. 2010. "Incapacitation and Imprisonment: Prisoners' Involvement in Community-Based Crime." *Psychology, Crime & Law* 16(7): 601–15.

Worrall, John L., and Robert G. Morris. 2012. "Prison Gang Integration and Inmate Violence." *Journal of Criminal Justice* 40(5): 425–32.

Young, H. Peyton. 1998. "Social Norms and Economic Welfare." *European Economic Review* 42(3–5): 821–30.

Zimring, Franklin E. 2008. *The Great American Crime Decline.* New York: Oxford University Press.

Index

Made in the USA
Middletown, DE
11 January 2020